MORE WRITERS & COMPANY

MORE **WRITERS**
& **COMPANY**

New conversations with
CBC Radio's

ELEANOR WACHTEL

VINTAGE CANADA
A Division of Random House of Canada

First Vintage Canada Edition, 1997

Copyright © 1996 by Eleanor Wachtel

Interview with Kazuo Ishiguro © 1996 by Kazuo Ishiguro
Interview with Alice Walker © 1996 by Alice Walker

Canadian Cataloguing in Publication Data

Wachtel, Eleanor
More writers & company

ISBN 978-0-676-97084-5

1. Authors, English - 20th century - Interviews.
I. Title. II. Title: More writers and company

PN453.W263 1997   823'.91409   C96-931009-9

Printed and bound in the United States of America

To everyone who cares
about CBC radio

Acknowledgments

My first thanks, again, go to Anne Gibson, Executive Producer of "Writers & Company," for her commitment and vision; she has been an inspiring presence. Also, my thanks are due to Damiano Pietropaolo, Head of Performance for CBC radio, for his dedicated and enthusiastic support of the program from its inception in the fall of 1990.

Making radio is a collaborative enterprise — the best and most exciting I know. I would like to acknowledge the talent and generosity of the program's producers: Sandra Rabinovitch and Larry Scanlan, who worked with me during most of the period covered in this book. In addition to the producers noted at the end of each interview, I am grateful to the show's current producer, Mary Stinson, for her wholehearted devotion to good radio (and good eating), to associate producer, Nancy McIlveen, for her energetic, cheerful and indispensible good works, and to her predecessor, Lisa Godfrey. Together we have worked with many able technicians in recording and broadcasting the interviews. They are too many to name here, but I do want to single out our former regular studio engineer, Larry Morey. The CBC's London and New York studios provide frequent assistance: Rebecca Penrose and Sue Phillips in London and Linda Perry and Donna Gallers in New York have been exemplary in contacting and welcoming guests.

My colleagues Shelagh Rogers, Susan Feldman, Angelica Fox, Paul Wilson, Michael Crabb, Rei Uyeyama, Kathleen Pemberton, and others on "The Arts Tonight" team, have throughout these years provided both stimulation and camaraderie. Outside the CBC, I am indebted to the indefatigable Greg Gatenby and his Harbourfront Reading Series and International Festival of Authors for bringing to Toronto so many fine writers.

His initiative enhances the experience of living in Toronto. I also want to applaud the enterprise of Eddy Yanofsky and the University of Toronto Bookstore for its lively reading series.

And I'd like to thank my good friend Irene McGuire, founder of Writers & Co, the Literary Bookstore, for allowing me to use the name for the show, and hence these books. When she abandoned us and moved to Tasmania, Michael Ondaatje suggested I continue the pattern and entitle this volume, *Tasmania*.

A number of people have been invaluable in helping to turn the radio interviews into this book. First, of course, the writers themselves who agreed to have their conversations appear between these covers; I feel gratified that no one who was invited refused. The ongoing encouragement of Boris Castel of *Queen's Quarterly*, Linda Spalding and Michael Ondaatje of *Brick: A Literary Journal*, and Derk Wynand and Lucy Bashford of *The Malahat Review* has been unstinting; a number of these interviews were first published in their pages. I am grateful for the expansive patience and good humour of my editor, Diane Martin, and the keen interest of Jan Whitford, Louise Dennys and Catherine Yolles. Special thanks go to Hedy Muysson for attentive transcribing, and to the spirited *adhoc* proofing crew.

The constancy, good will and affection of my family, friends, intimates are as necessary to me as oxygen. To them, I invoke Haruki Murakami's: "It seems to me, though, that you always understand very well what I can't say very well."

Finally, for crucial help in the preparation of this book — as with the first one — with editing, "keyboarding" and faith, my deepest thanks to Gayla Reid.

Since the first volume of *Writers & Company* was published three years ago, CBC radio has become increasingly and disturbingly vulnerable. To argue for this quintessentially Canadian medium would be superfluous were its continued existence not at risk.

Our many devoted listeners, especially those who've taken the trouble to write, fax, e-mail and phone, bring home to me the importance and vitality of CBC radio. I want to thank you here. You are the key part of this circle.

Contents

Introduction

I grew up in a house without books. But it didn't take me long to grasp the power of reading. I shared a room with my sister at the end of a long hallway; my brother's room was halfway down. On Saturday mornings, my mother would shout down the hall from the kitchen for us to get up, get out, do things. "In a minute," we'd answer, and turn the page.

Books came from the library or, one year, from a small bookcase at the back of my grade school classroom. In my class, you could write the title on a card and borrow one book at a time; I resolved to fill in both sides of the card. Growing up in 1950s Montreal, my reading was haphazard and I managed to completely bypass all of the children's classics, such as *Alice in Wonderland* and *Winnie-the-Pooh*. The English critic, Sir Frank Kermode, who grew up in the 1920s on the Isle of Man, recently told me about his own stumbling upon Dickens and "good" books only by accident, and never quite catching references to Eeyore. Exactly.

What I did know was that British books had a different smell than American ones. It must have been the glue or the binding. The children in those English books seemed more autonomous and adventurous, so I came to favour that scent. And although the very first thing I can remember reading on my own was pure description — the squeaking sound of a bear crunching along hard-packed snow (how atavistically Canadian) — I read for the stories. I only became aware of an identifiable author and voice a couple of years later when I encountered James Thurber and Edgar Allen Poe, "The Night the Bed Fell on Father" and "A

Descent into the Maelström." Laughter and fear. Each narrative style was so compelling and so distinctive. I wondered: Who wrote this? Were there other stories like it? I started to recognize names and I began to be curious about how these writers lived and what they thought.

I don't believe that the link between childhood curiosity and adult work is a simple one. But even now, if I had to say what I'm after in my conversations with writers, I'd find myself coming back to the intersection between the life and the work. And by that, I don't mean the autobiographical sources for the fiction. I'm not looking for equivalencies or even clues *per se*. It's more like trying to catch a glimpse of the writer's passion. What fuels the art? What informs the life?

This book is one of the outcomes of that fascination. I discovered long ago that the lives of writers, like any of us, are shaped by relationships with parents, siblings, lovers, children. But what I also found is that the most common thread, the one characteristic recurring most frequently among writers is their self-proclaimed marginality, their outsider status. It is something that most writers prize, even though it may be, or was, a source of pain or loneliness. It gives them license and perspective from which to reflect the world. Paradoxically, it is the writer's very marginalization that makes sense of the world for us. When I've done programs based on geography, interviewing writers from Ireland or Australia, from Africa or Western Europe, it's from them that I've found out about their society. That paradox — that writers claim their own experience to be marginal and yet are able to conjure the essence of their culture for us in their writing — is central to many authors' lives.

This outsider status is also a cliché: the loner, the bookish kid up in a tree. Yet as I make this tentative generalization about writers as outcasts, exceptions rush in. Even the nature of the marginality differs from case to case and what keeps me so absorbed is how different, and original, each situation is. On the face of it, Oliver Sacks' choice of career would seem like slipping into a warm bath. He was born into a family of doctors, studied at

Oxford, and became a professor of clinical neurology. His work is characterized by its deep humanity and his capacity to make empathetic connections with his subjects. Yet Sacks himself says he feels like a perpetual observer, "an outsider peering into the human condition wistfully but sympathetically," a "resident alien."

The Irish are good at exile. Joyce, Beckett, Edna O'Brien had to leave the country in order to write because they found it too oppressive or confining. William Trevor says he wouldn't be able to write if he were back in Skibbereen or Enniscorthy; he would be too comfortable. He has to lead an uncosy life. The writer has to be edgy, he says, on the outside of things, looking in. "It's a faint beginning of a rule." And though Trevor has lived in England for some thirty years, he insists he's still a visitor there.

Kazuo Ishiguro came to England from Japan when he was five. A *de facto* outsider, he argues that there are strong similarities between early 1960s Guildford where he grew up and his ancestral town of Nagasaki — the emphasis on politeness and etiquette, the emotional understatement, the two island cultures. But, he says, "I had a certain kind of distance." Growing up in a Japanese household in England enabled Ishiguro to discern that values are a societal construct, particular to a place and a people, customs rather than universal absolutes. This detachment is the hallmark of his fiction.

Indeed, whether it's across geographical borders or boundaries, as with Edward Said, Amitav Ghosh, Isabel Allende, Louise Erdrich, Jamaica Kincaid; or within themselves, as with Jayne Anne Phillips, David Grossman, John Berger, Harold Bloom, virtually every writer in this collection has claimed that feeling of being on the outside. Now it no longer surprises me.

What I wasn't expecting were the resonances, the effective "conversations" that seem to arise among many of these writers. People as different as Nicole Brossard and E.L. Doctorow invoke the idea of writing as transgression. Physical pain and its value or usefulness are examined by Louise Erdrich, Alice Walker and William Trevor. Carlos Fuentes, Jeanette Winterson, David Grossman and Amitav Ghosh talk about the importance of creating your own reality and perceptions of history and language to escape being bound by the visions (and versions) of others. Louise Erdrich and Jayne Anne Phillips describe how motherhood changes you irrevocably. Jane Smiley and Martin Amis discuss the nature and possibility of tragedy in fiction today. The impact of the colonial conquest is analysed by Edward Said, Jamaica Kincaid, Chinua Achebe, Amitav Ghosh and Carlos Fuentes, providing a "contrapuntal voice," as Said puts it, to the literary canon so passionately championed by Harold Bloom and Said himself, among others. The contrasts are tantalizing: Achebe and Said on Joseph Conrad; Bloom and Doctorow, both self-described misfits at the same inappropriate high school, unpredictably on opposite sides of the New Criticism.

These writers also provide so much that is inspiring and life-affirming from their position on the borders. In Carol Shields' commitment to writing as a form of redemption, redeeming the lives of lost or vanished women; in Chinua Achebe's valuing of endurance, when he says that struggle and story are enough; in Reynolds Price's insistence that he would choose the pain and anguish of spinal cancer and its debilitating effects rather than miss the experience; in Kazuo Ishiguro's determination that life be more than a fulfilling of basic needs, that it make a difference — in all of these one finds a hard-won wisdom.

I wasn't read to as a child. One uncle would occasionally tell stories to my sister and me. He'd always start by taking out a large pocket watch. I came to merge the sound of his voice with the movement of his hands as he spoke, and the ticking of the watch resting on his lap. Voice and story. They're what I've tried to capture in my conversations with writers and to preserve in this book. Alastair Reid, the translator of Borges and Neruda, recently wrote that "voice is perhaps the most essential and lasting incarnation of any existence." Here then are the voices, and the stories, of twenty-two of the finest writers in the world today.

MORE WRITERS & COMPANY

OLIVER SACKS

Oliver Sacks is most famous for two works. One is the wonderfully titled collection of his clinical tales, *The Man Who Mistook His Wife for a Hat*. The title case history was made into a chamber opera by England's Michael Nyman, and the book was an unlikely bestseller when it came out in 1985. The second is *Awakenings*, Sacks' account of his treatment of patients who'd suffered from a sleeping-sickness epidemic dating from World War I, and who were briefly brought back to life in the late sixties.

Awakenings was first published in England in 1973. Harold Pinter was inspired by one of the patients' stories to write a play. A documentary film was made, and then in 1990, Hollywood made its "major motion picture," with Robert de Niro as Leonard L. and Robin Williams as the shy neurologist. Sacks was pleased with the movie.

Oliver Sacks is an unusual and, in some ways, old-fashioned man in the nineteenth-century humanist tradition, who writes from a place where biology and biography intersect. He was born in 1933 in London, England and raised in a house filled with books. Both his parents were doctors — his father practising well into his nineties; his mother was physician to the Queen Mother. His three older brothers studied medicine as well. Sacks studied at Oxford, loves music and has a great belief in its therapeutic value. To give you a sense of the man: About twenty years ago, he seriously injured his leg while climbing a mountain in Norway. He writes about this in a book called *A Leg to Stand On* (1984). When he describes trying to get back down the mountain — a matter of life or death — crawling in some pain, he thinks of Nietzsche, Leibniz, Goethe and Mozart; he imagines conversations between Dr. Johnson and Wittgenstein — not in an abstract, cerebral way, but as people with ideas and art he can engage with.

What draws me to Sacks' writing is not so much the unusual neurological conditions he so vividly describes, but the compassion that he brings to the patients who have them. He doesn't think of these people in terms of their physiological deficits, but as whole and even advantaged in their own way.

When I met him in Toronto, he was warm and ebullient. He didn't stop smiling or moving his hands, playing with a pocket-watch chain on the table. When he talked about hugging Temple Grandin, an amazing autistic woman who's the subject of the title piece in *An Anthropologist on Mars* (1995), he hugged himself for emphasis.

WACHTEL You recently quoted a seventeenth-century writer named Thomas Willis, who wrote: "Nature is nowhere accustomed more openly to display her secret mysteries than in cases where she shows traces of her workings apart from the beaten path." What is it about nature's "secret mysteries" that draws you from the beaten path in your work?

SACKS I would put it the other way round, and say that I get attracted by strangeness, one way and another. I think there's something about the ordinary course of life which perhaps doesn't attract attention as much as a shooting star or a super-nova. Similarly, there may be something uneventful and seamless about health, so that you may not think of the enormous intri-cacy which is behind it, until you see a breakdown of some sort, or something unusual.

For example, last week I was talking to a delightful woman who was born totally colour-blind, or achromatopic. She has no cones in her eyes. She has never seen colour, she has no idea of colour. I think one may not be able to think about colour, what colour means in our lives and how the nervous system deals with colour, unless one chances to meet someone who is far from the beaten path, like this, and she shows one something of, as it were, the secret of colour.

WACHTEL So it's in the absence of something that you start to examine what its presence might be like.

SACKS Right. The absence or the excess or the unusual form which it takes.

WACHTEL You once described yourself as a reporter from the far borders of human experience. And you do write about people who in a way are almost exiles — the deaf, the blind, the autistic. Is that a useful notion?

SACKS I think very useful, both exile and imprisonment. I know certainly the original Leonard L. in *Awakenings* used both terms. He would sometimes speak of his body as a prison, with windows but no doors. But he also saw himself as being exiled from proper life and from other people. This can even happen within the body. For example, when I had my injury to a leg, the muscle and nerve injury which I describe in *A Leg To Stand On*, I lost all feeling in the leg, it was paralysed, and it didn't seem part of me, it seemed a meaningless object attached to me. The leg was in exile.

WACHTEL The leg itself? I got the sense of it as being like a for-eign object.

SACKS It was a foreign object, but you could also say it was in exile, or it was not where it should be. Normally we are so at home in our bodies and we so own them that I think things like this are unimaginable. But they can fairly easily occur. If you've ever had a dental injection, which puts part of the mouth out, or a massive one on both sides, you may feel that your jaw and your tongue are no longer your own. If you have a massive spinal anaesthesia, you don't just become numb from the waist down, you *vanish*, you end at the waist, you terminate there, and what lies below is not you, not flesh, not real, not anything, as if it were exiled from reality. It is very ghostly and unreal and strange.

It's very difficult to imagine this sort of thing, which is one reason I say — half-jokingly — that readers of the "leg" book should read it under spinal anaesthesia, if possible. Not something authors usually demand of their readers.

WACHTEL When I was reading it, it reminded me of the first time I read Kafka's *Metamorphosis*. I'd read a few pages, and then I would look down and check that my body was still intact, so it has that force. Apart from the great fear that instilled in you — that sense of being exiled from your leg or your leg being exiled from you — what did you learn from that experience?

SACKS I found it very fascinating as well, and I think the fascination fought the fear and conquered it, or at least confronted it. One saw how imagination and will alone are not enough, that you need sensation from the body in order to affirm that you have a body. Wittgenstein starts one of his books on certainty by saying: "Here is one hand, can it make sense to doubt it?" Normally, it never makes sense to doubt part of the body, but here the body is thrown into doubt. My good friend Jonathan Miller wrote a lovely book called *The Body in Question*. (Incidentally, he suggested the title *A Leg To Stand On*, but his own title would have been as good; he's very, very good at titles.) One saw how the body, how something which is normally taken for granted could become acutely questionable, and how you need a continuous flow of sensation and the nervous system processing it in order to have an image of the body. Not simply an image of the body but a sense of the place and time which contain it.

One of the very strange things — even with a spinal anaesthetic — is that not only do you seem to disappear from the waist down but you cannot remember being otherwise, as if you have an amnesia for the way you were, plus an inability to imagine it in the future. I think the whole nature of consciousness begins to emerge with an experience like this. So, although you might say it's just a peripheral injury, just a nerve-and-muscle injury, in fact something like this reveals qualities of perception, body-image, ownership of the body, personal space, personal time and consciousness, which are very deep indeed. I think one finds this again and again, that the seemingly eccentric little bypaths in fact are all windows into deep qualities of the human condition which one might not think of otherwise.

WACHTEL You once wrote that what you aspired to practise was a neurology of the soul. For a physician and a scientist, you use the word soul a lot. What did you mean there?

SACKS I probably mean something similar to what I was just talking about, in terms of consciousness and self-image. And perhaps I'm using the word illegitimately to mean the self and self-definition, the concept of self. I rather like the word, soul. It implies one's sensibility and one's relationship to other people; I think there's no other word as general as that.

WACHTEL Yet when you first became a doctor and decided to enter neurology, there was part of you that was attracted to the abstractions divorced from any human reality, the brainy, heartless side of the profession.

SACKS Yes, it's been a long trek. My original passions were for the physical sciences. I recently wrote an article about Sir Humphry Davy and the origins of chemistry, and it was such pleasure to get back to that childhood interest. After the physical sciences I moved into biology. I got into medicine rather tardily and rather reluctantly and wanting at first to hold everything at the level of physiology. I think this is not uncommon among some doctors and perhaps especially neurologists. Facing questions of individuality and suffering came relatively late.

WACHTEL When you say you moved into medicine reluctantly, what propelled you there? Obviously there was a remarkable number of role models; both your parents were physicians, your older brothers studied medicine. What tipped the scales towards medicine for you?

SACKS Obviously the family background was important. But my own path I think was dominated by curiosity, first about the physical world, about the "go" of things, and this curiosity gradually got to higher and higher levels until it was about human beings. I sometimes envy linguists and anthropologists and others — probably anthropology is the domain I feel closest to — but my path is one of looking at human nature through the accident of something happening to it.

I also want to say that the brain is the most interesting, complex and wonderful object in the universe, and it's a wonderfully exciting thing to study and be in contact with. I have nothing against kidneys and hearts and lungs — God knows we couldn't live without them! — but they are nowhere near the complexity of the brain. Perhaps most importantly of all, you can have a kidney or liver transplant; you can't have a brain transplant. The brain is *you*, not just biologically or genetically, it has all your experience, it's you. The notion of a physical object which is also you fascinates me above everything else.

WACHTEL Once you were studying medicine, how did you realize that the brain was the region you wanted to focus on?

SACKS I think I always felt that. Perhaps partly because as a child I had had so-called classical migraines, in which one can lose the vision to one side of the visual field or see very strange hallucinations, or have abnormalities of sensation or speech. I think I was forced precociously to see that, in a sense, the world as we know it is constructed by the brain. Also, both my parents trained in neurology, even though neither of them stayed in it. But neurological topics were very much dinner-table topics. I sort of grew up with neurology.

WACHTEL You also grew up with a strong interest in the arts as well as the sciences. Your ongoing interest in music and literature seems to spill over into your practice of medicine.

SACKS I suppose so, although I hesitate a little because it never entirely seemed to me that there was a division between the arts and the sciences. I've just been writing an essay on music and the nervous system, and about the neurology of music, neuro-musicology, or whatever one should call it. My parents were both very fond of biographies. I now love biographies, and I regard them as somewhat similar to case histories, or really the other way around: case history is a form of biography for me. I'm not too fond of C. P. Snow's notion of the two cultures. I have been lucky enough to grow up in a house and a time and place where things went together. But their going together may be rather suspect.

I remember when I first read *The Man with a Shattered World* by A. R. Luria, the great Russian psychologist. I thought it was a novel. After thirty pages I realized it was a case history and case-study and the most detailed I'd ever read. But it had something of the feeling of a novel, and a *Russian* novel at that. One feels that Luria himself must have grown up in that sort of tradition.

WACHTEL Why did you say that sometimes the connection is suspect?

SACKS I'll tell you. I took my first book to a medical publisher who had published one of my mother's books, a book she wrote on the menopause and which had been incredibly successful. When I took my book on migraine to these publishers, a very peculiar comment was made. They said, "The book is too easy to read. This may arouse suspicion. Professionalize it." Almost as if there had to be a realm of arcane language and deletion of emotion, which was the proper medical-academic realm.

This suspicion goes back a long way, really to the inauguration of the Royal Society in the 1660s. Thomas Sprat, its first secretary, stipulated that the language of contributions had to be free from ornament, from rhetoric, written in some objective, clear, universal language, uncoloured by prejudice or whatever. This is very complex. One way or another this could be understood as a delusion of objectivity, what has sometimes been called the "view from nowhere."

Yet, we are human beings, we form our own views, our own assumptions. Newton wrote in two styles. His *Principia*, a book of rigorous geometrical structure, a classical Archimedean structure, is not too accessible, you don't too often hear the voice and the man. And it's in Latin. His *Opticks*, which he wrote in English, is much more accessible; you hear his voice again and again. It doesn't mean it's bad science. It's very beautiful prose. I think Newton was a beautiful writer, but not in the least literary. It's the beauty of thought and depth and curiosity and passion.

I think one can have something which is both deep and accessible, and both scientific and literary, although I don't like the word literary. I think there should be some combination of — I don't know what to call it — dispassion with passion, objectivity with passion. I think there should be scientific writing which is good prose and full of passion, but never loses its balance and is never sentimental. This has nothing to do with either academic or popular, it's a much deeper definition of scientific thought and writing.

WACHTEL Some of the stories, whether they are fiction or non-fiction, that have moved me most in the last year are pieces I've read by you. In some instances they are hopeful, in some very sad. An example of a hopeful case would be a piece you wrote about Temple Grandin, an autistic woman who called herself "an anthropologist on Mars." Can you sketch her story for me?

SACKS Temple, at the age of three, was a rocking, screaming mute, severely autistic, likely to be institutionalized and likely to have a hopeless future. But then things went right. There was very excellent teaching, support and encouragement, and very delicate handling. She is now a biologist, an engineer and a professor in Colorado, the world's expert on the psychology of cattle and the building of various cattle facilities. She understands cattle better than anyone else; but her understanding of people, as she knows, is very limited, although she said she is studying the species very closely. It was partly in the context of studying the species closely that she said she feels like an anthropologist on Mars.

This is a highly intelligent woman. But, like most autistic people, the concept of other people, of other minds, and for that matter of her own mind, is never developed too well. Social relationships are very difficult. She can't read intentions, the complex play of motive and strategy and intention. She can't dissemble.

There's something ingenuous about her. It was immensely impressive and moving to see how, given both the peculiar strengths and the peculiar weaknesses of autism — and I think there *are* strengths as well, in terms of extreme concentration, tenacity of mind, remarkable memory — she is able to do very complex designs in her mind. She says she has a work-station in her head. She does complex simulations and then will make a blueprint. She brought out both the strengths and the weaknesses of autism so strongly and movingly. I was going to see her only as a bit of background for something else but I was so moved. I think originally she regarded *me* as a sort of anthropologist who had come to see her. The notion of personal relationship and friendliness is not easy for her to get.

WACHTEL I think that's something you're very sensitive to, empathetic. Getting at the emotional side of someone like that, you're able to document the degree to which she has overcome her inability to apprehend people's emotions, but at the same time you're so interested in connecting to the emotional part of her. I'm thinking of something she created called a hug machine.

SACKS She describes how as a child — this may be common with autistic people — she wanted affection, wanted to be hugged. But being hugged was overwhelming and out of her control. Sensations and feelings are not absent in autistic people. They're sometimes out of control — especially in childhood — so she thought she would like a controlled hug and a machine for administering it. Later, as an adolescent, and being of a practical turn, after seeing a thing called a squeeze chute, which holds calves still for injections or whatever, she designed a squeeze chute for human use, and in particular for her own use, which she called a hug machine. In her college days she had this in her room; she would crawl into it face down and the thing would administer a squeeze or pressure of, whatever — fifty pounds to the square inch. She thought of this partly as just comfort and security, but she also thought the hug machine somehow made her empathetic, made her think of other people. Here is this virginal, celibate woman, who has probably never had any sexual contact, who has this strange machine. She herself said, "I guess other people get this out of relations with other people." Her way of saying "other people" has this Martian quality.

WACHTEL And you got in there.

SACKS Yes, I got in there, and I rather liked it, I found it calming. Right at the end, I was so moved by something Temple said. Some barrier suddenly broke and she said that she wanted to have done something of importance. She wanted to transmit something. She couldn't do it genetically, but she would like to do it through ideas and words, to leave some impression on the world. Suddenly this woman, so estranged in a way, so exiled from all sorts of human concerns, felt this deepest concern, which perhaps all of us have, and she wept as she said this. It's very unusual for autistic people to weep like this. When I said goodbye, I said, "I don't know whether you'll let me or not, but I want to hug you." And I did. I think she hugged me back, I wasn't quite sure. I think in a way she did let me into her life a little bit, a little bit.

WACHTEL It seems to run through your work, this notion that a medical deficit, or what's described as a deficit, can nonetheless have certain advantages. Tourette's syndrome, for example, can provoke bizarre behaviour, but there's still vitality and intensity. Do people suggest that this Sacksian world view consists of finding silver linings in dark clouds?

SACKS Yes, and worse. It has sometimes been seen as a romancing of disease or morbidity. But I quote Temple herself as saying, "If I could snap my fingers and be non-autistic, I wouldn't because that's part of who I am."

A couple of weeks ago on the west coast, as I told you, I met an achromatopic woman, a woman born totally colour-blind because she has no cones in her eyes, only rods. This is a woman who has never seen colour, has never perceived colour, and who in a sense can't conceive of colour. There are some other disadvantages here — her visual acuity is not so good and she can be blinded by bright sunlight, but she can deal with that. She said, however, she does not regard the achromatopsia as an impoverishment or a defect. She said, "You may regard it as this; for me, my

visual world is rich, it is beautiful. I see innumerable shades and tones. You may say they're just grey. Grey is not a concept for me, any more than darkness is a concept for the blind or silence for the deaf." She spoke about the landscapes she loved. She does beautiful paintings, both of outer and inner landscapes. She said she is not pining for colour. I said, "Supposing you were offered colour? Supposing we could fix you?" She said, "Well, first I wouldn't know what the offer means, because I have no concept of colour. I hear other people talking about it, and it's sort of funny, as I don't know what they're talking about, although it is very real for them." She said that if colour could be given to her somehow, she thought it might be very disturbing; it would suddenly bring an irrelevant sensation, with no meaning and unassociated with anything else, to a world which was already coherent and complete in itself, and it might be severely confusing.

Sometimes deaf people use the word deaf in two different ways: deaf with a small d stands for medically deaf, auditory impairment, defect; Deaf with a big D means that one is a signer, one signs, one is part of a linguistic minority, one is part of a signing community, one is part of the Deaf tradition and culture with its own language, its own humour, its own perspectives, its own completeness. To the extent that this is so, deaf people may not be interested in hearing-aids, or cochlear implants, because this again would promise or *threaten* to give them something they could make no sense of, which carries no value for them, and which might disturb their world, as colour might disturb the world. So this lady was also saying she is Achromatopic, with a capital A.

WACHTEL I can see why this is where you get accused of romancing physical problems. There have been instances where the hearing parents of deaf children are so tragically wounded by the distance between them that they feel it's going too far, to see the silver lining in the situation.

SACKS It's very complex, or potentially complex, for hearing parents to have a deaf child. It's easier for deaf parents to have a deaf child. Deaf people and deaf children may have two identities, or two kinships. On the one hand there's their biological family, but there's also the family of the signing community, of the Deaf. If someone did hear, and they lost their hearing at the age of twenty, then if a cochlear implant will give them back their hearing, they obviously want it. There's no physiological difficulty, no moral or social difficulty. You're putting them back where they were. But to offer something which is totally new is complex.

WACHTEL There's a rather tragic example in the case of one of your subjects, Virgil, who had lost his sight when he was very young and then had it restored something like forty or forty-five years later.

SACKS Right. And his sight even in the first five years of life was poor and compromised, so he had probably never been a fully sighted person. I got a phone call saying that Virgil had had an operation two weeks before. He saw, and this was wonderful, except that he didn't know what he was seeing, and what the hell was the matter.

I think it was a simplistic notion that, if the operation worked, he would instantly be a sighted man, able to go out into the world as a sighted man; or, it might not work. What happened was neither of these. He was given his sight, but he could make no sense of it. He describes very vividly himself how, when the bandages were taken off twenty-four hours after surgery, there was a blur of colour and movement, out of which a voice came, the voice of his surgeon. He targeted on this. He knew that voices come from faces, therefore this strange, moving blur of colour must be a face. This is a man with no visual concept of a face. He has a tactile concept, but the tactile concept doesn't transfer straight away. Even with simple things, like geometrical figures, squares and triangles, a touched triangle is not the same as a visual triangle. This was a philosophical question right back in the seventeenth century. One saw that Virgil, who was so much at ease and assured in his touch world, was totally bewildered when he was presented with sight. He didn't have a visual world. His brain didn't know how to perceive and how to construct categories. Basic things like size and distance and perspective. He was bewildered by the fact that objects changed their appearance as one

moved. He was bewildered by shadows. So he had very great difficulties dealing with this. I think it was worse because he was unprepared. There should have been some discussion.

WACHTEL There are some old movies where, as soon as they remove the bandages, you can see!

SACKS This is the sort of notion I think we all have, and you have it in the Bible — there were all these miracles where one received sight. There's an interesting complex one where Jesus performed a miracle, and gave a man sight. And the man saw other men as trees walking. I think this a fascinating, enigmatic thing which almost suggests to me that he didn't quite know what he was seeing. Although one doesn't usually look to the Bible for clinical accuracy.

WACHTEL And Virgil's life was really undone by sight?

SACKS I think so. There were other problems. There have been a few cases of people in Virgil's position who have finally made a reasonably successful adaptation to the sighted world, at least in some ways. But there are other people who haven't. There was a famous case published about thirty years ago, where even a year after surgery, with 20/20 vision in a way, and high intelligence, and everything which one would think could adapt, the man could not adapt. He still couldn't recognize faces, was no longer able to work as a mechanic. He'd been an immensely gifted blind mechanic, and now he became a fumbling one. He used to go for bicycle rides with his hand on someone's shoulder, and cross the roads. He was a very audacious, sassy blind man; he became a timid, confusedly sighted man who was afraid to cross the road, and who said, "The gift has become a curse." He became very depressed and committed suicide. I don't want to romance being blind. Just to say that the whole thing is so complex; you have to look at the whole complexion of a life and the economy of a life before you intervene grossly and, as it were, medically, to fix it.

WACHTEL A sense of wonder permeates your writing. Has that wonder diminished in any way?

SACKS No. Sometimes, like everyone, if I have too much to do and don't have enough time, or if I'm forced to do things in particular ways, that oppresses me. But mostly I can get re-astonished, like a child. I was re-astonished when I spoke to the achromatopic woman. She said, "My world is fine." She also told me about an island of achromatopes, in the South Pacific, where this very rare — this is normally one in 100,000 — hereditary condition has become very common through isolation and intermarriage, so that now half the island's population is achromatopic. And I wondered, What's it like, being achromatopic? I thought of Wells' great story, *The Country of the Blind*. How do they dress? What are their buildings like? Their food? What's their art, their language like? Thank God I can still get astonished and pushed into wonder!

WACHTEL You sometimes talk of moments of solitude and regret. I remember reading about a course you were giving on mind and brain, where you decided to call it "Being Alive," because you'd been feeling half-dead and hoped it would encourage you.

SACKS That was back in 1985, '86. I do have my own desolate moments and moods. I think a little bit like Temple, although I don't think I'm autistic — I partly live for my work, or my work is my life. I rather dislike weekends. The vacuity, the abyss, the structurelessness of weekends frightens me somewhat. I'm rather glad when Monday comes along, and I can go to the hospital and see patients, or go to my typewriter.

WACHTEL A friend of yours — a *New Yorker* writer, Lawrence Weschler — has said that your remarkable empathy comes from your own sense of "remove." Does that sound right to you?

SACKS I'm not quite sure what Weschler meant. This again comes back to the recurrent notion of exile or the outsider. When I came to Canada yesterday, I had to show my card, as a resident alien. I never did become a U.S. citizen. This term "resident alien" slightly appeals to me. I think I always have felt something of an outsider, peering in to the human condition, wistfully but sympathetically.

Temple says, "I can really relate to Data." Data is an android in "Star Trek," who lacks empathy circuits and emotional circuits, and has a positronic brain. But he is wistful about organic creatures and human creatures. Last week, when I was on the west coast, I went to the set of "Star Trek" and I met Data. I was childishly thrilled!

I told him he was the hero of autistic people everywhere. I think he didn't know quite how to take that.

There is a remove, which both endlessly distresses and endlessly stimulates me. Sometimes I feel I'm not participating fully in life, that I'm a describer. Or that the detached, describing part of me is always there. Once, when I went with a friend to Japan, he said, "Stop thinking! Just take it in, just relax, just perceive things. You're like some enormous tractor in the Midwest. You're cogitating and churning things over and over in your mind." I think there is an odd sense of both remove and sympathy.

WACHTEL Were you able to stop thinking?

SACKS No.

WACHTEL It doesn't surprise me. As soon as you're told to stop, it's like, "Go in the garden, don't think of pink elephants, and you'll find a treasure." As soon as someone says, Stop thinking, it seems the mind would go into higher gear.

SACKS This may be part of the paradox of the describer — that there may need to be some remove so that things are not taken for granted. I like the anthropologist's term of the participant/observer, and there may be some sort of doubling like this. One also feels there may be a betrayal or treachery there; someone is participating and then they pull out their pen and write it all up.

WACHTEL I was reminded of how you described being in hospital with your injured leg. Your aunt came to visit you and brought Conrad's book, *The Rover*, and said there are two kinds of people: there are rovers and there are settlers. And you're a rover.

SACKS Yes. I think I'm always on the move. I love travel and I love the concept of travel. Also my concept of the mind and the nervous system is that *it* is a traveller. Again, this is in the nature of Edelman's theory, that the mind and the organism must form its own path and travel its own path. I think sometimes there are other precepts, which try to program one and fix one, genetically or culturally or otherwise. But I think all organisms — and especially human organisms — are built for adventure, travel, novelty and risk. That's what the wonder of life is about. And the danger.

WACHTEL I was just nodding along with that enormously affirming statement and then you startled me with the danger. Why danger?

SACKS Because things are not entirely in control, and you never know what's going to be round the next corner or over the next mountain. There's always anticipation, one perhaps tinged with a little apprehension, but I think it's worth it. I love to see the destruction of a theory as much as the creation of a theory. I think theorizing in science constantly builds in this cataclysmic way; it's not entirely a steady development. Einstein wrote a book called *The Evolution of Physics.* The first part is called the rise of the mechanical world view, and then there's the decline of the mechanical view and the rise of the field view. You see that the notion of field didn't evolve from the notion of clockwork. It's completely different.

I think some of the depressions I have, and one has, are sometimes because a world view, or the epistemology or theory, seems to collapse and you suddenly don't have a way of ordering the world. I think you have to wait patiently for a new theory to come along. I don't at all get a feeling of a continuously developing and evolving sense of the world. I think there are exciting discoveries, and then confirmations, and then you find an error and everything falls apart. There's a wonderful example of this with Wittgenstein. He describes how his first philosophy was punctured by a comment. He had this notion of the world as consisting of logical pictures, and then a friend asked him what the logical structure of a gesture was. Wittgenstein couldn't answer, and he said he felt his entire philosophy collapse like a house of cards. Then he was in a sort of darkness, an intellectual and emotional darkness, for seven years, until a new and very different philosophy, and I think one much closer to life, came into being.

February 1994
interview initially prepared in collaboration
with Larry Scanlan

KAZUO ISHIGURO

The Remains of the Day (1989), which won the Booker Prize and was made into a movie with Anthony Hopkins and Emma Thompson, is a virtuoso piece of writing: a perfectly controlled, sustained narrative of an aging butler reflecting on a lifetime of service. Set on an English country estate in the years leading up to World War II, subtly, inexorably, what leaks out is a tale of misplaced allegiance and self-deception. Kazuo Ishiguro has said that what interested him was not so much the quintessential Englishness of the butler; what *The Remains of the Day* really is, he's said, is "a study of the failure of emotion." And truly, this is Ishiguro's theme.

It holds true even in his next novel, *The Unconsoled* (1995), which in many ways is so different from his earlier work. At the most obvious level, it's twice as long as his other books, and it's set in an unnamed European city. Ishiguro's first two novels, *A Pale View of Hills* (1982) and *An Artist of the Floating World* (1986) were rooted in Japan, *The Remains of the Day* in England.

In *The Unconsoled*, the central character is a celebrated pianist of unknown nationality who arrives to give a concert. But the whole book resembles an anxiety dream: Apparent strangers expect things from him, people from his past appear, everything is without context. Time expands — a single evening can take 150 pages. And space contracts — he can travel on a bus for what seems a great distance, visit odd places, and then find himself in a café behind the hotel where he began. It's about missed appointments and missed opportunities, about disappointment and loss. If you recall E.M. Forster's famous dictum, "only connect," the response of *The Unconsoled* would be: "Impossible." In the detachment and disorientation of its hero, it too is about "the failure of emotion," of the inability to live inside feelings.

The Unconsoled proved to be a controversial novel because it asks so much of the reader: to share the anxiety dream of the protagonist, the relentless frustration, and ultimate emptiness. Initially, I found the anxiety so persuasive it was difficult to continue reading. I *worried* about all those missed appointments, those people waiting. But once I got used to the rhythm, and the certainty that things *wouldn't* be resolved, I read on with a kind of urgency. Ishiguro, "an extraordinarily perfect writer" — as he's been called — can only produce a compelling book.

Kazuo Ishiguro was born in Nagasaki in 1954, the son of an oceanographer. The family moved to England when he was five. He started off as a social worker — first in Glasgow and then London. His passion was rock music; in fact, he credits his becoming a writer with his failure as a guitarist and singer. I talked to him when he was in Toronto.

WACHTEL You've set most of your fiction in what appear to be recognizable landscapes — the first two novels mostly in Japan, the third in Britain. But in fact you've said that these settings are not intended to be realistic.

ISHIGURO I think what I was trying to get at was that I was not essentially interested in historical re-creations. My main purpose in writing those books wasn't to explain to readers what a specific point in history was like. I started off with the themes and the ideas and then thought, where could I set this particular story so that the themes and ideas came out most powerfully? Rather than taking contemporary Britain, which is where I was living when I wrote those novels about Japan, I said, why not take a period in Japanese history when things were in turmoil; because I was interested in the specific question, what happens if you give your energies and your idealism to something which turns out to be rather foul? As a novelist you have all these different worlds to choose from. You can look through history, you can location-hunt through history, and pick the place that suits you best. That's what I used to do. But gradually I came to feel a bit uneasy about using history in this way.

WACHTEL So despite the fact you were praised for the authenticity of the books, in fact they operated in a more metaphorical way.

ISHIGURO That's more to do with my motivation. Obviously, as a person of my age — I'm now forty — and someone who grew up in Japan and Britain, I don't have the same relationship to Japan before and after the war or Britain between the wars, as somebody who lived in that time. As a novelist, I was obliged to create an authentic-sounding, authentic-seeming landscape. But that's something that at a technical level, I could do. I went to libraries and just painted it up. It's a very different relationship to, say, someone like Primo Levi, who actually lived through some key moment in modern history and felt a need to communicate it. In many ways I was interested in the metaphorical aspects because naturally I'm interested most in what happens to me and the people I care about in my own life. And these people don't live in 1930s Japan or 1940s Japan; they live in Britain now. That was definitely one of the reasons I wanted to move out of a straight, naturalistic, realistic landscape and emphasize the mythic or the metaphorical aspects of my work.

WACHTEL Just to stay for a moment with landscapes that are literal, you were born in Nagasaki and you spent your first five years in Japan. What do you remember of Nagasaki?

ISHIGURO It's got to the stage where I almost have memories of memories, because when I was seven, eight, it was very important for me to hang on to my memories of Nagasaki, not only because I'd left behind a lot of people I cared about, but also because I grew up in England believing I was about to go back to Japan. It's not that my parents were kidding me; there was always the plan to return to Japan, so I was being brought up to live ultimately in Japan. I was being sent educational material from Japan — every month a parcel would arrive — and so there were things that would build these memories up into much more concrete images.

I had a very real motivation to keep my memories of Japan alive because they seemed relevant. It had to do with where I was headed, not just where I came from. And now it's got to a stage where, I think, I remember what I used to remember. They tend to be quite personal things, ordinary things: standing on the pavement with my grandfather looking at a film poster.

WACHTEL No one can hear the name Nagasaki without thinking of the bomb. At a certain time your mother told you about her experience of being there when the bomb was dropped. Do you remember what your reaction was to that?

ISHIGURO I grew up always knowing and not knowing about the bomb. I can't remember when I first heard the phrase, *genshi bakudan*, which is atomic bomb in Japanese. It's like it was always there, because people referred to, say, a building in Nagasaki and they'd say, that was built after the atomic bomb, or that bridge was there until the atomic bomb. I suppose because I was a young child then, adults wouldn't talk about the people who'd perished, but I knew that there was this thing in Nagasaki that tended to separate the past from the present. And I kind of understood, when I was about seven or eight, what it was. I remember, at my primary school in England, actually finding in an encyclopedia the fact that only two cities had ever been bombed in this way, and I remember feeling a weird sort of pride. I thought, oh, that's interesting, Nagasaki is one of only two places ever to have had this happen. I think that was when I realized that it was peculiar — not every city had an atomic bomb. I can understand that for people who don't come from Nagasaki, when they hear the word "Nagasaki," they immediately think of the atomic bomb. For me, Nagasaki is Japan, and it's the only Japan I ever knew; it's my childhood, my early childhood.

WACHTEL When you came to England, your family settled in Guildford. You've said that there's a surprising amount of similarity between Japanese culture and that of Guildford, England, where you grew up. How so?

ISHIGURO Guildford is a classic home-counties, middle-class English town, particularly in those days, in the early 1960s, when people were very concerned about being respectable. Looking back on it, I think it was a relatively easy transition. Of course there were these huge gulfs in language and customs, but some of the essential things were very similar. Both cultures don't like to be very demonstrative about emotions. There's an obsession with politeness and etiquette. They are both island people, the English and the Japanese; they have that in common. And so it wasn't that difficult. I think the gulf between, say, North America and Japan would be much greater than between Japan and England — certainly with that kind of middle-class, home-counties England.

WACHTEL You seem to have fitted in, adapted, assimilated, done what children do in new countries very readily. I was reading how when you were in your teens, you were great at ping-pong and then you hit an identity crisis. What was that about?

ISHIGURO I wasn't particularly good at a lot of sports. I tend to be a physical coward and I'm always scared of the ball. Cricket is suicidal with that hard ball. I felt drawn to ping-pong because it was the game the Japanese were reasonably good at. That was the start of my trying to discover my Japanese roots. In my early teens I thought: I'm Japanese, I'll get good at ping-pong, and the ball can't hurt me because it's only a little plastic thing. So that was positive, in terms of rediscovering my roots. But I had this problem of how to hold the bat. The Japanese hold it in a penholder grip, which I

discovered to my great cost is not simply genetic. It's a very natural way to hold a ping-pong bat, and one with enormous advantages over the Western grip only if you have the dexterity in your
fingers that comes from eating with chopsticks every day. I realized then, I suppose, that I wasn't a proper Japanese. I kept changing from one grip to the other, from the handshake Western grip
to the penholder grip. And there's a millimetre's difference in the
way you make contact with the ball. So although at one point I
was ranked quite high as a junior in Guildford, my career fell apart
because I couldn't decide whether I was Japanese or English.

WACHTEL It sounds jokey, but did it operate at a deeper level for
you during that time?

ISHIGURO Looking back now, I realize that that was the first time
I was quite keen to be seen as Japanese. Before that, I'd been quite
keen to de-emphasize my difference, except at certain moments
— if the other students thought I was a martial-arts expert in the
playground, I'd let them believe it. But I remember that I was
very keen on the idea that I should be the only person who could
hold the bat in this Japanese way. I think that's the first time I
recall wanting to do things in the Japanese style, rather than in a
way that perhaps came more naturally to me. It wasn't a big thing,
and certainly I didn't analyse it as such at the time, but I can see
that later on, when I first started to write fiction, there was an element of that same thing creeping in. I wanted to write about
Japan, I wanted to use my Japaneseness somehow in my creative
work, and perhaps it was the same impulse.

WACHTEL You didn't realize until you were fifteen or sixteen that
your family wouldn't be going back to Japan. How did that make
you feel?

ISHIGURO When you're a child, between those ages of five and
fifteen, you don't think about these things too much. You think
the world is in the hands of adults; they'll take care of it and it's
not your place to worry. We were always about to go back to
Japan. I suppose at some level I wasn't looking forward to going
back because I had all my friends here, but at some deeper level,
perhaps I was. Once again this is something I appreciate more

now than I did when I was younger. We had never as such
grated to England. We didn't actually land in England in 1960
saying, now this is going to be our home, so let's adopt these
customs; we were just visiting. I grew up in this rather odd way
where inside my home I had these Japanese parents who wanted
to keep Japanese values, and they were bringing me up in the
Japanese way.

My English friends had all these rules about life and the things
that were proper to do and things that were naughty, which they
actually believed to be absolute moral values. To me, because
they were quite different from what my parents said I should and
shouldn't do, they were just things that the English did. I remember that when I went round to my friends' houses, at times I
would pretend that the same things applied in my home as well,
but I knew that they didn't. So I had a certain kind of distance.
To me other people's values were customs. This was in rather stuffy
home-counties England — still very church-going, still rather
anti-child by today's standards — children weren't allowed into
the nicer parts of the house without knocking and so on, and this
was very different from the Japanese approach.

WACHTEL As soon as you talk about distance my ears prick up and
I think about the kinds of books that you've ended up writing
and the sense of detachment that your protagonists feel.

ISHIGURO I've always been aware that a society's mores can be
quite artificial constructs that don't carry over necessarily to a different culture, because that was actually my experience and at a
very personal, crucial level. So I think I perhaps have a heightened
idea of value systems as artificial things constructed by people.

WACHTEL Another thing that you've talked about in terms of
looking back is a recognition of the loss of leaving Japan for good,
leaving your grandparents for good, without being aware of it,
without having been able to say goodbye.

ISHIGURO I think this occurs at a fairly subconscious level for a
child. When you're that age, you don't think about the responsibility of things like saying goodbye. But at some deeper level it
did leave me with a sense of having let my grandparents down,

perhaps some sort of odd guilt. I should point out, my grand-parents were almost like my parents because we lived with them. My father wasn't around much in the earlier part of my life. I only really met my father when I was four because he was travelling a lot in America and in Britain as a scientist. So my grandfather was really like my father figure for the first five years of my life. I remember when we left Japan — the one thing I do remember — is promising that I'd bring a present back, as you do when you go on a little trip. I think I always held that as a kind of concrete thing, that I never went back and fulfilled this promise, that I never took back a little present from England, and I never came home.

In the meantime my grandparents grew old and died. Also that whole Japan that I had remembered seemed to fade away — not just in my head but perhaps in reality too. I didn't go back and become the kind of person I was expected to become. I sometimes think that by leaving Japan, leaving my grandparents, and turning into this odd sort of semi-Englishman, I've somehow let them down, and if they'd known, they might have been dis-appointed. There are all these kinds of feelings.

WACHTEL You were saying when you started to write, you set your books in Japan to draw on that Japaneseness in yourself. With your third novel, *The Remains of the Day*, you look to a very particular part of England and a particular time and place. What attracted you to write this quintessential British novel?

ISHIGURO As usual, my starting point was theme and, in many ways, *The Remains of the Day* is almost a rewrite of my previous book set in Japan, *An Artist of the Floating World*. In both cases you have an aging narrator looking back over a life he initially believes is one that he should be rather pleased about. But it grad-ually comes out that, because of the presence of fascism and that climate during the course of each protagonist's life, they are cru-cially flawed in terms of what they did and how they gave their energies and how they placed their loyalties.

I feel that in my first three novels I was covering this terri-tory. Each time I finished a book I thought, well, I know a little bit more about what I'm interested in in this territory, but it's not quite right yet, there's something I've missed out, or there's something I haven't done quite right. My second book is a kind of a refinement of the first, and *The Remains of the Day* is, for me, the definitive reworking of my second novel. To some extent, I moved it out of Japan because I thought having a Japanese setting was actually restricting the reading of my work. Japan is a rather exotic and alien culture to a lot of people. There certainly was a tendency to read my work and think, oh, it only applies to Japan. If my fictional world had a certain peculiar character to it, people would attribute that to the peculiarity of Japanese society or the Japanese mind or whatever. I felt increasingly uncomfortable about this, not only because I felt it was restricting me artistically, but also because I felt like a bit of a charlatan conveying a Japaneseness to the larger world, and I didn't feel I was qualified to do that. I don't know that much about Japan, you know; I've lived in England most of my life.

WACHTEL But you don't know that much about butlers. In a sense what you've done in each novel is pull off an imaginative feat.

ISHIGURO I felt that it didn't matter so much with butlers. I think it matters much more if you start to misrepresent a whole nation. I thought if you take something like a butler and make a whole world out of it and use the metaphorical implications, that's far more permissible because, apart from a few butlers who might say, no, no, you got this wrong or whatever, most people would receive it as obviously a metaphor. People wouldn't imagine that I'm fascinated *per se* with butlers and you should only read this book if you're interested in butlers. Whereas there was that problem with my Japanese novels. People tended to say, if you're interested in Japanese culture, read these books by Ishiguro, he'll tell you a lot about the Japanese mind. I don't know what the hell the Japanese mind is, but people seem to feel a need to decode Japaneseness. And I felt that that definitely limited the perceived relevance of my earlier work. I thought that moving into an English landscape would actually allow the book to travel into the universal much more easily. To some extent it did, but it was still set very much in a particular time and place.

WACHTEL By setting *The Remains of the Day* in the fifties but flashing back to the England of the thirties, you're tapping into both a modern nostalgia for ye olde England before, as some might say, it was ruined, and also probing a political dimension.

ISHIGURO I think that's an important point. It's not just that I was using the world of butlers, but that I was using a kind of mythic England. To some extent it's the England that's peddled by the tourist industry, the kind of England that is often used by the heritage or the nostalgia industry to sell tablecloths and teacups. It's also an England that people all around the world have in their heads from movies and books. I think if you use the words "an English butler," almost everybody has some kind of image that comes to mind. It's a stereotype, but I think people know that it's a stereotype. And it stands for a certain set of human qualities, this odd refusal to allow spontaneity to enter your persona. I thought I could use this mythical figure and play around with the associations of that stereotype. I was dealing with a mythical England, rather than a real England, and because it was something English, I think it was much more readily understood that that's what I was doing, whereas Japan is still a rather unknown, exotic place, and people can't distinguish between what is straight reporting and what is something that you're creating.

WACHTEL Certainly there are strong parallels, as you've said, between your second and third novels, between Stevens, the butler in *The Remains of the Day*, and Masuji Ono, the protagonist of *An Artist of the Floating World*. Both deal with a misplaced idealism. Why does that theme, that issue of compromised ideals, attract you?

ISHIGURO This probably does come partly out of my being Japanese. If you are German or Japanese, you do ask yourself, if you were just a few years older, if you were born just one generation earlier, what would you have been doing? If you come from the West, you still ask yourself, what would I have done had I lived through a period when everybody around me was caught up in this nationalistic or fascist fervour? Would I have stood against it or would I have gone with the tide? You ask that in an abstract way. I suppose I ask it in an abstract way too, but it's a little less abstract because you're talking about my parents' generation. And all you have to imagine is being just a few years older. If you were born just a few years before, what would you have done?

For me that question tapped into a lot of the things that were happening to me in England. I did grow up in that period of idealism — whether it was phoney idealism I don't know — but I did grow up very much influenced by the sixties and the early seventies, the time of radical politics on the university campuses. And a lot of my friends had this idea that we had to do something useful with our lives. It wasn't good enough just to get a job that would feed you and clothe you; you had to do something useful that would change the world for the better. That's an instinct that I still admire, and I think a lot of people have it, but at the time that was almost a creed of the younger generation.

I was committed to a lot of that: I worked with the homeless and so on. But after a while the picture starts to complicate, and you realize that it's not at all clear. You think you're doing something useful but, when you look at it more closely, you can see all the ways in which you could just as easily be doing harm. Increasingly, people I knew got into this dilemma. Take something like unilateral nuclear disarmament, which was the big thing in the late seventies and early eighties. A lot of people equated that with stopping nuclear war, but it wasn't as simple as it seemed. You're not just campaigning to make the world a safer place; you're saying that this particular strategy is more likely to succeed than another one. Was it better to disarm unilaterally? Or would that actually increase the likelihood of nuclear war? It's the same with working with the homeless or doing social work. You go in saying you're doing good, and then you look at it and it starts to fall apart in your hands.

So I had the experiences of the sixties and seventies, coupled with those thoughts about being Japanese. What would I have done if I'd been born a generation earlier? Would I have had the courage or the perception to stand above the climate of the times? And I thought, well, maybe I would have been like most people. So I chose to look at that period in Japanese history, and I used it to illuminate what was happening to me and my friends in England. In some ways it was an attempt to look back on the things we were doing and see what they might look like in thirty years' time.

WACHTEL So much of your work raises the question: What makes a successful life and what makes a failed life? What is a good life and what is a wasted life? Your characters tend towards some realization, and usually it's the realization of a failed or wasted life. What would you see as a good life?

ISHIGURO That's a very big question. When I was at a formative stage in my life, when I was an undergraduate, I was probably disproportionately influenced, as one is at that age, by people like Plato, who asked this very question at a philosophical level: What is a good life, what is a wasted life? Reading Plato made me realize that it's actually very difficult to know what a good life is. The more you look at that question the harder it becomes. But at the same time I felt that it was important that you didn't just despair, that you didn't go into a philosophical vacuum where you just said, because we can't clearly define a good life, let's just give up. Perhaps these definitions are pointless. I think at some instinctive level we all have an idea of what a satisfying life is, and if what we do falls short of that, I think we get very unhappy. I suppose that's what my early books tend to be about. It's not that these people feel they have failed at a theoretical level. There's a part of them that won't leave them alone, that says, you didn't quite come up to scratch.

As far as my protagonists are concerned, they think a good life is ideally a life that isn't just spent feeding yourself and clothing yourself and reproducing and dying, as animals do. Most human beings aren't like cats and dogs. For some peculiar, eccentric reason, we want to do something more. We want to tell ourselves that we contributed to something good, that we furthered the cause of humanity and left the world a slightly better place than we found it. We all seem to have a big need to do this. So even if we're doing rather trivial little jobs, as most of us are, we're determined to try and find some dimension to it that will allow us to believe that ours, although it's a humble contribution, is nevertheless a contribution to something larger and bigger. If there's a difference between my second novel and my third, I think my second novel did focus very much on this idea of having a useful life at the career level, the idea that what you did in life at that level could actually make the difference between a good life and a wasted one. But I suppose by the time I came to *The Remains of the Day* I thought there was another very important dimension to these things: it's important to actually lead a life that is fulfilling emotionally. If you don't allow yourself to love and be loved, perhaps it doesn't matter what you've contributed. If you don't do that, there's something wasted about your life too. *The Remains of the Day* is about the conflict between somebody wanting to contribute and turning his life into trying to achieve that end, but in this other dimension, the emotional dimension, not allowing himself to feel and love.

WACHTEL I'd like to talk about your new book, *The Unconsoled*. When you finished *The Remains of the Day* you said that you wanted the next book to come out of another side of you, "something more jagged and rough." What was that about?

ISHIGURO I felt with *The Remains of the Day* I had actually come to the end of something. I felt that it was the end of the project I'd started with my first novel in my mid-twenties, and I finished *The Remains of the Day* in my early thirties. And while I was happy enough with that, I felt that I had come as far as I could with that project and I'd become somebody else. The kind of voice that seemed to me correct and authentic when I was in my mid-twenties no longer felt like the right voice for me. I think it's quite an important thing for writers, or indeed, musicians or filmmakers, to keep asking this question: What is the right way to do things at this point? When you've already done two or three novels, there's a great temptation not to build things up from scratch but to take things down off a shelf from what you've done before. You get to a situation and you say, well, we've been here before, let's take method 489 off the shelf and apply it here. But it's very important that the voice that emerges is true to who you happen to be at the time. Although those earlier books are about life being hard to control, there's something about the tone that suggests life is something that is controllable and rather orderly, that you *can* look back and say, ah! that's where I took a wrong turning and that's the path I've come. Whereas by the time I got to my mid-thirties, paradoxically, things were looking more and more complicated to me and more and more chaotic, and issues seemed much more complex than they did to me when I was in my twenties. And this tone no longer seemed right for me. I'm not saying that other writers shouldn't write like that — it just wasn't who I was anymore; I couldn't write with that same voice. I wanted to write a book that contained some of the chaos and confusion that I felt.

WACHTEL I thought maybe you were worried that the very characteristics that *The Remains of the Day* was being praised for — this controlled, tidy, restrained life — were the things that ruined Stevens, so you didn't want to carry on in that way.

ISHIGURO There was that aspect too. I've had this odd relationship to my own style because I never consciously crafted style that much; I just write in a way that I think is the most clear, concise way. But then other people come along and say, oh, this is a very interesting style, it's very restrained and emotionally repressed, isn't it? That's obviously to do with your protagonist, isn't it? And I say, yes, but then I go home and think, Jesus, maybe this is just the way *I* am, maybe it's not Stevens the butler that talks like this, it's me! Sometimes I did worry that, if Stevens, this rather stuffy, emotionally repressed butler, went about writing a novel, he would actually write a book like *The Remains of the Day.* And yes, as you say, there was a fear that the very things I was talking about, the poverty of a life that is too controlled, did start to apply to myself and my writing. That certainly occurred to me.

WACHTEL *The Unconsoled* is set in an unnamed European city and you capture perfectly, I think, the feeling of a dream. It's not necessarily a nightmare but it's an anxiety dream. Why is that what you were after?

ISHIGURO For some years I've been wanting to give this a try. I wanted to tell a story of somebody's life in a new way. It has always seemed to me there are, broadly speaking, two standard ways in which you tell a story of a life: you can go through it chronologically — through childhood to adulthood, like *David Copperfield* — or you could take somebody towards the end of their life and gradually piece together the life through memory and flashback. That's what I did with *The Remains of the Day*. But I always thought, how about another method? Why not have somebody stumble into some kind of landscape: he would bump into people who are versions of himself at various stages in his life; sometimes they are versions of key people in his life, such as his parents and so on; sometimes they are people who are projections of what he fears he might become. So that by the time you get to the end of the book, by meeting this gallery of characters, you've covered his life.

It seemed to me that this is something we do in life anyway to some extent. But we do it in a very peculiar and pronounced way in dreams. I think most people are familiar with the way the dreaming mind tends to appropriate the physical characteristics of people you happened to bump into that day. You can borrow the same impatience that the dreaming mind has with the more superficial details. The dreaming mind is very impatient; it can't be bothered to think up some kind of convoluted reason why you get from this place to another place on the other side of the city. You just open a door in a room and you're there, in the next place. One of the challenges was to find an alternative set of rules that would apply in this rather dreamy world, because I felt it was very important — crucial, in fact — that there be a set of rules, that this world shouldn't be a place where *anything* could happen. It was very important that the reader, after perhaps an inevitable period of having to acclimatize, would settle down into a world where you could feel that there definitely were rules, and that there were still realms of the impossible in this world too. The typical reading experience of this book is that initially you think, oh, what the hell is going on?

WACHTEL What I think is so unusual about this novel, especially compared to your others, is that your main character is not grounded in his world — he just lands in it. In the other books the person grows out of the place, is indigenous to the culture, and here you have him plunked down in this European city. Of course that's part of what you want to do, you want him to be from nowhere and initially appear to suffer from a sort of amnesia. People know things about him and expect things from him that he doesn't know himself.

ISHIGURO He's a very different kind of protagonist from the earlier ones, largely because I wanted to capture this sense of confusion and being out of control. Although the life of Stevens the butler really was out of control, he narrates it from a position of relative control. He's got to a certain point in his life, he's very fixed there, and he has the luxury of being able to look back and assimilate things and try to evaluate the past. *The Unconsoled* is reported as it's happening. It's a kind of a chaos, and to some extent it reflects the way I feel my life is, and most of our lives are at some level. It's a story about a man without a schedule.

WACHTEL He *has* a schedule but he doesn't know what it is.

ISHIGURO Yes, he's got one. Well, somebody seems to have one but they haven't given it to him. He's too embarrassed to admit that he hasn't got it, so he pretends all the time that he knows what his next appointment is. He knows that he's got a busy few days, and that it's very important that he get to his next appointment, but he doesn't know what it is. First of all, he pretends he's got the schedule and he hasn't, but after a while he forgets that he's pretending; he comes to believe that he does know his schedule. This is the way a lot of us are obliged to blunder through life. Most of us are too embarrassed to admit that we don't have a schedule. We occasionally like to look back and say, I'm glad I did that there and, yes, I'm rather pleased I did this here, and, yes, I'm more or less happy about where I ended up. But the reality of it is, circumstances and other people's agendas have pushed in on your own and you have just crashed from one thing to the next. And this is how I felt, so this is what's happening to him.

WACHTEL But there's something much darker going on here too. I understand that you wanted to tell a story in a different way, and you certainly have, and that you wanted it to address the sense of your own life being more chaotic, more out of control. But while the world sometimes seems to take on a surreal dimension and absurd incidents occur — the townspeople eulogize a dead dog, a crudely amputated leg turns out to be wooden — the general sense of the place is dark, people's lives are anguished and genuinely painful, and all the relationships we see are unhappy. Is there something else going on in this world that you're not really addressing when you say, well, it's about a man without a schedule?

ISHIGURO That's right, yes. That's only one dimension to it. The dark side of this story lies slightly further back. For some time, like a lot of people, I've been wondering why people like writers do what they do, because it is a rather odd thing to do, to keep locking yourself up in a room and writing; it's a bit anti-social and a bit weird. Indeed, why do painters and musicians get so obsessed? And all these people, why do they do what they do? I know people who write novel after novel that will never get published. People who are otherwise quite busy somehow still find a couple of hours at the end of the day to write a little bit, even though they have to do a job and look after their children. I suppose I have to admit that I must be one of these people too, because that's what I do.

After a while you start to wonder, what is this all about? I came to a kind of conclusion that what all these people had in common was that they were slightly unbalanced. I don't mean in any crazy way. A lot of them are very able people and they get through life in a very good way. But at some fundamental level, their lives have been built on something that got broken way back — not necessarily a trauma, but something, some equilibrium got lost — in other words, some kind of wound that will never heal was received early on. And this business of locking yourself up in a room and trying to write novels for week after week has to do with mucking about with this wound, it seemed to me. You know at some level you can never heal these things, you can never fix these things, but a lot of this activity is nevertheless about caressing this wound. What you're trying to do is create an imaginary world that you have some control over, that you can reorder, and maybe that's some way of trying to go back, if only in your imagination, to try to fiddle around with some area of experience that you know is broken. The most you can often hope for — because you know that you can't go back and fix these things — is some kind of consolation, some way to caress the wound.

That idea lies at the heart of this book. This character isn't just a man without a schedule. He has always believed that if he became a good enough pianist, if one day he gave the most fantastic concert ever, he would be able to put right something that went wrong many years ago, and then everything will be happy again. I guess during the course of this book he comes to realize that it's too late, he will never be able to put that thing right, it doesn't matter how great a pianist he becomes. But in the meantime he has acquired a lot of prowess and he's taken on board a lot of baggage — other people's expectations of what he can fulfil for them, responsibilities that he feels obliged to discharge.

WACHTEL You say that he's looking for consolation, but of course your book is called *The Unconsoled*.

ISHIGURO I suppose in the end he remains unconsoled. If we take this slightly bleak view that sometimes we can never put right this thing, whatever it is, often even the consolation isn't there. We look for consolation in work, in a career, or in a relationship, but sometimes the very fact that you are obsessed with trying to heal this thing actually stops you getting a lot of the true consolation. I think Ryder ends up emotionally somewhat bound because of this need to fulfil his own personal agenda, and he is rather unable to love.

WACHTEL Do you know what wound you're addressing by locking yourself in a room and writing these bleak books?

ISHIGURO Well, here we're getting quite personal. There is a part of me that remains quite private, and there's a part of me that wants to invent when things start to touch on areas that might come too close to me in a directly autobiographical way. So when it comes to writing a novel, I shy away from tackling that head-on; I invent another wound for my characters. I have some ideas about it. I don't have any kind of trauma in my life, but it probably has something to do with a sense of having left something unfinished, or having led a different sort of life from the one I should have led — that's to say, not growing up in Japan and turning into this Japanese person, but turning into something else. It could be something to do with that, but it isn't necessarily of any interest to anybody else, and that's not the bit that I particularly want to share because that's peculiar only to me.

WACHTEL At the end of the day for most of your protagonists, what they're left with is so much imperfect understanding. Ryder says, "The truth is, the most I can do is to weigh up the evidence available at the time as best I can and forge on." Is that the best that he or any of us can do?

ISHIGURO Well, it probably is, isn't it? You could just go into this despairing posture of saying, oh, life's too difficult, I won't actually commit myself to anything. I think at a certain point you have to take what evidence you have and try and do something with it, and of course that means sometimes you go wrong. Your life might get more messed up or you might contribute to something that's actually not just a waste of time but actually evil. But I do have a lot of sympathy for people who feel that there comes a point when you can't just prevaricate and adopt this posture, you've got to move on. I think in some ways all my characters in my novels say something rather like that: there's nothing you can do other than to just act on the evidence you've got at the time. Of course it's a rather hopeless position, but what else can we do?

June 1995
interview initially prepared in collaboration
with Sandra Rabinovitch

CAROL SHIELDS

In 1993–1994, almost twenty years after her first novel, Carol Shields became an overnight success: *The Stone Diaries* won the Pulitzer Prize, the National Book Critics Circle Award and the Governor General's Award for Fiction; it was short-listed for the Booker Prize; and Shields was named 1994 Author of the Year by the Canadian Booksellers Association. The novel was an international bestseller, catapulting Shields onto the pages of *Entertainment Weekly* as well as *The New York Times*, and to bookstores in Sydney as well as London.

Born in Oak Park, Illinois in 1935, Carol Shields published two volumes of poetry before her first novel, *Small Ceremonies* (1976). *The Stone Diaires* is her twelfth book. When Shields turned fifty, her writing turned a corner. The titles tell all. Before: *Small Ceremonies*, *The Box Garden* (1977), *Happenstance* (1980), *A Fairly Conventional Woman* (1982). After: *Various Miracles* (1985), *Swann* (1987; originally published as *Swann: A Mystery*), *The Orange Fish* (1989). "You get older and braver,"

Shields says. "Braver about what you can say *and* what can be understood."

Her first four novels presented recognizable pictures of middle-class, domestic life. Shields is expert at evoking the feelings and concerns of ordinary people — their ambivalences about their jobs, their families, their mates. Her characters think. They try to be nice. They may discern some uneasiness around the edges of their lives, but they cherish the safety of the familiar. Shields is witty, often ironic, always affectionate, with a delicacy and subtlety of language.

With Shields' collection of short fiction, *Various Miracles*, the lid came off. She began to experiment with different ways to tell stories. She flouted conventions against literary coincidence, building the title story on a series of "miraculous" circumstances, creating an imaginative interweaving of events that lead to a playful "trick" ending. The book's epigraph is Emily Dickinson's "Tell all the truth but tell it slant." Shields bends its meaning a little. In Dickinson's poem, the truth is so brilliant that if we look at it directly we'll be blinded. Shields interprets this obliqueness as an invitation to experiment with a range of narrative approaches — omniscient, direct, fractured. In *The Stone Diaries*, it takes her to a kind of fake biography of a twentieth-century woman, complete with family tree, photographs, letters and lists. It's a remarkable — and moving — construct.

Carol Shields lives in Winnipeg. She's married, has five grown children and a number of grandchildren. I first met her in Vancouver. In late 1987, when *Swann* was published, I elected to edit a special double issue of *Room of One's Own* — the Vancouver feminist quarterly — devoted to Carol Shields. The issue featured a long interview that stretched over several days. The tone of this is quite different from the briefer radio conversations that I came to conduct later (with *The Republic of Love* [1992] and *The Stone Diaries*). For this volume, I undertook to merge all three interviews, to include some of the personal flavour of that earlier, leisurely conversation. Among other things, Carol Shields is a friend and I admire her enormously.

WACHTEL Let's start at the beginning — growing up in Oak Park, Illinois, home of Ernest Hemingway.

SHIELDS When I was there, it was an exceedingly WASP suburb of Chicago. What a place to grow up! Like living in a plastic bag. There were 750 students in my high-school graduating class and we were all white, every one. I always knew something was wrong with it, but I never knew what it was until I went away. What was wrong was that it wasn't enough. It was all very good, it just wasn't enough. Everyone went to church. Almost all Protestant, though there were a few Catholics. That's what I thought a mixed marriage was.

In some ways I feel my childhood was very uneventful. We had a predictable family, the usual aunts and uncles and extended relatives. There was only one death, my grandmother's. But I didn't like her very much and didn't know her very well, so it just happened.

WACHTEL Did you live in a ranch home?

SHIELDS No, in this kind of suburb there were no ranch homes. The houses were built around 1910; in fact, Oak Park is famous for having these lovely Frank Lloyd Wright houses, which I did not live in, but I certainly lived in a house of the period. I lived in a big old white stucco house.

WACHTEL What did your parents do?

SHIELDS My father managed a candy company. He disappeared downtown every day to work. For a long time, I didn't know what he did. My father had three years of university, then had to quit when his father died. My mother was a fourth-grade teacher. She stopped teaching when she had children because she wasn't allowed to continue. Then she went back after the war when there was a teacher shortage and taught until she retired. She had two years of normal school, then teacher's training college; it wasn't a degree. In later life, she was obliged to go back and get her degree. So my parents were semi-educated people.

My mother's parents were born in Sweden — there were eight children, four of them born there. She was at the tail-end, one of twins: Irene and Inez. It's such an exotic name, Inez, I can't imagine where they got it. She never liked it because the Midwestern pronunciation was "Inis."

WACHTEL Did you have any sense of what your parents' expectations of you were? Did they expect you to have a career?

SHIELDS My mother said to us once — very solemnly at the kitchen table — that she had failed Latin in high school. She told us so we would not feel that if we failed anything, it was the end of the world.

They wanted all of us to go to university — my sister and I, as well as my brother. Although I went to college and majored in English, I also got all my teaching qualifications at the same time because they insisted on that. They encouraged my brother to go into engineering, those were the days of engineering, and my sister did primary school teaching. My sister and I each had a degree, but we knew we would get married and have children. The lives of middle-class girls in my era were highly predictable but nevertheless — and this is sort of a Depression thing — we were told that we must "have something to fall back on." No way did anyone ever think of a career.

WACHTEL When you were young, what did you think you were going to be when you grew up?

SHIELDS I was writing even then. I was encouraged by my teachers, and my parents too. They were very excited when I got something in the school paper. But I never thought that I would have anything professionally published. Even though in my high school yearbook I was the one who was going to write the novel, I never believed that for a minute. I'd never met a writer and it just seemed far too difficult a thing to be. It was like wanting to be a movie star. But it seems to me I was always involved with language, right from the beginning. I think it may have had something to do with being short-sighted — this is just a theory. For me, learning to read was the central mystical experience of my early life. Realizing that those symbols meant something and that I could be part of it was like an act of magic.

I was always a book-oriented kid. One of the things that was important to me was story hour at the library which lasted, in our town, up until grade eight. People still told stories for older kids and I almost always went to that. That combination of drama and narrative was something I loved. We had some books at home; we had a set of encyclopedia and so on, but we didn't have a lot. One thing I had was all of my parents' old childhood books, so I read all of Horatio Alger for example. I wish I had those books now.

WACHTEL Do you think Horatio Alger had an influence on you?

SHIELDS No. But I'm certainly drawn to those books and actually — this is how random a reader I was — I even enjoyed those *Dick and Jane* readers. Being a middle-class child, I certainly didn't find them alien — Jane especially, with her little white socks — I understood Jane. Jane was very sturdy, knew her own mind, I always thought. And I loved the way that Dick was good to her, protective of her, so unlike most brothers. Everyone was terribly good to everyone else. There were no bad intentions there at all. It was so nice.

WACHTEL Did that ring true to your own experience?

SHIELDS No, surely not. It was a kind of fairy tale, even though all the middle-class signs that I recognized were there. But this sort of extraordinary goodness is very appealing to children.

I loved fairy tales for a long time. Then overnight, I didn't like them any more and wanted stories, very realistic stories, about kids in school. I remember the first adult books that I read. One of them was *A Tree Grows in Brooklyn*. It was quite a shocking book when it came out. Then I read a book by Edna Ferber. Once I started reading even these not very good adult books, I never read children's books again. It was like a door opening.

WACHTEL Into a more cosmopolitan world?

SHIELDS My own world was probably less safe and ordered than I thought it was. I don't know about my own parents' insecurities. I do know they were both timid people, so that instead of their having expectations for us, the expectations came to a large extent from the school system. Oak Park schools were very wealthy. We were all in classes of about twenty. Until I got to high school, I never had a teacher who was not an unmarried, middle-aged, bosomy woman. They were wonderful women and very caring. It was a kindly system, but limited. Imagine growing up near Chicago, just a few blocks from where James T. Farrell of *Studs Lonigan* had grown up. He was never mentioned in high school. I didn't even know anybody who lived in the city of Chicago. I had no idea what the outside world was like. I suppose I thought that the books I read were the unreal world and mine was the real one, but in fact it was just the opposite.

WACHTEL So you went to high school in Oak Park, and then you went away to college?

SHIELDS Yes, as almost everyone did. It was the next step, I put very little thought into it. I just sent off for all kinds of catalogues, and I chose a school that looked like a "Father Knows Best" college — small, very conservative. You'd have thought I would have wanted a taste of the world. If I have any regrets, it was that I didn't plunge into something more bravely. Why didn't I go to the University of Chicago? I would have loved it. It was a mistake, in a way, for me to go to Hanover College. So much of it was a waste for me. I even belonged to a sorority, and I was bored with that, but I wasn't brave enough to stay out of the system. I think I'm one of those people on whom education was wasted. I was much more interested in falling in love and going to dances, although I did some reading. One lucky thing happened. I went, during my third year, to Exeter University; it was a great surprise, and wonderful to get away from the sorority house. I was in a totally different environment where we were not spoonfed. I remember my advisor at Hanover had given me a sheet to take to my professor in England. It was huge and had little squares in which he was to give me daily grades. When I showed it to my professor in England he looked at it, then tore it into four pieces and threw it away. We were on our own in England. To go to lectures or not. People took their subjects seriously. This was all a revelation to me, that people would sit in the dining hall and talk about Christopher Marlowe. It was wonderful.

WACHTEL You met your husband in England?

SHIELDS Yes, he was from Saskatchewan on a graduate fellow-ship. I met him that year, but I did go back and finish my degree. I had a baby the first year we were married.

WACHTEL I guess at this time you gave up any idea that you were going to be a writer.

SHIELDS Except for one thing. When she first met him, my mother mentioned to my husband Don, "I hope you're going to encourage Carol to keep on writing." Don looked blank. We were engaged to be married, and I had never mentioned to him that I had done any writing. I forgot about it for a while. I was just interested in being in love and having a house — the whole *Ladies' Home Journal* thing. That was all I wanted. I can't believe it now.

My husband remembered this, and after I had my second child, he said, "Why don't you do something? There's a course at the University of Toronto in magazine writing." So I went to that class. I can't remember much about it except that a woman lectured to us once a week — there were about forty of us — and she had a big hat which she never took off. She came in, lectured away, and I remember she said, "When you send in a manuscript you should use a paper clip and not a staple." That's all. Towards the end of the year, she wanted us to actually write something and so I wrote a short story. Then I forgot about it. In the middle of that summer, she phoned and said, "I've sold your story to the CBC." I couldn't believe it. So over the next few years when we were in England — my husband was doing his Ph.D. at Manchester University — about once a year I would stir my stumps and write a short story, and I always sold it — to the CBC, or to the BBC, without too much trouble, which you'd think would have encouraged me. In fact, I was pretty relaxed about it all and instead of doing more, I was having French lessons and taking an interest in politics.

And of course, I kept having more children. Small children are hard work and I can remember being tired a lot, but I can't remember having the kind of frustrations I've read that women with young children can have. I hadn't started really writing so I never felt, at that time, that the kids were keeping me from it.

When I got back to Canada I thought a little about what I would do, but then I had another baby. I belonged to a "Great Books" discussion group. I was involved in my neighbourhood with other young mothers. I always resent the disparaging of coffee clatches because the women in my neighbourhood were enormously supportive of each other, in a very real sense.

Around this time, I was conscious that the women in the fiction I read were nothing like the women I knew. They weren't as intelligent. There was a real gap. And they weren't as kind. I was reading fiction where women were bitches or bubbleheads. I was reading mainly novels and non-fiction. Then I read a review of a book by Philip Larkin. It was such a positive review that I went to the library and got the book. I loved it. I thought, "Good heavens, this man is being honest." It really was a wonderful revelation. I thought, "I'm going to write some poetry." At that time, the CBC had a competition for young writers. I was twenty-nine; thirty was the cut-off. All spring, I had this little baby crawling around, and I wrote seven poems. I worked and worked on these poems. It was the first time in my life that I took my writing seriously. In fact, I mailed them off the day before the deadline, and I can remember coming back from the mailbox and Don saying: "Well, it's nice to have you with us again." I must have been totally absorbed in that. I won the competition. I can remember Robert Weaver phoning and saying: "We're really pleased because none of us has ever heard of you."

WACHTEL And then you tripped over Susanna Moodie. How did that happen?

SHIELDS When we went to Ottawa and my husband joined the University of Ottawa, I realized that I had this free tuition. Being very thrifty about these things, I decided I'd better take advantage of it. I signed up for an M.A. in Canadian Literature. I started in 1969 and there were hardly any mature students in the system. The graduate advisor took me aside and said, "We have not had much success with part-time, married women." I didn't care. A couple of years later, women were coming back in droves and they were having enormous success.

One of our essays was about Susanna Moodie and I decided I would do my term essay on her. Even so, when it came to the thesis, I was going to do P.K. Page because I liked her poetry. I even interviewed her when she was in Ottawa, staying at the Château Laurier. I talked to her about some of her poems and I asked her what one of the poems meant. She said, "Oh, I haven't the faintest idea." At this time I was rather severe about these things, and I thought, "If she doesn't know what it means, why am I going to try to figure it out?" Since then, I've met all sorts of poets who don't understand their writing, and I've written things myself I don't quite understand. I thought, "If I'm going to do this, it had better be an act of love, something I really want to write about." I remembered this essay on Susanna Moodie and I decided I would look at the work we never look at in Canada — all those horrible novels she wrote.

WACHTEL What was it about Susanna Moodie that attracted you?

SHIELDS When I went through all those old novels, there were recurring themes, and the most interesting was the male/female one. Moodie always pays lip service to the supremacy of men, but if you look at her novels, without exception, the men are weak and the women are strong. You get a recurring tableau of the supine male and the woman nursing him back to health. You see this again and again, all the way through; I think it's utterly unconscious.

WACHTEL You've said that you didn't think of yourself as a feminist in those days — the early seventies. How did you become a feminist?

SHIELDS I can remember when I was first married and living in a little apartment in Vancouver. It was the first week of our married life and I was in the kitchen cooking and I thought, "Why am I doing this? We've never discussed it." But it was only a flicker. The process was very gradual. A lot of my experience of what a woman's life could be came from reading fiction, not from reality. Reading Betty Friedan's *The Feminine Mystique* made an enormous difference to me. I went to hear her speak at the University of Ottawa. I didn't have many models of women who were doing much.

I've always been interested in the lives of women and I've never doubted that they have value. But I can't really remember when I became a feminist. I think I'm one of these women in between, too late to be an old-style woman and too early to be a new-style woman. I'm always going to defer to men to a certain extent and I can't get over it. I regret that.

WACHTEL How did you come to start writing your first novel, *Small Ceremonies*?

SHIELDS I was offered the first job of my life. This is when I was still writing my thesis. I became the editorial assistant on a scholarly quarterly for two years, *Canadian Slavonic Papers*. With small children, I did this job at home in my own little work room. The journal was edited at Carleton so I'd go in but most of my work was at home. It was what people call a "jobette." I did that for a couple of years and then I finished my degree [in 1975]. I had all this material left over from my thesis on Susanna Moodie that I couldn't use because it was too conjectural. So I thought I would try to do something with it. And that became *Small Ceremonies*.

WACHTEL But you'd never written a novel?

SHIELDS Oh yes, I had. I had tried to write a novel during the early seventies. I dropped out of the university for one term. It was kind of a literary whodunit. I sent it to a few publishers and they all returned it, but they wrote very nice letters. So I thought I would try again. *Small Ceremonies* went very easily. I wrote two pages a day, every day, and at the end of nine months, I had a novel. And it was published just as I wrote it. It was so easy to do, it was wonderful. It was a very happy time.

WACHTEL When you wrote *Small Ceremonies*, did you know what you wanted to say in your writing?

SHIELDS I wanted to write a novel about a woman that I would recognize, who had a reflective side to her life. I wanted to show a woman who had good friends. And I wanted to use some of the Susanna Moodie material. I had a very strong sense of connection with the past. I wrote about this sense of history in another novel, *Happenstance*; I think it's something that some people have and some don't, like having an ear for music, which I don't have at all. But I do have this other feeling where I connect with historical events. I feel myself a part of them. I'm surprised when I meet people who don't know where things occur on the time line. I'm interested in the connection we have with the past, and particularly with women in the past.

WACHTEL *Small Ceremonies* is about a biographer; do you know what it is about biography that interests you?

SHIELDS I think it's the only story we've got. The only story with a nice firm shape to it is the story of a human life, but so much of it is unknowable. I like fiction because fiction can go where biography can't. It can go where most of it happens, which is inside the head. It's where nine-tenths of your life goes on. So I can see the weaknesses of biography, but I'm very attracted to the shape of it. I love novels that cover very long periods of time so that a person's life can be traced.

One of the interesting things about Susanna Moodie is the silences in her work, the things she doesn't say. You can try to fill in those spaces, but how do you retrieve that? How do you retrieve someone who is dead and try to build up with the nib of your pen a personality who was, in a sense, voiceless about things that mattered?

WACHTEL In filling the gaps, how do you know what's authentic?

SHIELDS I don't know if it's authentic. But I do think that the things she leaves out are the authentic parts of her. And the other parts are not. It's like reading a negative. It's marvellous. And in a way, it's a little bit like the resurrection of Mary in *Swann*. How can you ever know anything about a person who's been so effectively erased from the world?

WACHTEL So you just sent off *Small Ceremonies*?

SHIELDS I sent it to three publishers — McClelland & Stewart, Macmillan and Oberon — the people who'd sent me the nice rejection letters before. They all sent it back and I was fairly discouraged. But we were getting ready to go to France so I was distracted by other things. I thought maybe I could cut it up and make short stories out of it. Ever practical.

WACHTEL Reminds me of my mother making pillow cases out of old sheets.

SHIELDS That's an excellent analogy. Then I went to the bookstore to look for more publishers. I sent it to McGraw-Hill and they eventually accepted it. It was wonderful. The week I turned forty they phoned to say they were going to take the novel, my two professors said they were going to publish my thesis, and we were on our way to France — all in one week.

WACHTEL Did you then think you were going to be a novelist or was this simply a novel you had written?

SHIELDS I thought, "I'm going to be a novelist all my life."

WACHTEL Did you write while you were in France?

SHIELDS I started *The Box Garden* the first or second day we were there. I had a kind of post-partum feeling and I was missing the people in *Small Ceremonies*. I remembered that there was a sister that I'd alluded to a couple of times. I thought maybe I'd start with her. It seemed so easy to flow into it because I already knew the family. Again, it went quite easily — not quite as easily as the first one, but it was also finished in nine months.

I had a lot of doubts about certain things that I did in that novel, even as I was doing them. I should have listened to those doubts. The editor of *Small Ceremonies* had told me that there was not much happening in that novel. I took this as a set of instructions that I should make something happen in my next book. That's why I decided to put police and a pseudo-kidnapping in *The Box Garden*. You can imagine how much I know about these things. I wouldn't do that again.

WACHTEL Your next novel, *Happenstance*, was an apparent shift, a shift in locale to Chicago and to a male point of view.

SHIELDS One of the things that puzzled me about the two books I'd already published was that they were being called "women's books." So I decided to pick up the gauntlet and write something from the male point of view. I wrote it in the third person, though, instead of the first. That book took me a little longer. I had a few problems with it. I started writing in the wrong place. With the other books, I started on page one and worked my way through — exceedingly methodically. With this one I went a certain way and realized that the children were going to be more important so I had to go back and introduce them.

Then I had to do a kind of replating of it when I was finished because I realized I'd made Jack into a kind of buffoon. I don't know how that happened. I wanted him to be a man who was trying to be good in a world in which it's not always easy to be good, and feeling his way, and being occasionally foolish as we all are, but not continually. I felt I was mending — I had this darning needle and I was going through to keep the tone towards him the way I wanted it.

WACHTEL Did you find it difficult to write from a male perspective?

SHIELDS I didn't think it would be. I really do think that men and women are more alike than we admit. I think they speak differently, they use language differently, so I was trying to pay attention to that. Also the withholding of language. I was very interested in friendships between women and friendships between men: What do they mean? What do these silences between men mean? Does this mean that the friendships are superficial? In fact, I never quite resolved that one. I think my position in that book was that no, the friendship was genuine, but there was a lot less shared.

WACHTEL Why did you locate *Happenstance* in Chicago?

SHIELDS I was going to write a short story about this man and set it in Chicago. McGraw-Hill tried very hard to get me to change it to Toronto because they didn't feel that this typified an American family — it was far too gentle. That was ridiculous because I'd grown up in a family which was like that. My father never fired a gun in his whole life.

WACHTEL Then you turned around and wrote a book from the point of view of Brenda, Jack's wife.

SHIELDS People asked me whatever happened to Brenda when she went away, so I wrote *A Fairly Conventional Woman*, which was great fun. I love writing about the fifties and trying to recover the way we thought during those years, and I loved fitting those two novels together. It was like a game. I remember once the editor phoned and said, "Hey, you left out the cheese sandwich they ate at their meeting." So I put in the cheese sandwich. I had also changed her dress size, so I had to fix that. I loved working on all the timing and details. I was also very interested in the way we share memories, how different they are. I wanted to write about two people who were more or less happily married, but who were in fact strangers to each other and always would be, and the value of the strangeness.

But the main thing that I wanted to write about was a woman's discovery that she was an artist and what that does. Nothing had prepared her for this sense of herself. Most reviewers missed that and thought it was about a woman on the brink of an affair. That was the red herring; but a lot of people bought it, and I have to take responsibility for that myself.

WACHTEL There is an uneasiness expressed by a number of your women characters — these are women who are mostly okay but they're not as happy as they think they should be. There's a sense of something missing. Is that a starting point for you?

SHIELDS I suppose it's a universal perception, that kind of existential angst that we all carry around with us like a big lump. I love the Chinese expression, "double happiness." That's what we really want, double happiness, not just single happiness. And we can't get it. A lot of people say I write optimistic and happy books. I'm not always optimistic and certainly not always content, but relative to many people I must be, otherwise I wouldn't be hearing this all the time. You can't live in this century without having a sense of loss somehow.

WACHTEL We were talking about safe and ordered worlds, but there is in your books, *Swann*, for instance, both surface order and safety, and also a glimpse of — horror is probably too strong a word for it — but something dark and chaotic underneath.

SHIELDS I think it's true; it doesn't matter how well insulated you are, you're going to get glimpses of that chaos. They're frightening. It is a kind of angst when you suddenly feel you're alone and powerless and nothing makes sense. It's the opposite of those other equally rare transcendental moments when you suddenly feel everything makes sense and you perceive the pattern of the universe. I think we all get a few of these minutes. I'm very interested in finding language to record them. They are what poets are always trying to write about, what Byron called "the everlasting moment."

WACHTEL Your fiction took a more experimental turn in 1985 with *Various Miracles*. What happened?

SHIELDS I discovered the old storyteller's voice, the omniscient narrator. I'd never tried it before and I wanted to. I thought I would write a book of short stories, because you're not bound to one particular voice. I could tell stories from close up or from far back. I wanted to tell stories from children's points of view. I wanted to do all the narrations. The other thing I realized as I wrote those stories was that I could get a little bit off the ground and let the story find its own way. I decided to let that happen, let it go where it seemed to go, even if it didn't make any naturalistic sense.

WACHTEL You mentioned the idea of numinous moments. Do you think of yourself as spiritual or religious?

SHIELDS I'm not religious. I was brought up in the Methodist Church and for a while I went to the Quaker meeting. I do believe in these moments, though I don't know where that belief comes from. Not from any spiritual centre. I think it comes from the accidental collision of certain events. I think the English language is very poor in its vocabulary to describe mysticism, so a lot of this never gets talked about. Or only clumsily, or by people that we think are only marginally sane. Or it's sometimes discoverable through poetry.

WACHTEL Does it come from a yearning for some kind of connection?

SHIELDS I don't know if it's so much a yearning; I think it's more of a celebration. When you experience one of these moments, it's like a great gift of happiness. Of course, everyone would like the moment to go on and on and on, like an endless orgasm. But it doesn't. It doesn't happen again the next day or the next. You can't order these things into being. You can't say, "Today's the day I'm going to have a transcendent experience."

WACHTEL You've written about the reassurance of domestic life, about couples and families, but I don't think I've ever come across your arguing more persuasively on behalf of love and coupledom than in *The Republic of Love*.

SHIELDS In that novel I was interested in what had happened to the whole idea of the love story, the great seizure of passion, the story we read from the nineteenth century. Something has happened to the love story; it's become a little bit flabby in our century. It's been done to death by pop-song lyrics, greeting-card verse, and the cynicism that's collected along the way. Nevertheless, I still think it's the thing that distinguishes a human life. I think it's what makes us larger than we are, it makes us better than we are. It's everlastingly mysterious.

I wanted *The Republic of Love* to be a book about what love means at the end of our century, what the search for the other means. To show that the love story of serious fiction isn't really in the mortuary drawer, as it were, that it's still happening all around us. This novel gestures all the time towards the nineteenth century and the idea of the romantic story, in which you have a cycle of attachment, a disruption of that attachment and then a reconciliation.

WACHTEL You call your novel *The Republic of Love* because love is democratic. As you say, it's not a kingdom; almost everyone gets a chance to say, "I love you," and to hear those words said to them.

SHIELDS That's always surprised me, thinking about it, because here is this precious commodity, love, this mysterious commodity, nevertheless it is very widely spread; almost everyone gets a chance to experience it, to love, to be loved. Not all these relationships work out, but everyone gets a little bit of it.

WACHTEL This seems to be a republic where people often lose their citizenship.

SHIELDS I do have quite a bit of faith in the endurance of love. We always hear about the divorce statistics, for example; what we never hear about are the endurance statistics, which are also amazingly impressive. If we look at it the other way around, say, fifty per cent of marriages survive, that seems an extraordinary achievement. None of that ever seems to find its way into fiction. It sounds stunningly boring, of course, when you talk about the endurance of love — maybe there's a better phrase — and no one pretends that an enduring love is uninterrupted. I think love has always been disrupted and renewed. But do you remember what the Venerable Bede talks about? — pre-tenth century — it's a wonderful image: that our life is such a little thing, it's like a bird in the darkness suddenly finding a way into the banquet hall and flying through it and looking down at all the banqueters and then flying out the other side. And I always thought how much better it would be if there were two birds flying together.

WACHTEL I want to turn to your latest novel — why did you decide to call it *The Stone Diaries*?

SHIELDS That was a major compromise between me and the publishers. We had a terrible scramble for titles right after the book was finished. My original title is so unmemorable that even I can't recall what it was, but we came up with this. I also liked *The Stone Curtain*, but no one else did.

WACHTEL I'm asking because to me it has quite a lot of resonance because of the stone that works its way through the book, in terms of people's names and quarrying, and it appears everywhere, but diaries...

SHIELDS Yes, *diaries* is problematic because it's much more of an autobiography than a diary, and of course it's an *unwritten* autobiography — she never sits down and writes. This is the autobiography, or diary, that she carries in her head, this construct of one's self that we all carry around with us.

WACHTEL I like the idea that this novel is an unwritten autobiography.

SHIELDS Which is actually written by me, so it's this postmodern box within a box within a box, but the inside box is empty. This is the image I had of it all the way through.

WACHTEL Tell me about her, this autobiographer Daisy Flett Goodwill. It *is* a kind of biographical treatment of her life, which spans most of the twentieth century.

SHIELDS I didn't start out with a full idea of who she was, I started with this tiny little baby, and as the novel went forward, starting with chapter one, chapter two, chapter three — it doesn't always work out so neatly — she grew in my mind and very gradually she became this person.

WACHTEL Did you have the circumstances of her birth in your mind? They're very dramatic.

SHIELDS Oh yes. For years I have collected newspaper accounts of women who were pregnant without knowing they were and then suddenly wham! from stomachache to childbirth. Of course I was also interested in women dying of childbirth and why they did. There are all sorts of reasons but to have a baby in 1905 was almost like entering a lottery; your chances of losing your own life were very great. And I was interested in my mother's generation, not so much my mother's life as the world that she inhabited. I'm told this is something that happens to people at a certain age: we want to go back and feel out the surfaces of our parents' lives.

WACHTEL Let's move forward into the century. You started with 1905, day of birth; you're moving into, as you say, chapter one, chapter two, and you lay the book out that way.

SHIELDS Yes, the writing of the book went well, because I had this structure right away. I was going to lay it out in the usual biographical chapters — childhood, youth, love, marriage, motherhood, and so on, right down to death. Ten chapters. That seemed to make the writing of the novel easier, to have it compartmentalized. But I wanted all the titles to be just slightly askew so that each one reflected not what was in the chapter, which would traditionally have been there, but something quite other. The image I had in my mind was that I was slicing into this life at more or less approximate ten-year intervals and seeing what was there, like a still life in a sense.

WACHTEL You said you didn't know, yourself, who she was when you began. How did you figure it out?

SHIELDS These things are hard to pin down. In many ways, she is like so many women of this century who became, in fact, nothing.

Their lives did not hold many choices. They were this huge army of women, they were mainly voiceless, they were defined by the people around them. And that became the trick of writing this novel, to write a biography of this woman's life, but it's a life from which she herself is absent.

WACHTEL You've worked with this before — the idea of the invisibility of a life. I'm thinking of *Swann*, where there are all these people, this little battalion of researchers and friends and scholars and whatnot, trying to piece together an essentially in-visible woman, Mary Swann. Is it only women's lives that are invisible in this way, that go unrecorded?

SHIELDS I think women's lives much more than men's. You only have to read the obituaries. There you see men defined by their professions or by the organizations they belong to — the Knights of Columbus, or president of an insurance company or something like that — but women's lives are almost always defined by the people around them, wife of, mother of, loving grandmother of, and I think you disappear a lot faster if you don't have any of your own identification tags. Women do these disappearing acts. I'm sure there have been loads of women this century who haven't even had a social security card to remind people of who they were. And you certainly see it in graveyards, you see "Loving Wife," and sometimes not even her name. Men disappear too, of course. I have this impulse to see fiction as a form of redemption, to redeem what otherwise might be lost.

WACHTEL You have said that Daisy's inability to express herself is the true subject of *The Stone Diaries*.

SHIELDS Not only her failure to express herself but her failure to *want* to express herself. It's an absence of wanting. All she does with her life — this is her life's work — is fill in these biographi-cal gaps, which she does through acts of imagination. For exam-ple, you can't imagine your own birth, or you can't *know* your own birth or your own death; but you can imagine it. In the case of my own birth my mother used to talk about it and it used to embarrass me terribly. She would say, "Oh, you just slipped out like a lump of butter." I used to say: "Oh, Mother! Don't say that!"

I know some of the other facts of that day, but the rest you fill in, I suppose, if you think about these things at all. And of course in Daisy's death scene, in her final coma, she is simply imagining the kinds of things that people will say after she is dead, or what will be left over from her life. These little bits and pieces of lists and scraps of conversation form part of her death scene.

WACHTEL Is that why when she dies her last words are "I am not at peace"? Because her existence wasn't "authentic" or "actual"? — I don't really know which word to use.

SHIELDS I see the book in a certain way as the nineteenth-century novel turned upside-down — those novels where the whole book is a search for meaning, and then meaning is discovered. But in this case it's a search for meaning or authenticity and it isn't found. That's the modern part of the book, I suppose.

WACHTEL Although when I finished the book, I didn't feel sad. There is a poignancy, there is pain recounted, but at the same time, paradoxically enough, it feels as if she had a full life.

SHIELDS Yes, I felt exactly the same way, and this is, as you say, a paradox, that in fact she did have most of those strands that we want in our life, but she didn't know it.

WACHTEL Your earlier novel, *The Republic of Love*, was a fairly unabashedly romantic love story in some ways. Love in *The Stone Diaries* is something else, although a number of characters speculate about it. At one point Daisy's husband thinks about his life with Daisy and comes to conclude something like "Love is a word trying to remember another word." What does that mean?

SHIELDS Romantic love, which I would love to think happens to everyone, doesn't happen to Daisy Goodwill. It's another missed connection. She misses it in her first marriage and she misses it in her second.

WACHTEL I think one of the saddest lines in the book is where, near the end of her life, she recalls that no one ever said to her the words "I love you, Daisy." There's something terrible about missing that.

SHIELDS Whether or not Daisy knew real love in her life is in some ways immaterial. What matters is that she didn't know that she knew real love; there was no resonance from it if it did occur. This is how she sees herself, and so this becomes the reality, of course. And what does it mean? When I was writing *The Republic of Love* I asked all my friends about love and their feelings about it, but we were never able to actually pin it down. In terms of vocabulary, love is simply in a basket with a lot of other words which are exaggerations or diminishments of that word.

The Stone Diaries isn't a "feel-good" book the way *The Republic of Love* was. Who's to say why? It's probably because I'm a little older, I've seen a little more, and one does inevitably get a little darker as you get older.

WACHTEL One thing that's very distinctive about this book is the fact that Carol Shields the author is having a lot of fun, "just fooling around," as the narrator says. She talks about a doctor, "whom I'm unable or unwilling to supply with a name." At another point she asks, "Have I told you such-and-such?" What are you doing here?

SHIELDS I'm reminding myself that I'm writing this and Daisy Goodwill isn't, although she is the "I" of the narrator. She looks ironically at her life occasionally, but she's not a particularly ironic woman. And it *was* fun. I have to tell you that, like most writers, I find writing hard work and what I love is *having* written rather than the actual writing. But I loved writing this book. I never wrote anything with greater happiness. It seemed to me it was about something important and it seemed to be going well, and I gave myself permission to do just what you're mentioning, to have a little fun, and to recognize the fact that the novel form — my favourite form, my chosen form — is a lot roomier than I'd ever thought. In fact, you can put anything in it, you can stretch it in any direction you like, and more or less get away with it.

1988, 1992, 1993
*parts of this interview were initially prepared in collaboration
with Sandra Rabinovitch and Peter Kavanagh*

WILLIAM TREVOR

You'd think it would be hard to love a writer who breaks your heart. Yet I bought and gave as presents copy after copy of "Reading Turgenev" (published in *Two Lives*, 1991, and short-listed for the Booker Prize). Whether he's writing a novel or a short story, William Trevor is a marvellous storyteller. "Probably the greatest living writer of short stories in the English language" was Stephen Schiff's assessment in a *New Yorker* profile. Trevor has "layers of sympathy for his characters interlaced with layers of irony about their foolishness." But the overriding feeling in a William Trevor story is regret. There may be wit, but oh, the sadness, the missed opportunity, the circumscribed life, the inability to say what you really mean. Yet Trevor writes so well, with such richness and precision, that the pleasure is all ours.

    William Trevor was born in 1928 in County Cork to Irish Protestant parents — "lace-curtain Irish." His father was a

banker, moving the family from town to town in the south of
Ireland; Trevor went to thirteen different schools as a child.
After Trinity College, Dublin, he worked as a teacher and a
sculptor, and then wrote advertising copy for a London agency.
His early novel, *The Old Boys* (1964), won the Hawthornden
Prize and launched his literary career when he was thirty-six.
The book was adapted for television and radio, with Evelyn
Waugh declaring it "uncommonly well-written, gruesome,
funny and original." And, after twenty-one books, there've
been many other prizes since, including the Whitbread Book
of the Year Award — three times, most recently for *Felicia's
Journey* (1994), which also won the £20,000 *Sunday Express*
award. In tracing the downward despair of a young woman
who leaves her small town in Ireland for England in search of
the man who fathered her child, *Felicia's Journey* illustrates
Trevor's characteristic empathy for women, especially rural
women, and for the victims of the "Troubles." When asked
once if he thought the "well-developed sense of tragedy" in his
work was "informed by the crisis-bound state of Ireland," he
said that more likely it came from childhood.

I met William Trevor when he was in Toronto with his collection of autobiographical pieces, *Excursions in the Real World*
(1993). He was, as reputed, mild, unassuming and charmingly
elusive.

WACHTEL What does it mean to be an Irish writer? Is there particular baggage attached to that label?
TREVOR Not for me. I think of myself as a writer and I think of
myself also as an Irishman. I don't think of myself as an Irish
writer; I don't think there is any such thing.
WACHTEL But you edited an anthology of Irish short stories and
there are bundles of literature that seem to come under the rubric
of "Irish writing."
TREVOR Yes, there are, and I did edit that book. "Irish writer" is
a label which is a very natural one but I think it's fairly meaning-

less. The reason that I edited that book is that I'm meant to know a certain amount about Irish short stories. An English or a Canadian person could have edited it just as well, if not a great deal better.

WACHTEL Is there a national character, though? Are there qualities that are integral to being Irish? I think at one point in the introduction to your memoir, *Excursions in the Real World*, you talk about an Irish sensibility.

TREVOR There are things, I suppose, that make you Irish. But I think that those "Irishisms" don't add up in the end. My wife, for instance, comes of an Irish family but she was born in London, and she seems to me to be much more of an Irish person than I am. I think I have possibly reacted against my Irish background; I'm rather cagey and careful about it.

WACHTEL What does that mean when you say she's more Irish?

TREVOR Well, she has that Irish enthusiasm and — I hate to use the word "blarney" because she might hear me saying it — she has that effervescence which I associate with Irish people and that great friendliness and a natural sense of hospitality, which English people don't have. She also has red hair.

WACHTEL Now we're really getting into cliché. Are there other things that go into the reality of being Irish? Is there something about the geography or the history or the weather that makes the Irish identifiable?

TREVOR I wouldn't think the weather makes all that much difference, but I see what you mean. The history of Ireland certainly is a point around which to identify in some way, and in a sense you are what you were as a child. Childhood is very important. You take in so much as a child, especially physical things, the physical appearance of places — those images never leave your mind and never leave the imagination.

WACHTEL You write novels and you write short stories, and you once said that the novel was an English form and the short story an Irish one. Why is that?

TREVOR What people have said, and I think I have said it myself, is that when the great Victorian novel got going in England,

Ireland wasn't really ready for it. If you can imagine England at that time, it was a peaceful, quiet country, and when war was made it was not on English soil, it was on the Continent somewhere. So people were well-to-do and prosperous, and there was plenty of time for sitting down to write great long novels and there was plenty of time to read them, and to watch cricket and to do all those things they do in England. Ireland was very different. Ireland was a disaffected country. It had a repressed religion. It had a repressed language. At any moment almost anywhere there could be trouble — rebellions, small rebellions. There wasn't that feeling that you need to have for a novel to thrive, that feeling of endless time, of the pleasant afternoons never coming to an end. Ireland was poor and distressed, and what happened there was that the old oral tradition kept going longer than it had in England. I think that's as good an explanation as any other.

There is of course another one, which simply is that there is a flair which Irish people have for doing things in short bursts. If you watch the Irish playing, for instance, rugby football, they're marvellous for five minutes, absolutely beating the hell out of preferably the English, and then they fade and there is nothing left. But that short burst, like doing a hundred metres rather than two miles, is something they are good at. I think this runs through Irish life a great deal. There is this huge enthusiasm, this feeling that you put everything you've got into something, and I think you see that sometimes in Irish fiction. The English are much too cool for that. If you watch the same game and see how the English do it, you'll notice they're more calculated. I think the English write in that same cool way, and of course they have written the greatest novels anyone's ever written, in my view.

That is the other theory, that we can do things in short bursts. I sometimes feel that myself. I have said that my own novels are in fact a series of short stories which are knitted together so that nobody notices. I think there are a few other Irish writers you could say the same thing about. I like, for instance, James Joyce's stories better than anything else he wrote. But the ease with which Jane Austen and George Eliot and Charles Dickens wrote is something which is, I think, tricky for us.

WACHTEL One critic suggested that you escaped the peril of your birth; you were able to work even in the shadow of such impressive predecessors as Yeats, Joyce, Beckett and O'Casey. How intimidating was that peril? Were you even conscious of that shadow of greatness?

TREVOR No, you can't really be conscious of that. It's the very opposite of what all art is about. Art is doing something simply because something isn't there, because there is a vacuum and you want to put something in it. There is no story: you make a story.

WACHTEL You grew up as a member of a Protestant minority in Ireland. Did that put you on the edge of being Irish?

TREVOR Yes, it did. When I used to be asked this question twenty years ago, I'd say, nonsense, it made no difference at all. In fact, looking back to it now, with a greater perspective, I realize it did make an enormous difference because, as a child, as a person, you were outside the pale: you were different from most of the people; you went to a different church; you belonged to a tiny group. That is very similar, in fact, to the position that's occupied by fiction writers, or indeed by any artist: we are all, I believe, outside society because society is our raw material; it's what we work with, it's the territory which we use. In order to see it and to work with it, we've got to be outside it.

WACHTEL Why did you change your mind about the importance of your Protestant background?

TREVOR Because I couldn't see it clearly. I could remember no instances in which people were prejudiced, for instance. I was brought up in County Cork. We were a small, not terribly well-to-do, lace-curtain, Protestant family, and I didn't come across any unpleasantness or pressure of any kind. I went to the nuns as a child; I was very fond of them. The next school I went to was a Methodist school, which I hated. It seems to me it was perhaps because of those experiences that I later said, well, there wasn't really an awful lot of difference. Now I see that there was a difference. It certainly affected my writing. It has *helped* to allow me

to withdraw myself in the way I have to do in order to write —
to be a stranger, which I think is the only way *I* can do it. I'm
only speaking for myself.

WACHTEL You go back to your childhood, at least in the first part
of the essays in *Excursions in the Real World*. Tell me about your
family. What do you remember most clearly from being a child?

TREVOR I was brought up in a little seaside town called Youghal,
in County Cork. I remember, very distinctly, the fishing boats
going out at the beginning of the season and some of them not
coming back. There was a high rate of drowning in those days. I
remember faces of people to this day. But what I remember most
of all and what affected me greatly as a child was my parents' very
unhappy marriage. That was carted around the south of Ireland
from small town to small town when my father got another job
in the bank as his career advanced.

WACHTEL Do you think that's affected the way you write about
marriage now?

TREVOR We're talking now about more than fifty years ago, and
I don't think you would be much of a hand, really, at writing
fiction if you hadn't put that into its place by now. I don't think
it affects the way I write about marriage. I've known so many
other marriages since, and invented quite a lot, and I've had one
myself and all the rest of it. I think it's a bit of luggage which you
carry around, the way when you travel you sometimes have luggage which is not quite necessary but it's there all the same. It's
just a part of the past.

WACHTEL You moved around a great deal as a child, to something
like a dozen different towns. Do you think that added to a sense
of marginality or dislocation?

TREVOR It did add to that dislocation, because what it meant was
that when we arrived in a new town, the friends of the old town
weren't there any more, and especially, I think, my parents would
have had to get to know new people. It's not so bad for children;
children make friends more easily and it doesn't really matter very
much, but I think for my mother in particular it was enormously
upsetting. On the other hand, my father needed the promotion,

he needed the money, so he had to go along with it. I think it did actually add to that business of being marginalized because we were doubly strangers — we were not just Protestants in a Catholic world, we were well outside even the Protestant centre.

WACHTEL You evoke that time vividly in *Excursions in the Real World*, and there's one detail that you toss off that I want to ask you about. You mention being taken to Cork as a child to have your tongue cut, as you say, "to rid me of my incoherent manner of speaking." It sounds like something from another century. What was that?

TREVOR There's a little bit under your tongue which ties it down, and children used to have that cut in order to give the tongue greater flexibility. When I was young I suffered from the awful Irish difficulty with the words "this," "that," "these" and "those" — *dis, dat, dese* and *dose* — and that was put down to the poor formation of my tongue. It was clipped with something that looked like a nail-scissors by a doctor in Cork, and I was given, I remember, two shillings as a reward.

WACHTEL Was it traumatic?

TREVOR No, I don't remember it being so because it was so exciting to get such a huge sum of money, and it didn't really hurt all that much, but it's something I do remember all the same.

WACHTEL In your reminiscences of those early days in your life, and particularly the school days, you write quite fondly of a series of eccentric characters and you reflect on the nature of eccentricity. Was school your first full exposure to the eccentric?

TREVOR I don't think so. Eccentric is probably too strong a word, but there were a lot of interesting people on the streets of these towns, and as a child one would somehow or other get into conversation with such people. At school one saw eccentrics at closer quarters, so they impinged more. That's why they're in that book.

WACHTEL Tell me about Frig Allt and what he taught you. You have this wonderful line where you say, "He died the way he lived: he was somewhere else at the time."

TREVOR Poor old Frig Allt died. He stepped out of the train on the wrong side and ended up on the electric rails. He was a very

forgetful man. He was at the time working on the poetry of
Yeats, which he'd done for a long time. While he was teaching us
French, he used to teach sometimes from outside the classroom.
He would open the windows and teach from the fresh air outside. He liked to behave in an odd manner to see if people
noticed, sometimes because he found his fellow teachers a dreary
lot and wanted to wake them up. He was a very attractive man
with a great big pipe, I remember, and I was very sorry to hear
that he had died. He had his accident when he was quite young,
with his edition of Yeats unfinished. But it has been finished since
and in fact it's very well known.

WACHTEL One thing that comes through strongly in your reflections on childhood and people that you've known in *Excursions
in the Real World* is a love of cinema. Why?

TREVOR That goes back to childhood, and to this day I love the
cinema. It was absolutely marvellous to go and see Clark Gable,
Spencer Tracy, Loretta Young and all the rest of them. Imagine
Hollywood brought to the screen in Skibbereen! Such sophisti-
cation! And such good stories. It was like walking into a kind of
paradise. I still wander into a cinema anywhere in the world and
hope for the best — don't often get it nowadays, but you still
hope for the best and there still can be that great excitement at
the cinema. Although I've written for the theatre, it's never meant
quite the same as the cinema, and I think that has to do with
childhood experiences and the gurgle of excitement you get as a
seven-year-old or an eight-year-old.

WACHTEL You've remarked on a number of occasions that if you
had not left Ireland, you probably wouldn't have written. What
would have prevented you, do you think?

TREVOR I think I'm one of those people who have to lead an
uncozy life. Living in Skibbereen or Enniscorthy, or one of the
small towns, I would have gone on being cozy, which I think is
anathema for the fiction writer. You've got to be edgy, you've got
to be, again, on the outside of things looking in. You quite often
feel — I always do — that I don't belong. I think that's a fiction
writer talking, I don't think it's a person talking.

I've always rejected the dictum that young writers should write about what they know. I think that is nonsense. I think young writers should write about what they don't know, should experiment far more. If you can make something of what you don't know, then you can go on afterwards to combine what you don't know with what you know very well indeed. And writing is like that. Writing is a much messier business than people imagine it is. You've got to create raw material in the first place, and out of the raw material you cut out a short story or a novel, leaving huge areas absolutely unused.

I think it's true to say that if there is the faint beginning of a rule, it is that writers do tend to move about a bit — and not just Irish writers. Irish writers always quote Shaw and Wilde and Joyce and Beckett as people who went away. English writers have done the same thing. Somerset Maugham is an example. So is Graham Greene. Their travelling was a great help to them in their writing.

WACHTEL It seems especially true of Irish writers. You mentioned, I think, Richard Ellman commenting on Oscar Wilde, James Joyce and Samuel Beckett, that they had to leave because they had to "remake themselves in unfamiliar air."

TREVOR I think that's beautifully put and wish I could have said it myself.

WACHTEL You have said you feel more at home in Italy than anywhere else, but then you add, "and not being able to speak Italian helps." What do you mean?

TREVOR It's another way of saying the same thing. It's the fact that if you don't speak the language, you're even more of a stranger, you're more outside. I'm not sure if I would still say that I feel more at home in Italy than anywhere else. I don't feel particularly at home anywhere. I say to myself I feel enormously at home in almost any small Irish town; I imagine it mightn't be permanent, and that there would be a feeling of claustrophobia such as you can only get, I think, as you get older. I think that might very easily happen in Ireland.

WACHTEL Do you feel at home in Devon?

TREVOR I never feel at home in England at all. I *like* not feeling at home. There's no claustrophobia in England because I don't belong there. I don't take part in political arguments in England because I'm a visitor and it would strike me as impolite.

WACHTEL You've been *visiting* there for about thirty years?

TREVOR I have been visiting there for about thirty years and it suits me nicely. It's the same as Joyce felt when he wandered about Europe. It's exactly the same feeling — he had the same thoughts.

WACHTEL You have a lot of empathy for your characters but you seem determined to keep yourself out. You once said, "I don't come into my fiction at all," and as a reader I would agree. Why is that?

TREVOR There are two ways of answering that, and neither of them will be very satisfactory. I think that I do come into fiction in the sense that physically, as a person, the author must come into his fiction because he's the only yardstick he has. I describe someone's pain or someone's happiness: I can only go by what I myself have experienced in terms of pain and happiness. But I have no interest in myself otherwise: I don't want to explore myself on paper. Sitting here talking to you, I am more interested in hearing your answers to my questions than in answering yours. Whether that's a personal thing or whether it's a fiction writer's thing, I simply have no idea.

WACHTEL In a review of your collection of short stories, the American writer Reynolds Price speculates on what he describes as "the writer's primal scene." And this is how he describes yours. He says, you can't open a page of a story, however disparate all the stories are, and not see somewhere "a boy of twelve, say, at the edge of a lush field or patchy lawn in a country far from the world's great noise, his grey eyes fixed in a just and merciless (though not unkind) gaze at a family whose faces are taut with the pain of hiding their most urgent needs and the dread of losing their long-hid yearnings." Do you recognize that?

TREVOR Up to a point, yes. But only up to a point. I would say much more simply that I go after the stories, I find stories like a miner finds a mineral. I don't think it's always a boy with his grey eyes. The analysis of how I do it or what the story is about is of no interest to me whatsoever. All I'm aware of is the fact that I want to tell stories and I've been telling stories for quite a time, and I'm going to go on doing it until I can't any more. I'll find them anywhere. There's a sort of terrier feel about that; it's like a terrier rooting out a rat. That's another way of putting it. Less pleasant than a miner. It's an obsessive thing.

I think all writing is obsessional. Quite often a story begins from something you read in the newspaper, for instance. You read about a fact or a person, and then you begin to think about a total stranger and, say, nine months later you realize there's a story, and you wonder where it came from, and then you can track it back to that point. I think that's of no interest whatsoever to anyone else. It's a technical thing, it's part of storytelling, it's a bit of craftsmanship.

WACHTEL There's so much sadness in your stories.

TREVOR There is a certain amount of sadness. But there's also some happiness in my stories. Sometimes people don't notice it but it's there.

WACHTEL I think, for instance, of the novella "Reading Turgenev." It's beautiful but it's pared down to the essence of sadness.

TREVOR Yes. But that young girl really ends up with quite something, you know. She's not a totally forlorn creature. She has got an awful lot if you think about it, though she made a very foolish marriage. She married a man who wasn't nasty or unpleasant or anything like that; it was just a bad marriage, and somehow or other her whole life opened up and she ends up alone and, people might say, in a horrible situation. I wouldn't describe it like that; I would think that there's enough going on in her head and in her life as she sees it to make her a reasonably happy woman. I don't think of her as an unhappy person at all. The sisters of the man she married are two very unhappy people, but that's another kettle of fish. Mary Louise has been given something. She has the memory of a marvellous experience, which most of us don't have.

WACHTEL Something opens up and then it closes very quickly, and what she's left with is only memory for thirty, forty years.

TREVOR Yes, but who really can say that they have as much as that? She had a lot. Not enough, but a lot.

WACHTEL You were saying earlier about your being the person who's felt the feelings that the characters in some way or other feel because you're the one imagining them. If there is no pain that the characters feel that you haven't felt, is it William Trevor's melancholy that we're finding here?

TREVOR He is a melancholy old bloke, I think. But I haven't experienced all the distress that happens to be in my fiction, or indeed all the happiness that is in my fiction. How could I? The imagination has to begin to work too. Where imagination is really very limited is about things like physical pain. Even to remember your own physical pain as an exercise is a hard thing to do, hard to remember how awful it was when you had a toothache or a nasty cut on your hand, but you have a fairly good idea.

WACHTEL What about this melancholy fellow?

TREVOR Well, I think melancholy is a rather good thing. I think we need to take a second look at a lot of words we use as "bad words." I think guilt is a good thing; I'm not against guilt, I think people should feel guilty. People used to say, especially about twenty years ago, that guilt is insidious, that it destroys people's lives. It needn't destroy people's lives. It can in fact refresh people. It can give them new perspectives. It can make them see themselves. Guilt's not so bad. Melancholy is not so bad. Life is not just all the glossy good things like feeling great. The only useless experience in human life is physical pain because it gives you nothing. Even in the death of someone you're very fond of there can be something. I have a friend at the moment who is dying. I was speaking to his wife just before I came over here, and I could hear in her voice that her coming to terms with the fact that he's dying had calmed her enormously. I don't want him to die: he's a very old and good friend of mine, but he will die shortly, and she knows that, and she doesn't want it to happen, but there is this little compensation of being able to come to terms with the inevitable. That's part of the human spirit. I think this is probably in my fiction quite a lot.

WACHTEL The central character in the novella "My House in Umbria" writes romance novels and she actually gets stuck trying to write a book called *Ceaseless Tears*. I was wondering if this is a little self-mockery.

TREVOR I'm sure it is, yes. I would hope there's a lot of self-mockery in what I write, and certainly I think that Mrs. Delahunty does contain a certain amount of mockery, and not just in that title. *Ceaseless Tears* is the kind of title she'd use anyway.

WACHTEL You do seem to be a great believer in "you make your bed and you lie in it," and in so many of your stories, no matter what you do, that bed is uncomfortable.

TREVOR Yes, it's uncomfortable. I think it's uncomfortable some days or some nights, but it's not uncomfortable all the time. I probably have a certain distaste for the feeling that everything goes along smoothly all the time, that people live happily ever after. That is simply not true. And my business is the truth. I love the truth, I hate lies. One of the odd little things that fiction writers discover is that they can detect lies in real life. It's probably because all the time you're writing, you're saying to yourself, I wonder if this is believable or not, is this really the truth that I'm writing? Somebody tells you some ordinary little white lie, and you're taken aback all of a sudden because instinctively you realize you're being lied to. What's being said wouldn't work on the page.

WACHTEL I was thinking about a couple of stories, "A Friendship" and "Old Flame." Both of these stories are about marriage and adultery, and in both stories the adulterer decides to stay married, not to go off with the other person. I thought, I wonder if William Trevor subtly leans towards the notion that you should stay in the particular bed you've made. Then I thought back to the story "Lovers of Their Time," and in that instance the adulterer leaves the wife and goes off with the lover. Whatever choice you make, things turn out badly.

TREVOR I wouldn't put it like that. I would simply say that with those two stories you mentioned that is what happened on these particular occasions. In the one called "Old Flame," for instance, the couple were so old that wanting to part would have been absolutely ludicrous because the love affair took place about forty years earlier, so keeping together, as they kept together, was the natural thing to do. It wasn't a great gesture of any sort. He behaved rather absurdly in keeping a dead romance going; she forgave him. It's about that absurdity and forgiveness, and being able to live with both. It's about old age offering a kind of clarity, which isn't in the least destructive. It's about compassion in old age, which comes from clarity also.

WACHTEL But he'd had a choice much earlier. I think so many of your characters have that. There's a moment in their lives where they have some sort of choice and then that moment shapes the rest of their lives.

TREVOR Yes. The story, "Old Flame," doesn't tell you very much about the choice. When you read that story, as we see him now, as an old man, there's a feeling that he actually did the right thing because he thinks to himself, I wouldn't have got on with her particularly well. In the other story you mentioned, "A Friendship," in which they stay together, in fact it's not so simple because, although there is adultery in the middle of that story, there's absolutely no reason to suppose that that marriage will stay the way we leave it. It's not about a marriage, it's about a friendship. I think that you as a reader might wonder: Well, is that going to work out? Or is the friendship so much better than the marriage that somewhere or other it will come back and destroy the marriage? I actually would hope it would because I don't think the marriage is happy, and the friendship was a particularly good one.

WACHTEL You write frequently about women, from the perspective of women, about what one critic described as "the well-behaved battleground of female stoicism." What attracts you to the female mind and emotions?

TREVOR That's simply because I'm not a woman myself. If you write out of curiosity, as I do, you really want to find out. And not being a woman, it seems very obvious to me that you would try to get inside a woman's skin, as it were, and do it from a woman's point of view. I know about being a man. When I first wrote, I was in my very early thirties, and I wrote about a gang of people who were in their seventies and eighties. I didn't know what it was like to be old. I had no idea what I was writing about, but I was guessing all the time, and to me that's very exciting. It comes back to what I said earlier concerning writing about what you don't know.

WACHTEL But by now, having written about women for so long and so well, you must feel that you do know them.

TREVOR I would never know them as well as any woman can, but it still won't stop me from going on writing about them. I'm very fond of the company of women. I like talking to women and I like listening to women. Often women's points of view are quite different from men's. I love listening to stories, I love listening to gossip, and women's gossip is good. It's not that I don't like the company of men. I have written quite sympathetically about men too, I think, from a man's point of view — though not nearly as much as I've written about women, from a woman's point of view. I write more about men now, and I write more about children now than I did in the past. I don't write about old people much, just once in awhile, because now I know about being old myself. I would really like to write about three-year-old children, but I don't think I could.

WACHTEL You've written a lot about women who live on farms, women with few opportunities. You return again and again to the farm, the rural setting in Ireland. And the women on these farms live lives of seemingly very quiet desperation. What draws you to them?

TREVOR That background is one that I knew fairly well in Ireland, and something must have registered there, some iota of sympathy when I was very young. Also, I happen to like the remote farmhouse as a setting. I actually come from that particular stock myself. Both my grandparents were small farmers. But I really don't know the answer to your question. I see exactly what you mean and I'm sure there's a better reason for my obsession than the one I give.

WACHTEL The world of Irish maids shows up as well, and it's such a hard place.

TREVOR Yes. A lot of those maids came from small cottages or small farms, and the two things are related. It's that business of being trapped. And also, in a way, it's about wanting to honour those people. I have great respect for them, and I'm aware of that as I write about them.

WACHTEL It's just over thirty years since you made the switch from being a sculptor to being a writer, and you have suggested that it had to do with the growing abstraction of your sculpture, that the people were disappearing. Do you know where the people in the sculpture went and where the people in the stories arrived from?

TREVOR The people in the sculpture presumably went into limbo and waited there for me to change my tack and start to write about them. When I first began to write stories, I wrote fast and I wrote a lot. The stories came one after another, and I think there must have been some little multitude of people whom I had rejected. But more important for me was the fact that I didn't like what I was doing as a sculptor. I'd been a sculptor for sixteen years and to wake up one day and find that you actually don't like the look of what you are doing is a nasty experience. So I just stopped altogether. It happened that I worked in an office in those days and didn't have an awful lot of work to do, but I had a typewriter and so I just began to write. I hadn't written very much before. I've still got some of the sculpture and still don't like it. Everyone makes these false turnings that end up in a cul-de-sac, and that happened to me. I'm sure it's good in the end. Always everything that happens to you is good, I think, in the end.

October 1993
interview initially prepared in collaboration
with Peter Kavanagh

EDWARD SAID

Edward Said is complex. When I try to describe him, I find myself stringing together a number of apparently incompatible labels and phrases. He's a Christian, Palestinian Arab whose father served in the American Army during World War I. An academic who's lived in the United States for the past forty years, he was an outspoken member of the Palestinian National Council from 1977–1991, yet he mistrusts nationalism, criticizes Saddam Hussein and defends Salman Rushdie. Educated at Princeton and Harvard, a professor of comparative literature, Said loves the very novels in which he discerns racism, imperialism and parochialism.

Said's international reputation was established with *Orientalism* (1978), a controversial and disturbing book. In this exploration of the West's attitude to Islam and the East, Said described "a web of racism, cultural stereotypes and dehumanizing ideology." Among other things, Said politicized what had previously passed as simply "comparative literature." The book became the subject of symposia and was translated into fifteen languages.

His 1993 book, *Culture and Imperialism*, is characteristically ambitious and erudite. As one reviewer put it, "Said is one of a handful of great cosmopolitan humanist critics." Said analyses the work of Austen, Thackeray, Dickens, Eliot, Kipling, Conrad and others, and argues that the golden age of the English novel was organically linked to the building of the British Empire, that the justification for imperialism was embedded in the cultural imagination of the West. And Said goes further. He scrutinizes the literature of these former colonies and maps out a history of resistance, and a literature that reflects this. Here, he goes beyond the ground covered in his most famous book, *Orientalism*.

Said continues to combine cultural criticism with political analysis, as evidenced by the two titles he produced in 1996: *Representations of the Intellectual* (originally delivered as part of the BBC's Reith Lectures), and *Peace and Its Discontents: Essays on Palestine in the Middle East Peace Process*. In 1992 he was diagnosed with leukemia, which he says simply spurs him to speak out more. It also prompted him to visit Jerusalem, his birthplace, and to begin a memoir of his life before 1967.

Edward Said spoke to me from his office at Columbia University on February 26, 1993, the day the World Trade Center was bombed.

WACHTEL You've said that your background is a series of displacements and expatriations which can't ever be recuperated, that the sense of being between cultures is the single strongest strand running through your life. I'd like to trace some of these displacements, starting perhaps most logically with where you were born — in Jerusalem, in what was then Palestine. Did you feel between cultures even as a child?

SAID Yes, I did. I was born in Jerusalem, my father was *from* Jerusalem, but he was a rather strange, composite creature. He had lived in the United States before he was married, having come to America in 1911 or 1912 to escape the Ottoman draft. They were going to take him to fight in Bulgaria, I think. He was sixteen or seventeen at the time, so he ran away and came here, to the United States. And then, through inadvertence or wrong information, he got into the American army, which he believed was going to send troops to fight against the Ottomans. In fact, he originally joined the Canadian army, and then didn't stay because he realized they weren't going to send him to the Middle East to fight the Ottomans; he joined the American army and he ended up in France, where he fought and was wounded. He then became a U.S. citizen and around 1919, a year or so after the war, he went back to Palestine and shortly thereafter went into business with his cousin. In the late twenties he established a branch of their business, which was books and office equipment, in Egypt. So actually, when I was born in Jerusalem in 1935, my parents were commuting between Palestine and Egypt. I didn't spend a huge amount of time in Palestine or, for that matter, anywhere really; we were always on the move. We would spend part of the year in Egypt, part of the year in Palestine and another part of the year in Lebanon, where we had a summer house. In addition to the fact that my father had American citizenship, and I was by inheritance therefore American and Palestinian at the same time, I was living in Egypt and I wasn't Egyptian. I, too, was this strange composite, and that is my earliest memory.

WACHTEL You've also talked about being a minority within a minority.

SAID Both my parents were Protestants in Palestine. That really meant that they were separated from the overwhelming majority of Christians, who were of course a minority in an essentially Muslim society. Most Christians in the Middle East — or at least in the Levant — are Greek Orthodox, but my parents were the children of converts from Greek Orthodox. My father became, through his father, an Anglican — an Episcopalian — and my mother became, through her father, a Baptist. It's one of the serendipitous things about the missionaries. When they came to

Palestine and Lebanon and Jordan and Syria in the 1850s, they were tremendously unsuccessful in converting either Muslims or Jews to Christianity, which was what they came to do, and they ended up converting other Christians from the majority into these new sects.

WACHTEL As a child, what did that awareness of being between cultures mean to you?

SAID I'll tell you the honest truth: it was miserable. My strongest continuous memory as a child was one of being a misfit. I was incredibly shy. I was terribly anxious and nervous about my relations with others, since I was sort of envious of their being Muslim/Egyptian, or Muslim/Palestinian, and I always had this sense of not being quite right. In fact my next book is going to be a memoir called *Not Quite Right*. I felt always that I was being made to pay for it in one way or another.

I forgot to add an important component to all of this, which is that I always went to English or French schools, so in addition to my problematic Arab identity, there was this other fact of my education where, by the time I was thirteen or so, I knew everything there was to know about English history, let's say, or French history, and next to nothing about the place I was living in. That was the style of education. So it was a perpetual discomfort. My family compensated for this by creating a cocoon around us. We were unusually different and each of us — my four sisters and I — had different kinds of gifts. And so the result was that we lived in a make-believe world that had no relationship (a) to reality and (b) to the history and actuality of the places we were living in.

WACHTEL I can see why you might be a little bit daunted by some of the company you were keeping. As I understand, when your family fled to Cairo in 1947, you spent a few months at a posh boys' school known as "the Eton of the Middle East," where the other students were people like the future King Hussein of Jordan and the actor Omar Sharif.

SAID At the time of course I didn't know that he was going to become an actor. He was the head boy of the school; he was about four or five years older than I was, and he was rather flashy and daunting in the sense that he used to take it out on smaller kids like myself. Prefects in those schools were actually allowed the privileges of masters. There was a lot of beating, caning. I got caned the first day I was in school for talking in prayers or something equally horrendous. But it was a really mongrel atmosphere with all kinds of people, most of whom we knew only by their last names. Omar Sharif — that's his stage name — was Michel Shahoub, so we called him Shahoub, and I was known as Said. All the masters were English, and they treated us with contempt. It was a continuous war between us and them. It was the last days of the British presence in Egypt and they were the last remnants of this rather scraggly empire by then. So all in all it wasn't very happy, and after I was there a few years I was kicked out.

WACHTEL Why?

SAID The euphemism was "misbehaving," which really meant causing a rumpus in the classroom, endlessly annoying the teachers. My impression, looking back on it now, is that the teachers were shell-shocked veterans of World War II. If they turned their backs on the class, it would be like an enormous war — we were incredibly sadistic — and they'd dissolve in shakes and epileptic fits, that sort of thing. They were British and didn't understand what we were saying in Arabic. An important fact here is that when you arrived at the school you were given what was called a handbook, which had a list of rules, and the first rule was that English was the language of the school and if you were caught speaking Arabic or any other language, you were either caned or given lines or detentions. So we used the language, Arabic, which Muslims spoke, as a kind of assault on the teachers, and they of course didn't understand this. After a few years of that I was thrown out, and my father decided that, although they would have taken me back, my future in the English system was not bright. So I was shipped off to the United States to a disastrously unpleasant puritanical boarding school in New England, where I experienced for the first time the beauty of snow. I'd never seen snow before.

WACHTEL But the school was disastrous?

SAID It was terrible. I should note, by the way, that all along I was very clever at school, and got good grades, so they couldn't completely banish me. At the school I went to in New England — I'd rather not mention the name because it's quite a well-known school — you had to get up at an ungodly hour and do things like milk the cows, and there was a lot of evangelical stuff. I had been so fantastically well-trained in the English system that when I came here, to the United States, it was academically a lark. But the rest of it was quite bad. And there, too, I fell afoul of the system. My impression of it was that I was frowned on for my character or absence of it, something of that sort. So, although at the end of two years I graduated as a senior with the highest average in the school, I still wasn't named either salutatorian or valedictorian. When I tried to inquire, I was told that I didn't meet the moral requirements. And I've never forgiven them that particular infringement on my achievement.

WACHTEL You describe your book, *Culture and Imperialism*, as an exile's book. So you're really a creature whose current interest is very much controlled by the conflict between the culture in which you were born and the culture in which you now live. Do you think that in a sense we should all be intellectual exiles? You seem to see exile as a salutary thing.

SAID I don't know any other condition, to tell you the truth. I'm fifty-seven years old. I went back to Palestine last year, after forty-five years. I took my children and my wife came along, and the four of us trudged bravely around and visited the West Bank and Gaza and all the rest of it, and then we went and saw the house where I was born. And you know, it was patently clear to me that I could never go back. It was nice to be able to visit it after all these years; it wasn't so nice to see what's become of it, from my point of view, because it's irrecoverable in some ways. What must it be like to be completely at home? I don't really know. I suppose it's sour grapes that I now think it's maybe not worth the effort to find out.

WACHTEL Initially, I think you tried to keep literature and politics relatively separate. On one side would be academic study of

English literature and on the other your political concerns. I think you led what you called a "very schizophrenic life." How did you find a way to bridge these interests?

SAID The fact is that all of us live in the world. I suppose it was just a matter of time and the right event. In my case it was during the 1967 War. I'd been this well-behaved academic; I'd done all the right things — gone to college, gone to graduate school, got a Ph.D., got a job, had fellowships, written books — and then in 1967 the world I knew completely fell apart. More of Palestine, or the rest of Palestine, was taken by the Israelis — the West Bank and Gaza — and I suddenly found myself drawn back to the area. I've never taught the literature of the Middle East — I've taught some Arabic books in translation, but basically all my work has been in Western literature. So I started to accommodate myself to the somewhat repressed or suppressed part of my history which was Arab. I did several things: I started to go back to the Middle East more often; I got married in the Middle East to a Middle Eastern woman; and then in 1972–1973 I took a sabbatical year in Beirut, and for the first time in my life undertook a systematic study of Arabic philology and the classics of the Arabic tradition. By that time the Palestinian movement had been involved in a catastrophic clash with the Jordanians. Because a lot of my family lived in Jordan, I had been in Amman visiting relatives in 1970. When I was there I saw some friends of mine from college, Palestinians, who had gone back and joined the movement. It was quite a shock to see them there and realize that they, too, had gotten involved. Gradually, after the movement moved to Beirut — my family lived in Beirut by that time, in the seventies — I got more and more involved in the politics of the Palestinian struggle. That naturally honed my interest in issues of dispossession, exile, the political struggle for human rights, the struggle to express what is inexpressible, and a whole set of things that since that time have moulded my work. My book, *Orientalism*, really came out of that experience.

WACHTEL *Orientalism* is one of your most influential books, and what you do there is look at how the Arab or Eastern world is represented in and by the West. And basically it has been misrepresented.

SAID All representation is misrepresentation of one sort or another, but I argue in *Orientalism* that the interests at work in the representation of the Orient by the West, were those of imperial control and were the prerogatives of power. I tried to show that the invasion of the Orient, beginning with Napoleon at the end of the eighteenth century but continuing as Britain and France spread into the Orient, coloured and indeed shaped the representation. Far from it being objective or scientific, as a lot of the professors of Oriental studies used to say in the nineteenth century, especially the Germans but also the British and French, it was really a function of power and continued control over populations that they were trying to rule.

WACHTEL But the resulting images — the caricatures of the inscrutable Orient, the mysterious East, the evil and terror of the Arab world — why were they necessarily created?

SAID I think ignorance played a big role. There was an hostility that prevented what I would call the normal exchange between cultures. One of the things that is quite amazing is that there is a rather stubborn continuity between European views of Islam in the twelfth century and European views of Islam in the eighteenth, nineteenth and twentieth centuries: they simply don't change. First of all, I argue there's no such thing as Islam, pure and simple; there are many Muslims and different kinds of interpretations of Islam — that was the subject of another book called *Covering Islam*. There's a tendency always to homogenize and to turn the other into something monolithic, partly out of not only ignorance but also fear because the Arab armies came into Europe and were defeated in the fourteenth and fifteenth centuries. So there is that long-standing sense. Then of course they're part of the monotheistic trilogy. Islam is the latest of the two other great monotheistic religions, Judaism and Christianity, and there's a sense in which the closeness to Europe of the Arab and Islamic world is a source of great unease. Nothing is easier for people to deal with something that is different than to portray it as dangerous and threatening and to reduce it ultimately to a few clichés.

That's what's really appalling, that the whole history of this creation of the Orient involves a continuous diminishment, so that now, for example, in the Western press, the things you read about Islam and the Arab world are really horrendously simplified and completely belie the two or three hundred years of close contact between Europeans and to some degree Americans on the one hand and Arabs and Muslims on the other. It's as if they've always been standing on opposite sides of some immense ditch and all they do is throw rotten food at each other.

WACHTEL And that isn't changing?

SAID No, I think it's actually getting worse. At times of crisis, such as during the Gulf War and also on a continual daily basis in the media in America, the clichés are getting less interesting and less forgiving and less "true." They correspond less to any conceivable human reality. Islam in the West is the last acceptable racial and cultural stereotype that you can fling about without any sense of bad manners or trepidation.

WACHTEL Why do you think that is?

SAID There are many reasons for it but I think the main one is that there's no deterrent. No Western, or let's say North American person, knows very much about the Islamic world. It's out there, it's mainly desert, a lot of sheep, camels, people with knives between their teeth, terrorists, et cetera. The cultural heritage, the novels and other books that appear in English, are never paid attention to. There's nothing to prevent people here from saying what they wish. On the other hand, the Arabs and the Muslims haven't really understood the politics of cultural representation in the West. Most of the regimes in the Arab world are basically dictatorial, very unpopular, minority regimes of one sort or another; they're not interested in saying anything about themselves because it would expose them to justified criticism. The myths about America and the West in the Arab world are equally clichéd: all Americans are oversexed and they have large feet and they eat too much. The result is that where there should be a human presence there's a vacuum, and where there should be exchange and dialogue and communication, there's a debased kind of non-exchange.

WACHTEL One of the apparent contradictions or complexities in your own life is that, although you've been a member of the Palestinian government-in-exile and you're a champion of Palestinian liberation, you're uneasy with nationalism.

SAID Nationalism can quite easily degenerate into chauvinism. There's a tendency when you're attacked on all sides — particularly in movements like the Palestinians', where we really don't have too many friends — to fall back into the fold and end up by fraternizing or sisterizing with your kind, and everybody who isn't of your ilk, who doesn't think like you, is an enemy. This is especially the case for Palestinians living in the Arab world. It's completely understandable. There was a time when to be a Palestinian was a great noble thing. But the Arab world is now a much reduced place, and there is poverty, economic and social disintegration, so the Palestinians now enjoy a problematic status, to say the least. And people are tired of the struggle that's gone on for so long. Of course on the West Bank and Gaza, there's been a lot of talk about collaborators and agents, and the secret manipulation of Palestinians by the Israelis. People are understandably suspicious because we're talking about the dangers of loss of life. But in general, nationalist movements actually work on that model; they tend in time to grow smaller and more particular and more homogenous. Look at what's happening in Yugoslavia, where what used to be a multicultural state, a multilingual state, has degenerated into "ethnic cleansing." The same happened in Lebanon, where a pluralistic society, with Christians and Muslims, in the end became a perpetual daily bloodbath of people killing each other "on the identity card," as they used to say in Lebanon. If you were asked for your identity card and if you had the wrong name or the wrong religion, you were shot on the spot or your throat was cut.

I'm afraid that the unpleasant aspects of nationalism are also surfacing in societies like the United States, and maybe in Canada also. You have all these different ethnic communities who are now beginning to feel that the problem is how to preserve, against the depredations of the others, their own identity. Identity politics becomes separatist politics, and people then retreat into their own enclaves. I have this strange, paranoid feeling that *somebody* enjoys this — usually people at the top, who like to manipulate different communities against each other. It was a classic of imperial rule. In India, for example, you got the Sikhs and the Muslims and the Hindus dependent on you and suspicious of their compatriots. That is all part of the process of nationalism. In that respect I find myself very unhappy with it.

WACHTEL I can see that the complexity of things puts you in an awkward or a very acrobatic position, because you have to walk two sides, not only politically but also in terms of your raising issues of multiculturalism and "the literary canon." On the one hand you're an advocate of inclusivity and opening things up, and at the same time you are a defender of the literary canon.

SAID I'm a defender of what I would call good work. The main criterion for me in judging a novel or a poem or a play isn't the identity of the person who wrote it. That's interesting, but it's not the major issue. If that person happens to be of the "right" colour or gender or nationality, that doesn't necessarily mean that it's going to be a very fine work. You've probably heard of this Palestinian woman, Hanan Ashrawi, who was the spokesperson for a PLO delegation. She was a student of mine and she wrote a dissertation under me on the literature of the West Bank under occupation. And one of the things that she discovered in writing this was that being Palestinian and writing about the travail of being under occupation doesn't necessarily produce good poetry or a good novel. That's the point, and it's a very important one to make.

I'm not saying it's not subjective. The determination of what constitutes good work is profoundly subjective. It really has to do, for example, with things like pleasure. I've maintained a long battle with people who talk about objectivity, especially in the media, because obviously everything is based on relatively subjective interpretation. We're really talking about discriminations that you yourself make. In a sense, quality is profoundly subjective — it can't be legislated from above; it can't be that somebody tells you, this is a great book and you'd better believe it, or it is a great book because I say it is. It has to be achieved by a process of investigation and analysis. I think the closest we can come to a rule about great as opposed to not-so-great work, aesthetically speaking, is that great work repays much reading and much rereading and continues to deliver a certain kind of agreeable or pleasurable sensation, whether through enlarged consciousness or enhanced taste and sensibility or whatever, and a lesser work doesn't. We have all had that experience. You read a Danielle Steel novel — and I do, actually — you don't necessarily want to read it again, but if you read a novel by Dickens, you want to return to it.

WACHTEL You quote Walter Benjamin where he said that every document of civilization is also a document of barbarity, and in a way that's what your book *Culture and Imperialism* is about.

SAID Right. A great work doesn't necessarily mean an innocent work, or a work that's completely unaffiliated with anything that we would call sordid. When *Culture and Imperialism* came out in England, there was a tremendous storm of reviews, a lot of them insulted by the notion that somebody as pristine as Jane Austen — whom I talk about at some length in my book — had anything to do with empire and slavery, even though the evidence is not invented by me, it's what she herself talks about. I don't say that Jane Austen is a lesser writer because of that. I just say that almost all works of art, like all human beings, are connected to what is unattractive and barbaric in some instances. It's really particularly noticeable in these canonical works of the nineteenth century in Europe. We're connected to the practices of slavery and empire largely through what they said about them. So I don't think it's a problem to discover that. The question is: once you've discovered it, what do you do? Do you suppress it and say, well, it doesn't really matter, or rather — which is what I'm saying — do you try to hold it in your mind and say, well, that's there too.

WACHTEL You say you don't want to be reductive, but how do you avoid reading literary classics as colonial or imperial propaganda?

SAID I don't read them that way. In the book I said it would be wrong to reduce these classics to a long list of instances of imperialism, or to say that they're all imperial. They're not; they were part of an imperial culture and part of a process which, as the theorists of empire have said, involved not only the most sordid practices but also some of the best aspects of a society. A lot of very brilliant people were involved in empire: great artists, like Delacroix; great writers like Flaubert. Of course the nature of the involvement, the degree of the involvement, is different in each case, and their view is quite different. They're not all the same, that's why there are so many analyses in my books, both in this one and in *Orientalism*. I'm not trying to make the point that they're all imperial, but that they give different views of the imperial world in their work. They elaborate it, they refine it, they ascribe certain kinds of sensations and pleasures to it, in the way that Kipling does, for example, in *Kim*.

WACHTEL You make a very far-reaching claim, though, that the novel and empire-building were inextricably linked, that the novel didn't simply reflect what was going on, but that imperialism and the novel somehow fortified each other.

SAID It is a rather far-reaching claim, but I think it's true.

WACHTEL How does that work?

SAID Well, in the following way. The first English novel of note is *Robinson Crusoe*, and *Robinson Crusoe* is incomprehensible without the imperial quest. He leaves England, he's shipwrecked, he finds himself on an island, and within a matter of days, a couple of hundred pages into the novel, he is the master of everything he surveys. And then you realize that what this island has done for him is allow him to create his own world. In other words, imperialism at that level is associated with a certain kind of creativity. Later, at the end of the nineteenth century, John Seeley said that the central fact of England, the central fact of English culture, of English identity, is expansion. This is not true of every society. My argument is that in the nineteenth and twentieth centuries, England was in a class entirely by itself. The idea is a very strange one: you're sitting in London — let's say you have a little apartment in Hampstead — and you get up in the morning and say, "I control the lives of a hundred people," because if you break down the relationship between the population of England and the population of India, which England controlled for over three hundred years, it really meant that every English person was in control of a hundred or a hundred and fifty people. That fact has to be taken into consideration, *plus* the fact that in no other Western society has there been such unbroken continuity in the imperial tradition as in England, and in the writing of novels. There is no Italian novel before 1860 or 1870. There is no German novel until well after 1870. There is no Spanish novel, with a few exceptions, in the nineteenth century. I'm talking about continuous. The English novel begins formally, according to most literary historians, with people like Defoe in the early eighteenth century, and continues in an unbroken way through the eighteenth, the nineteenth and the twentieth centuries.

WACHTEL But are you seeing causality where there's only synchronicity?

SAID No, I don't say causality, but I say that there's accompaniment. All of the great novelists of the nineteenth century make allusion to the facts of colonial control, such as immigration to places like Australia or America or Africa. The same is true, to a lesser degree, of France. My argument is that the facts of imperial control have an imaginative side to them which is part of the structure of identity. Most novels are really about the creation of a fictional identity, who am I? I am Pip, for example, in *Great Expectations*, or Tom Jones, the foundling. He's found in a bed at the beginning of the novel; at the end of the novel we know who he is. The novel is really a form of acculturation and accommodation, the accommodation of a self to society. Part of this process is that the identity is bound up with imperial reaches. In the case of Jane Austen's *Mansfield Park,* for example, the slave plantation that Sir Thomas Bertram owns in Antigua is used to finance the estate in Mansfield Park, in England. That's the kind of thing I'm talking about, that there's a kind of an imaginative projection in the fiction, in the narrative, that suggests that England is tied up with its overseas colonies in different ways. We're not talking about the same thing over and over again; each novel is slightly different, inflected differently.

WACHTEL Is it too innocent to see it as plot?

SAID It's not innocent at all: it *is* plot. But why that plot and not others, you see? All novels involve choices on the part of the writer, and the fact is that this was a subject ready at hand; it was part of the intellectual, imaginative, emotional property of the English. If you read a German novel, it's a completely different thing. There's no talk about our territories, and we can't go to India; it plays a different function: exoticism or something of that sort. In England it's a place you can go to because we're there, like in *A Passage to India* or *Kim*, or some of Conrad's works. It's literally everywhere. The fact is that the British were nearly everywhere, when you think about it for a minute. By 1918 a small group of European powers were in control of eighty-five per cent of the world. What could be more natural than that possession, which is an historical experience, also becoming part of the imaginative experience? I think it does. I'm saying: it's there, what do you make of it?

WACHTEL What do *you* make of it?

SAID I think you have to see it as part of something bigger than itself. My point is that this experience is part of reading the English novel. I'm not saying it's the most important part but it's an important part. One also has to remember, which most people don't realize, that these places that Jane Austen or Kipling talk about have had a history beyond what is enacted in the novel. In 1814, when *Mansfield Park* was published, Antigua was a plantation colony of England, but most people who read the novel say, oh yes, well, there it is. But the fact is that that experience continues and Antigua is liberated, becomes independent.

There is a whole literature coming out of the Caribbean, written by people such as V.S. Naipaul and George Lamming and a whole school of Caribbean writers who in fact see the imperial experience in its past — as slave colonies — from a completely different perspective than Jane Austen. What I'm saying is that the fullest and most interesting way to read people like Jane Austen or later Kipling, who writes about India, is to see them not only in terms of English novels but also in terms of these other novels which have come out. You can read them contrapuntally, to use the metaphor for music. They're going over the same history but from a different point of view. When you read them that way you get a sense of the interdependence of these normally quarantined literatures. There's nothing more exciting and interesting than that, because it puts you in touch with great writing. It also puts you in touch with the notion of contest, that a lot of culture involves the struggle over territory of one sort, figurative or real. And it puts you in touch with ideas of human liberation, that people don't endure colonialism for a very long time. I'm sure most people who read Jane Austen know very little about what happened to that place that Sir Thomas Bertram went to. She doesn't say very much about it either, because *she* didn't know what happened; it was just a place where you went to pick up the money and come back to England. You go; if there's a slave revolt, as there was in the novel, you fix it and then you come back. To leave it at that is not to have a very accurate sense of what's going on out there. In a certain sense if you just leave it at that, you're perpetuating the bias of that earlier novel. Other great works — such as *The Black Jacobins* of C.L.R. James, for example — could be read against it or with it, if you like.

WACHTEL It seems as if some of the Victorian novelists just took a very utilitarian approach to empire in terms of plot.

SAID Exactly. But the argument that I make at the very opening of *Culture and Imperialism* is that the world has changed now: it's no longer Indians in India, English in England, and travelling around. The fact is that, for example, most of the European countries today are not pure countries made up entirely of white people. There's a very large Indian community in England; there's a very large Muslim and North African community in France, in Germany, Sweden and in Italy and so on, and the world has become largely mixed. Why are these people in France from North Africa? Largely because France was the imperial master, and when these people are running away from depredations they come to France — they're Francophonic, they speak French. The world is a mixed world. My sense of it is that what used to be utilitarian in the nineteenth century is now no longer the case, and there are critics who write in English who are not English. When Conrad wrote *Heart of Darkness*, for example, he assumed — obviously wrongly, but that was the bias of the time and I can't blame him for that — that no African could read what he wrote; he wrote for English people. But the fact is that there are now Africans who read *Heart of Darkness*, and what they see in *Heart of Darkness* is very different from what Conrad's white contemporaries in the 1900s saw, and *their* reading has become a factor in the novel. So the novel opens up in a way that Conrad and Dickens and Jane Austen and others never even dreamed of. This is to be welcomed because it shows you a new side of the work and enables you to see things that you couldn't have seen before.

WACHTEL Why is Conrad one of your favourite writers?

SAID I've always felt a tremendous affinity with him because he was Polish and left Poland at the age of about sixteen, lived for a time in Switzerland and France, learned French, and at the age of twenty or so, began to write and learn English, and lived in England and became a member of the British Merchant Navy, serving on sailing ships for fifteen or so years, and then he settled in England. When he became a writer he was in his forties, I think. He remained a Pole; he was outside the English centre, in a sense, although he wrote a marvellous English. He had this strange sort of exilic consciousness; he was always outside any situation he wrote about, and I feel that affinity with him. His angle on things is completely unlike anyone else's in the period. He was very friendly with people like Henry James and John Galsworthy, and they were wonderful writers too, but they don't provide you with that strange prismatic sense of dislocation and above all, skepticism, especially the skepticism about identity and settled existence that Conrad does. Conrad is one of the few novelists in English to write in a masterful, although in some cases objectionable, way about places like Indonesia, Malaysia, Thailand, Africa and Latin America. He was really an internationalist of the imperial period.

He's a very complex figure, and I don't pretend to suggest that my interest in him is entirely because he shares a roughly similar background. Not at all. He's a great novelist and there is something astonishingly complex and brooding and rich about him that makes me keep wanting to come back to him. Nobody really sees things quite the way that he does. I suppose another affinity is that he writes English like somebody who is not a native-born English speaker, and I find that endlessly fascinating. The syntax is slightly off in Conrad; the adjectival insistence is rather peculiar. There are a number of things like that which on a gut level are very interesting to me.

WACHTEL Another aspect of your far-reaching claim is to say that imperialism more than any other literary theory, Marxism, deconstruction, or the new historicism, is the major determining political horizon *vis-à-vis* literary theory.

SAID The notion of a global setting in literature comes from the imperial experience. People have global empires — the British and the French certainly did — and now, in the twentieth century, the United States has succeeded to the British and French hegemony. Therefore, it would seem to be lacking in seriousness in the study of culture not to take this larger horizon, this framework, into account. All I'm doing is saying there is a connection. I'm not saying that the connection is simple or direct or causal; I'm saying there are lots of interconnections and interlacings — interdependencies, I call them — between the two spheres. Insofar as imperialism had a global reach, has a global reach, then it is the backdrop or the stage setting for the enactment of some of these literary structures, cultural structures and practices.

February 1993
interview initially prepared in collaboration
with Lisa Godfrey

ISABEL ALLENDE

It's more than twenty years since General Augusto Pinochet overthrew the elected government of Salvador Allende, who died during the struggle. It was a military coup that ended a 150-year-old tradition of democracy in Chile. Allende's niece, Isabel Allende, decided to stay on in Chile with her family, because she thought it impossible that the military could stay in power. "We had absolutely no experience in dictatorship," she says, "no experience in repression. I had never heard the word torture applied to an actual situation. I always thought that torture was something that happened in medieval times, in the Inquisition."

But two years after the coup, it was clear that Isabel Allende was in danger, so with her husband and two children, she sought refuge in Venezuela. She was able to continue to work as a journalist and then, when she was almost forty, she started to write fiction. It began as a letter to her grandfather who was almost a hundred and close to death. She reassured him that he'd always be alive in her memories. That letter grew into a five-hundred-page manuscript, *The House of the Spirits* — a saga of three generations of a Latin American family, first published in 1982 and released in English in 1985.

Isabel Allende was hailed as the first woman in the all-male club of Latin American "magic realists." But Allende takes as a compliment any suggestion that her work resembles that of Gabriel García Márquez. She also embraces criticism that her work is a mix of melodrama, politics, feminism and magic realism. "Another 'bad' thing," she says, "is that I'm very sentimental."

Allende is a compelling storyteller. Her books — which include *Of Love and Shadows* (1984/1987), *Eva Luna* (1987/1988) and *The Stories of Eva Luna* (1989/1991) — have sold ten million copies in twenty-seven languages. (*The House of the Spirits* was made into a movie with Meryl Streep, Jeremy Irons, Glenn Close and Vanessa Redgrave.) In 1993, Isabel Allende published her first novel set mostly in the United States, *The Infinite Plan*. Subsequent to this conversation, although clearly she was working on it at the time, Allende produced her first non-fiction book, *Paula* (1995). A moving story about the death of her twenty-eight-year-old daughter, it is also a social history of Chile and an autobiographical account of Allende's eccentric family and of her own experience. *Paula*, too, began as a letter, this time addressed to her daughter.

Isabel Allende lives in northern California. She spoke to me from Washington, D.C.

WACHTEL I'd like to begin with politics. If we look back to the time before the coup in Chile and the death of your uncle, the president, how would you have described yourself politically?
ALLENDE Neutral. Not interested. I come from a very political family, and maybe that's why I didn't like the idea of it and was never involved. I wasn't really interested in spite of all the things that were happening in Chile at the time of Allende. I did not participate in his government. After the military coup — that is,

forty-eight hours later when the curfew lifted — I realized what was going on in the country, and that no one could remain neutral at that point. I think that many people in the same situation experienced that sudden awareness.

WACHTEL Growing up in an upper middle-class family, was it surprising to be identified as a socialist?

ALLENDE Yes. I lived in a neighbourhood where the socialist was probably me, although I wasn't a socialist in the sense that I did not belong to the party. But I voted for Allende, I was related to him and I sympathized with his government. And later I opposed the dictatorship openly. I experienced a lot of hostility and so did my family. So eventually I had to leave.

WACHTEL You've talked about how your life was divided in two: before and after the coup. Can you tell me how it affected you?

ALLENDE I think that before I was in a state of innocence. I thought that life was great, that it was like a game, that you were always playing roles and having fun; and I was a playful person. After the coup I realized that there was a dimension of violence and brutality always present in our lives, in everybody's life. Sometimes that violence has one face, sometimes it has another face, but it's always there, and you have to deal with it sooner or later. Only a handful of very privileged and lucky people can go through life without ever experiencing it, without being aware of it. And that violence has many forms: it begins with poverty and injustice and inequality, but it can also have the face of the military coup — war, rape and crime of all sorts.

WACHTEL I know what you mean when you say that only a lucky few can get through life without actually having to confront that reality. I would say in Canada most people still live in that kind of innocence. What does it mean to have to reckon with violence like that?

ALLENDE I think that first of all you have to admit that this violence is perpetrated by human beings, and I'm one of them, so that possibility is also inside me. I'm no different. Given the circumstances, given the right excuse, I can behave as brutally as any of them.

WACHTEL Do you really believe that?

ALLENDE Yes, I do believe that, and I have that awareness in my heart, so I'm always watching myself, asking myself, what is my motivation, why am I doing this, and trying to be very clear about who I am and why I am here, because I know that this dimension of evil and violence is present in every human being. Even the most civilized, given the circumstances, behave like the Germans did in Germany and like the most pacific Chileans behaved in Chile. I'm always scared of that part of myself, and because I know that it is present in me, I know that it is present in everyone. It's something that I fight against not only as an individual, but in the community.

WACHTEL Have you thought about going back to Chile?

ALLENDE I do go back every year but I don't live there because I married an American and we have a life in California. Life is so ironic. I was waiting for democracy to return to my country so I could go back with my family, and by the time I could return, I had a life here.

WACHTEL Does this mean you feel split, divided?

ALLENDE I have lived most of my life in foreign places. I'm used to never fitting in and being marginal, a foreigner. When I was a child, my parents were diplomats, so I grew up saying goodbye to places and people. Finally, when I was fifteen, I was sent back to my grandfather's house because there was violence in Lebanon at the time; the Marines disembarked in 1958, and my parents thought that I would be safer in my grandfather's house in Chile. I remember that when I arrived there, I said, I'm never going to travel again; I'm going to stay here forever. Then in 1973, we had the military coup and in '75 I left. I have never gone back to live there. And I have never belonged in any other place, because in Venezuela, although I lived there for fifteen years, I never really belonged. Now I feel very much a foreigner in the United States. I'm used to it.

WACHTEL Why did you never feel at home in Venezuela?

ALLENDE Because I was looking south. I was always expecting the soldiers to go back to their barracks and call elections and that

I would go back. I never thought that I had immigrated to Venezuela; I felt that I was an exile, and when the circumstances changed in my country, I would go back.

WACHTEL It's interesting the way you say you've spent your life saying goodbye to places rather than hello. Is that true of living in America now? Or does marrying an American mean that you are saying hello to the country?

ALLENDE Yes, in a way I am, because this is the first time that I came to a place by my own choice. I was on a hectic lecturing tour, like the one I'm on right now, and I met a man who had read my second novel. We just locked in and I stayed with him. I moved into his house. I didn't know the rules at the time: I didn't know that you are supposed to date eight times before you touch. I didn't know that you never mention the word "commitment" and you never move into somebody's house without his permission. But as I didn't know the rules, I did all the wrong things and I ended up marrying him.

WACHTEL Do you feel any discomfort living in a country which in some way was responsible for the overthrow and death of your uncle?

ALLENDE On the contrary. I feel that I have had a wonderful platform to speak from that I did not have before. I could have yelled my ideas in Venezuela and no one would have heard them. Here I'm in a privileged situation. I go to universities, I talk to the press, I very often meet my readers; and I have an opportunity to tell them who we are, what happened in our country. I feel I'm like a bridge between these two cultures. I have one foot in Latin America and one foot here. I can speak both languages. I can understand both cultures. I have been travelling all my life. So I'm a privileged witness to what happened in my country and a privileged spokesperson because I can do a lot here.

WACHTEL You're living in California and your most recent novel, *The Infinite Plan*, is described as your first novel set in America. Is California really America?

ALLENDE That's a very good question. If you go to the Midwest or to New York you might ask the same question. This is such a huge country and there is so much diversity that it's very difficult to say what the United States really is. All the races of the planet live here, you can hear all the languages, smell the smells of all the foods, hear all the sounds of all the music. It's an amazing place! California is the west of the west: you can't go further without falling into the Pacific Ocean. People tend to go west when they're running away from bad memories or running after some crazy utopia. So it's a place of weirdos and lunatics and poets and rebels and great ideas and sunshine. It's a wonderful place, and it's part of the United States. When I moved to the United States six years ago, my publishers were horrified. What was I going to write about now? No more magic realism, no more women with green hair. I said, what are you talking about? I'm moving to California. The truth is that I've never been in a stranger place.

WACHTEL   Given the themes that dominate your work, I was struck by a line in *The Infinite Plan* which describes California as a place where, even today, every possible formula for avoiding the anguish of life proliferates. That does seem like a different locale from the one that you were accustomed to writing about.

ALLENDE   Yes. But that's just an illusion. You cannot avoid pain. You cannot avoid the risk of life. People think they can, and in California people think that they can be forever young, forever beautiful, forever thin: no cholesterol, no fat; organic chicken. The truth is that life's not like that at all. Sooner or later you have to face those taboo words — death, pain, old age, violence, defeat — those are unavoidably part of life.

WACHTEL   You've said that in your first novel, *The House of the Spirits*, you overcame hatred and a sense of nostalgia; and in your second, *Of Love and Shadows*, you overcame anger. What was the underlying emotion that you were working through in *The Infinite Plan*?

ALLENDE   Curiosity; and love, I suppose. I would have never written this book without coming to the United States and I came here because I fell in love with a man. I was in awe of everything I saw at the beginning — and I still am. I thought, how can people take these crazy things for granted? By trying to understand the place where I was, I felt the need to write about it because that's my way of feeling it inside me. The only way that I can exorcise the demons and welcome the angels and explore myself is through writing.

WACHTEL Next to love, destiny seems to be the strongest force in your writing and in your life.

ALLENDE I do believe in fate. I think that you are born with marked cards. Why are you born in this place or that, from this race or that one? Why are you born healthy or sick? Why are you born a man or a woman? All those things determine your biography. There are changes that you can make, right or wrong decisions that you can make, roads that you take, but ultimately, there is a lot that is given to you, and that's fate, destiny.

I feel that much of my life has been determined by events that I cannot control. Let's take the military coup, for example, or the fact that my parents divorced and my mother married a diplomat, things that determined certain very important aspects of my personality and my life — and my children's lives, for that matter. What could I do in those circumstances? Not very much. I had few choices. So when I write and when I live my own life, I try to feel that sense of destiny in my gut; I want to know what my belly is telling me. I very often take decisions guided by instinct, more than reason or logic or common sense. I trust my instinct because I think there is a way that my instinct or my dreams or my unconscious tune into that part of me that is destiny. I know it sounds very South American, but if that could be explained with technical words, you would be impressed. As soon as I met my husband, I trusted my instinct and I thought, well, I have nothing to lose; I'm forty-five, if it doesn't work I can only go back; I like this guy and I think that he's part of my destiny. So I just moved into his house.

WACHTEL You have this great line, which is, "If something's not true at this moment, it may be tomorrow."

ALLENDE Yes. And it has happened in my life. It happens all the time. I'm very careful with my own words and with my writing because I feel that if I say the wrong thing, it will probably happen. Not that I can make things happen, but if I'm saying it, it's because in a way, unconsciously, I know about it. Sometimes — and right now I'm living in one of those moments — something happens and my reaction is very passionate, and I do something that everybody thinks is crazy, and I know inside my heart that it's crazy now, but in two, three or four years I will look back and say, well, this is why I did it. When I moved in with this man, I knew inside myself all the time that it was the right decision.

Let me give you another example. When I wrote my collection of short stories, I wrote about a little girl who's trapped in the mud. That really happened. In 1985 there was an eruption of a volcano in Colombia, a mud slide that covered a whole village, and a little girl called Omaíra Sanchez was trapped in the mud for four days until she died. We could see her on our television screens because television crews from all over the world went there, but they couldn't fly in a pump to pump out the water and save the girl. At the time I saw this little girl's face on my TV, I didn't know why I had an immediate connection with her. I could never forget her. I followed every step of her agony until she died. I had a photograph of her on my desk for years, and she haunted me. I was always asking Omaíra: What's the message? What do you want to tell me? What is it? Why are you so important in my life? When I wrote *The Stories of Eva Luna*, I decided to exorcise that terrible ghost by writing "And of Clay Are We Created." I could not get her out of my heart. I still didn't know why I had written it and why I was haunted by the girl.

Last year, my daughter fell into a coma — she was in coma for a year — and she eventually died in my arms. Then I realized why I had been so impressed by this girl. I was being prepared for what was coming. My daughter, like Omaíra Sanchez, was trapped in a body, trapped there in a long agony, and I witnessed her agony and her death. Omaíra taught me about love and about patience and courage and the dignity of death. In December 1992, when my daughter died, I realized why Omaíra had been so important. Now I know what the message was. So I trust my instinct.

WACHTEL In your novel *The Infinite Plan*, mothers play a key role in a number of different settings: real mothers and adopted mothers and mothers who abandon their children. How important is the mother to this story?

ALLENDE I suppose that she is as important as my mother is in my own life. The longest relationship and the most important in all my life is my relationship with my mother. When I became a mother, everything changed for me for ever. I can never think of myself in terms of an individual. I am part of a group and the group is my children and I, and now my grandchildren and I. I think that's why mothers are so important in my writing.

WACHTEL You and your mother seem to have an unusual relationship, even when it comes to your writing. Can you say what role your mother plays in the life of Isabel Allende the novelist?

ALLENDE Well, first of all, I write a letter to my mother every morning and she writes back. In this uninterrupted correspondence, somehow we register life. I feel that if I have not written it to my mother, it has not happened. So even now when I'm on a tour, I write on planes, in hotels, because if I don't, I would forget that I ever lived that experience. On the other hand, when I finish a book, when I think I'm finished a book, I send it to my mother because she's my only editor. I send it by courier to Chile; she reads the book, takes a red pencil, gets on the first plane and comes to California. Then we lock ourselves in the dining room and fight. We fight for a month at least. By the time she leaves, of the six hundred original pages I had, I have, say, fifteen left. So I have to write the book again, with all her insights. I don't do everything she says, but she helps me in very important things: with language — the fact that I'm writing in Spanish when I'm living in English has made my vocabulary really weak at this point, and she helps me with that. She also helps me because she has an eye for clichés. She has a sense of irony and a good sense of humour. And she's always pushing me deeper and deeper. She wants to know more about the characters; she likes complex characters. Nothing in black and white: she wants all the shades of grey. It's great to have her because as I write in Spanish, I can't have an editor in this country. Editing as it's done in the United States is unknown in Spanish publishing houses. They accept or reject your book, but no one will say, look, add a sex scene on page forty. They don't interfere with the writing.

WACHTEL How does your mother relate to this American novel?

ALLENDE She thought that I was crazy. She said, imagine if an American comes to Chile, lives here a few years and writes a book about Chile. We would hate him. How can you be so arrogant, to write a book about the United States when you've just arrived! And I said, Mom, that's the difference between Chile and the United States: they're more flexible here.

WACHTEL What happens if you disagree with your mother's view of something?

ALLENDE It depends. Sometimes we disagree because I'm just being stubborn, but inside my soul I know that she's right. My mother, for example, reads a story and says, I like this story, it's not bad, but this is a shitty ending. And I know that she's right. She can't tell me why she doesn't like the ending, but I know that that's something I have to work on, and so I do it. Then there are a lot of other things I know she objects to. For example, if I write ironically about the pope, I know she will object to it. I don't even pay attention to that. I don't even show her the sex scenes because she will object to them as well.

WACHTEL Your stories are often about great passion, strong women and great sexual desire. What attracts you to that?

ALLENDE As I understand sex, it's the ultimate, the most perfect form of communication. When you really love someone, and it is very special because you can only do it with your partner, with a man — or with a woman if you're lesbian — but you don't have that kind of communication with your children, with your mother, with your friends. It's only with that person whom you allow into the inner circle of your own soul. Sex is an expression of that. That's why I like it. I try to create the feeling or the atmosphere of eroticism, but I don't go into many details. When I write about violence I do the same. I try to create the sense of terror, of horror, but I don't go into details. I'm a real expert in torture; I can describe anything you want, but I don't in my books. It's more effective if you don't, if you let the imagination of the reader write the other half.

WACHTEL Not only in this novel, but in all your books, you tell marvellous stories. It didn't surprise me that the idea of Scheherazade and *The Thousand and One Nights* would strike a chord with you. What do you see as the role of the storyteller?

ALLENDE I think that the storyteller is a story hunter. She doesn't make up stories. She goes around asking people about their lives. By repeating the stories, their lives, you end up tapping into the collective dreams, the collective fears. Why is it that humankind has this need for stories? People sometimes ask me: do you think that books will exist in the next millennium? And I say: maybe the form won't, maybe we'll have other things instead of books, but stories will be with us forever because they're part of our soul. I think that the role of the storyteller is just repeating the story so the people who hear it can find some particles of truth that will illuminate their own lives.

WACHTEL You've described yourself as an old-fashioned storyteller. You've talked about how you've tried to be modern and understated, but that you need people to be raped and beheaded. Why is that?

ALLENDE I don't know, maybe because my life is like that. I hate minimalist literature, minimalist anything. I like abundance, baroque things, extremes. My life has been determined by the fact that I'm always pushed to the limit. There is a lot of complexity and diversity in my life, and all that richness that I have become used to appears in my books. It's very difficult for me to write in a simple, understated, ironic, British way — very difficult. Things happen in my life, my private life is like an ongoing soap opera. Most of the things I write have maybe not happened directly to me but are part of the experience of my life. I come from a weird family, also. I had several uncles who were totally crazy. My grandmother was a clairvoyant and she experimented with telepathy all her life — and actually, it worked much better than the Chilean telephone company. With a family like mine you don't need to stretch your imagination. You have magic realism right there.

WACHTEL When you went back to Chile when you were fifteen, and lived in your grandfather's house, were you conscious of the abundance of the environment in which you were living?

ALLENDE Yes, I was always conscious of the things that were happening in my family and around me. I was also conscious of the fact that I lived in a society that was like a cake of many layers. In the same household you had a part of the house that belonged to the family and another world that belonged to the servants, and there was an invisible boundary between these two places in the same house. We ate the same food but in a different form. And that created something very uncomfortable inside me; I could never cope with it. I think that I never fitted in. All my life I have never fitted in, and I've always been aware of the contrasts and the strange things around me.

WACHTEL People talk a lot about magic realism, and of course it's something you have been identified with, and the idea of the surreal or ghosts. When you talk about this other dimension, what does it actually mean to you?

ALLENDE I think that often those spirits or those magic elements stand for passion, obsessions, emotions — strong emotions — myths, legends, the overwhelming power of history and nature, and all those things that are present in our life that we tend to ignore. In literature, they are wonderful devices, and when we give a space to them, they enrich the text enormously. But in *The House of the Spirits*, the ghosts in the house were really the passions of the family. Most of the time the spirits are tongue-in-cheek. It's not that I really believe in the ghosts, but I believe in innumerable forces, unknown forces, that somehow control our lives and we don't know the rules, we don't know how to handle them, and therefore we ignore them. But they are there.

WACHTEL I love the idea of ghosts being tongue-in-cheek.

June 1993
interview initially prepared in collaboration
with Peter Kavanagh

CHINUA ACHEBE

The first book I ever read by a black African was *Things Fall Apart* (1958) by Chinua Achebe. I read it more than twenty-five years ago, just as the Nigerian civil war was winding down, a conflict often referred to as the Biafran war, because Biafra was the name of the breakaway Ibo nation. That was the first time in my memory that Africa became associated with the horrific image of starving children with distended bellies. Casualties were very high — most of them Ibo civilians who starved to death after federal forces blockaded the rebel-controlled area.

Things Fall Apart provided a rare and original picture of Ibo society in the late nineteenth century. By focusing on a single village and its leader, the novel illustrated Nigeria's early experience of colonialism and British rule. The book was translated into thirty languages, and was adapted for stage, radio and television. It was the first novel by an African to be taught to African secondary students throughout the English-speaking parts of the continent. By the late sixties, when I caught up with it, *Things Fall Apart* had come to be recognized as the first classic in English from sub-Saharan Africa, and Achebe became known as the "father of the African novel in English."

Achebe followed *Things Fall Apart* with three other novels in quick succession: *No Longer at Ease* (1960), *Arrow of God* (1964) and *A Man of the People* (1966). But when the Biafran war began in 1967, Achebe, himself an Ibo, stopped writing novels. Even when the war ended in 1970, Achebe wrote poetry, short stories and essays, but not novels. In the early 1980s, he became directly involved in Nigerian politics — first as deputy national president of the People's Redemption Party, and then as president of his town union in Ogidi. Finally, in 1987, twenty-one years after his previous novel, Chinua Achebe wrote a dark political work of fiction called *Anthills of the Savannah*. It was short-listed for Britain's Booker Prize.

With more than ninety million people, Nigeria is Africa's most populous country. It won its independence from Britain in 1960, but this oil-rich state has been run by the military for all but nine of those thirty-six years. In June 1993, the presidential elections were declared invalid and the generals maintained control. Recently, Nigeria has attracted international attention for its execution of writer and activist Ken Saro-Wiwa and its effective expulsion of Nobel Prize winner, Wole Soyinka. Both Soyinka and Achebe have been campaigning for human rights in Nigeria.

Six years ago, Chinua Achebe was gravely injured in a car accident on a highway in Nigeria. The circumstances were unsettling and a military vehicle was said to be involved. Achebe spent six months in England undergoing operations and therapy and then, still close to death, he was moved to the United States. In fact, the American doctors who examined his X-rays didn't think he'd survive.

But today, at sixty-six, Achebe continues to write and teach. In his novel, *Anthills of the Savannah*, the traditional storyteller says, "It is only the story that outlives the sound of wardrums and the exploits of brave fighters. . . . The story is our escort; without it, we are blind."

Chinua Achebe spoke to me from his home in Annandale, New York, where he teaches at Bard College.

WACHTEL You have said that your father revered books and hoarded paper and that, when he died, the family made a bonfire of his life's accumulation of paper. It's a striking image; did it feel strange to see all that he had saved go up in smoke?

ACHEBE In retrospect, yes it did, but it wasn't archival material, it was old church magazines and the like. We needed space. You know, even though I'm a writer, I don't like paper. When my table is full of paper, I always get rid of it. It's a matter of temperament. You are right, though, looking back, one should save what can be saved. But I do think there's too much paper in the world.

WACHTEL So your father's legacy to you was a love of literature and a revulsion for paper.

ACHEBE Yes, that's right. It's a nice paradox.

WACHTEL You were born in a village in eastern Nigeria to Christian missionary parents, and you've talked about "living at the crossroads of culture." Can you give me a sense of the early days in your life with those two influences, the Christian and the traditional Ibo?

ACHEBE It's not easy to put into words. It's like being in two worlds or being at the confluence of two rivers, but it's never quiet at the confluence. The image of crossroads is a good one because crossroads are a place where there's a lot of traffic, not just human traffic but also spirit traffic. So it's a very powerful location. That's the idea I was trying to convey. Christianity was new, strange in many ways, but it is powerful, and so is the traditional life of the people. When I was growing up, we had already passed the initial meeting, which involved fighting at times — actual battles. Things became more settled, and the advantage was that you saw a bit of the past and a bit of the future. That was where you stood. Of course, being of the Christian party, the missionary party, I was not really supposed to pay much attention to the traditional; what they did was thought to be heathenish and I was not supposed to be interested in it, but I *was*, and so it was an advantageous position.

WACHTEL You've written about how on one arm of the cross in this crossroads you sang hymns and read the Bible, and on the other there was your uncle's family, as you ironically put it, "blinded by heathenism, offering food to idols." As a child, which one were you more drawn to?

ACHEBE The one which I was not supposed to see. The fact that it was forbidden was part of the attraction. I wasn't evaluating the two. If anyone had asked me, I would have said that the Christian faith was the right one. But I was curious about what was going on in the other place.

WACHTEL Which impulse do you feel most strongly now?

ACHEBE The traditional, because it is the underdog; and of course I've learned more and more about it. I was not exposed to it, nor was anyone in my generation. It was not taught in the schools, so it was always something half understood. Now that I have had time and years to look at it, I have discovered profound truths and profound significances that are very valuable, and so I'm in a position to look at Christianity from the position of traditional religion.

WACHTEL Would you describe yourself as speaking three languages — Ibo, English and Nigerian pidgin?

ACHEBE I've never really described myself that way but you are right. Nigerian pidgin is something we all pick up. I didn't grow up with it; it's more a language or dialect of the cities but, as one grew up, one encountered it and picked it up.

WACHTEL You use it quite a lot in your novels. How your characters speak seems to depend on a number of things: their class or level of education, the context and how intimate they're feeling. Is this something you consciously do?

ACHEBE Yes and no. A closeness to life as it is lived is very vital for me. What I try to achieve in my novels is as accurate a version of events as would happen in real life. That's an aspect of realism that I think is valuable, so that then you can delve into magic or whatever you do.

WACHTEL Ibo proverbs figure prominently in your novels. Did they always resonate for you, even when you were growing up?

ACHEBE Yes, I loved them. The language of the Ibo people, their imagery, is all very picturesque and I always found it, and still find it, very moving. A simple example: In English we would say, "Two heads are better than one." The Ibos would say, "Two heads, four eyes." They always bring in a picture so you see it at once — it's not just that it's better, they tell you *how* it's better.

WACHTEL There's a line in your first novel that "proverbs are the palm oil with which words are eaten." It's a very vivid image. There's another one that you use and I think the idea of it is implicit in several of your novels; the English translation is, "To every man his due." What does that mean to you?

ACHEBE It's extremely central to my understanding of reality, and it is so important to the Ibo that they say it in many different ways. The world is very complex, that's what they are saying. We must be aware of that complexity, and not just be aware but actually recognize it in the way we behave, by according to every reality its own respect. You are not expected to admire or to love every thing, but you are expected to recognize that that thing has its own validity. That is what is meant by "To everyone his due."

For example, if you entered a hall in which Ibo elders were assembled for a meeting, if you came in and there were many, many people seated, the polite thing would be to shake hands with everybody and call them by their chosen names, not the names which they were given at birth but their titles. Everyone who becomes a titled person takes a new name, and you are supposed to know that and address them that way when you meet. Now, that's how you should deal with this crowd. But it's impossible! It would take the whole day if you were to go around shaking hands with everybody there and calling them by their names. So what you do is greet them generally and say, "To everyone his due," which means you recognize everyone's title.

WACHTEL Your first novel, *Things Fall Apart,* was published thirty-five years ago. It sold more than three million copies, and it's been translated into thirty languages. How does it feel to be described as "the father of African literature in English"?

ACHEBE Oh, I don't mind that. I don't mind that at all! It was certainly not in my mind when I started writing. It's one of those amazing and gratifying surprises, the way that my work has grown. Actually, the figure that my publishers give is not three million but eight, and it's still spreading — right now it's spreading very fast in the Far East. So I'm very happy and of course humbled by this, and that's all I can say, really.

WACHTEL You've said that one of the reasons you became a novelist was to tell the story from the inside. Do you remember how you felt when you first read books like *Mister Johnson,* by Joyce Cary, which was actually set in Nigeria, or when you read Joseph Conrad's *Heart of Darkness,* set in what was then the Congo?

ACHEBE That's a long story. I encountered Conrad before I was old enough to see what was going on and so it didn't make the kind of impact that it would have made if I had been older. It was only when I re-read it at college, as an undergraduate in the English department at the University of Ibadan, that I began to realize what was happening there. Joyce Cary was different. The Joyce Cary was a later book; it was published in the forties, so I read it for the first time in college. Not just my response but the response of the whole class was quite definite: we didn't like what Joyce Cary was doing. I remember it was interesting because our teachers were all English and we were all Nigerian, and our teachers thought it was a marvellous book. In fact, it is still called by some people in the West the greatest African novel. It's just amazing. One of my colleagues shocked our teacher by saying that the only moment he enjoyed in the book was when Johnson was shot. That was a very drastic response, but it conveys the exasperation that we Africans feel when we encounter this kind of mindless racism.

WACHTEL When you first read *Heart of Darkness,* and you say you were too young to understand it, did you identify with Marlowe?

ACHEBE You identify with whom the author wants you to identify, that's what fiction does; and until you are strong enough to break away from that, you don't see what's going on. I believe this is the problem with professors in the West today who don't see racism in *Heart of Darkness*. They are still reading like young boys and girls who are fascinated by the sound of adjectives and the creation of emotion, a cheap emotion, with fear and stereotype. But when you become experienced with literature, you should be able to get rid of that response.

WACHTEL Do you buy into what's called "appropriation of voice," the argument that only a black African is truly able to write about black Africa?

ACHEBE No, I don't. I think anybody can write about any place, even places they have never visited. Kafka wrote about America without leaving Prague. But a good writer knows just what kind of story to write about the place you don't know deeply. There are many different levels on which a story can move; you don't have to be an expert about place.

WACHTEL You were what's sometimes called a "been-to," in that you studied in Ibadan but you also studied in London. When you came back to Nigeria, just before independence, what were your hopes or expectations?

ACHEBE Actually, I wasn't a proper "been-to." I went to London, to the BBC school, for less than one year. I was already working; I was not a young student. Although it was an important experience, to spend seven months in Europe, it wasn't really formative. But as to what that period meant, it was a time of excitement — it was four or five years before our independence, and independence was very much in the air. We all felt happy and excited and hopeful, optimistic. It was the optimism that at last we would be on our own again and take hold of our history and manage our lives. It was a heady moment. About a year after I came back from London, Ghana got her independence; Ghana was the first in modern Africa. And it was so exciting! We were not Ghanaians, we were Nigerians, and Nigerians and Ghanaians tend to be rivals, yet the independence of Ghana felt like our own. People stayed up till one a.m. in the morning, which was twelve midnight in Ghana, to hear the handing over of power. So it was that kind of heady, excited feeling.

WACHTEL You once described your first novel, *Things Fall Apart,* as "an act of atonement, the homage of a prodigal son." What did you mean by that?

ACHEBE What I meant was that being a Christian, being educated in things of the West, being a university graduate and all that, one really shouldn't be any of those things. Our business should be to restore what was lost, to take on the task of redefining ourselves. That is what I tried to do in my writing, and I see that as a kind of service which is demanded of us by Africa, because we betrayed her in doing all these other things. My father, for instance, was one of the first generation of Christians; he abandoned the faith of his fathers. I'm putting it rather strongly so that what I'm trying to say will be clear. In actual fact, one's life doesn't stop because you've become a Christian; there are even some advantages in getting acquainted with another culture and all that. But basically, we were led into accepting that what our forefathers, our ancestors, had done through the millennia was somehow misguided and that somebody else who's come from afar could straighten us out, that He was the Way, the Truth and the Life, and that we had been sunk in blindness. That's an outrageous thing to accept. In retelling, in redefining ourselves, we are making amends for this betrayal.

WACHTEL Yet I think one of the reasons that *Things Fall Apart* is so successful is that you don't romanticize the old Africa.

ACHEBE No. Making amends doesn't mean glorifying. It simply means giving to everyone his due, you know, that salutation. This is due to Africa. At no point in the history of Africa, at no point was it inhabited by people who were less than human — we have to be absolutely strict about that. You must give it its due. Then, having said that, you have to recognize that things were not perfect. Things were not supposed to be perfect. God did not make a perfect world. The Ibo people have a different notion of creation. They have a notion in which God is constantly having a conversation with humanity on how to improve the environment. It was not finished in six days; we have a role to play. So we recognize the fact that things are not perfect, things are not even good. But that does not mean that this place is less than a human habitation.

WACHTEL Between 1958 and 1966 you published four novels, including your post-independence political satire *A Man of the People*. Then in the late sixties, from 1967 to 1970, there was the Nigerian civil war, which is sometimes called the Biafran war. You've described the war as a watershed for you. Can you talk about what happened to you during that time?

ACHEBE If we go back to that spirit of euphoria I described, when we got our independence — the feeling that we were new people, that we were reinventing ourselves — all that hope and promise seemed smashed in the catastrophe of the civil war, in which Nigerians set upon one another and people were massacred in the thousands, hundreds of thousands. It was a war in which perhaps a million people died in the short period of two-and-a-half years. It seemed as if everything we had planned for and looked forward to was going to be taken away, and that independence itself was perhaps a hoax. It was a very savage war. Beginning to deal with that reality was very difficult.

I was quite involved in the war, not in the sense of going to the front or anything, but it was close, it was close to everybody. Everyone lost friends and relations, their homes; we all became refugees, running from one place to another. So at the end of it you had to reassess what you'd been doing in this redefining of yourself. You realized that it had perhaps been too optimistic, and that now you had to look more closely at what happened. And that was why I virtually put aside the novel I had been planning. Actually, I didn't put it aside, the novel just refused to come. Again and again I wrestled with this novel that I'd had in mind for years, and it just wouldn't make itself available. I realized that this was understandable, that what had happened to us was so devastating that we couldn't just get up and say, now it's business as usual again. Some people thought, when the war ended and the leader of Biafra and the leader of Nigeria were seen embracing, that the whole thing was over. That's not true. You don't lose a million people and shake hands and just go back to business as usual.

WACHTEL   Was there a way in which you felt you had to heal yourself as well?

ACHEBE   Yes, and I wasn't sure just what to do. One of the things I did was leave the country, though not right away, I felt that my role during the war was so well-known that I couldn't run away. If there was going to be any punishment, it would be right that I would be one of those punished. So I sat around for two years after the war ended and when it was clear that I could go away, then I left the country for four years.

WACHTEL   What was your role during the war?

ACHEBE   I was more of a traveller. I travelled to the United States, to Europe, to other parts of Africa, and spoke about what was happening. I gave lectures, but I always came right back, to the fighting itself and to the war. And my family was there, my wife and three little children. My role was described as diplomatic in some places, but that's a very grand way of putting it, because I didn't really have any official position. I was simply a writer who travelled and spoke about what was going on.

WACHTEL   More than twenty years elapsed between the last novel of your earlier period, *A Man of the People,* and the publication of *Anthills of the Savannah* in 1987. The poet in *Anthills of the Savannah* is a man poised between action and reflection. At one point he's addressing a group of students and, in answer to a question about what the country should do, he says, "Writers don't give prescriptions, they give headaches." When I read that I felt it was *you.* Is that true?

ACHEBE   Yes, I think you are right. Just at that point, as long as you don't take it that that character is me: no characters of mine are allowed to be me. They may reflect, they may share some common ideas here and there with me. On that point, yes, that's exactly what I would say in that circumstance.

WACHTEL   That whole dilemma of action or reflection seems to be one that you have alternated between in your own life. You were involved in actual Nigerian politics in the 1980s. Then you published a novel. Do you find yourself going back and forth on this issue?

ACHEBE Yes, I think there's an inevitable seesaw position for someone like me, because you get so frustrated that things are not working out, and you want to go in and do something. Then you find that it isn't really in that kind of action where your best work can be done. I discovered, for instance, that party politics was really going to be a waste of my time. I got into it because I felt so desperate to indicate that, out of all the bad leaders we had, this particular man was least bad and our people should know that and recognize it. There is a certain amount of value in that kind of work, but it's time-consuming and it's also energy-consuming. In the end you say, no, I really should be writing my books. So one does alternate in that kind of desperate way in our situation, and our situation is very desperate.

WACHTEL The novel *Anthills of the Savannah* is in some ways a very political book. It's set in a fictional country called Kangan, but it feels as if it's probably not a very distant relation from a country like Nigeria, and it's a place where corruption is everywhere. Have people in Nigeria ever criticized you for being disloyal to your country by painting such a bleak picture?

ACHEBE They have on and off, yes. But Nigerians are very critical of themselves, generally. I think you will find more people who regard me as a truthful witness and as a seer and prophet rather than as somebody who is disloyal. You will find some who take the other position, maybe among the leaders, but even there I'm not so sure. Nigerians tend to recognize their faults, and it's amazing that we don't do very much with that recognition.

WACHTEL Has there been any personal price that you've had to pay for being a writer who speaks the truth?

ACHEBE Oh, little ones. I wouldn't really bother even to discuss them because I got off very lightly. For instance, at the end of the Biafran war, someone who was on the other side, who was very powerful on the federal side, told me that I personally gave Nigeria more trouble than all the other Biafrans put together. That was of course an exaggeration, but even so I got off very lightly. Having one's passport seized is not something one can complain about when one could have been charged with high treason. I think by and large my political work has been accepted as valid and valuable for Nigeria.

WACHTEL You were involved in a terrible car accident in Nigeria in 1990, which necessitated surgery and many months of therapy. Did you ever feel that the accident wasn't an accident?

ACHEBE We have not bothered to pursue any investigation along those lines, but it did cross our minds. There were a few strange things that happened just before the accident. But we are very lucky, we are very lucky that it wasn't worse than it was, and so we have simply left it there. Also, the outpouring of love and sympathy that we saw, from all over Nigeria, makes it unnecessary for us to pursue what happened.

WACHTEL What is your physical condition now?

ACHEBE It's more or less where it was when I left the hospital. I broke my spine and so, as you know, I am a paraplegic. I'm in a wheelchair and it looks as if that's the way it's going to be.

WACHTEL The anthills of your novel's title, *Anthills of the Savannah,* stand as a powerful metaphor, some indication of hope. Can you tell me what that metaphor means?

ACHEBE It's about hope, promise, but most importantly it's about memory. The grassland, the savannah, is generally consumed by a fire at the end of every year in the dry season, and all the grass is burnt. If you came there you would see nothing except these anthills dotted across the landscape. That's all that survives until the rains return and the new grass comes up. But that new grass wasn't there when this disaster happened, it doesn't know anything about it, and if it's going to find out what happened last year, the only person it can ask is the anthill, that's all that was there. So that's the image. It's hope, it's survival, and it is memory, because if you survive without knowing who you are, then it really doesn't make any sense. You have to be told the importance of the story. It's the anthill that has the story. If the grass is wise, it will ask, what was it that happened? And then the story will be told.

WACHTEL Nadine Gordimer has described you as a moralist and an idealist, but it would seem to me that your idealism has had to weather some very difficult things over the years. How is your idealism faring these days?

ACHEBE It's still alive and well because without it the business of the writer would be meaningless. I don't think the world needs to be told stories of despair; there is enough despair as it is without anyone adding to it. If we have any role at all, I think it's the role of optimism, not blind or stupid optimism, but the kind which is meaningful, one that is rather close to that notion of the world which is not perfect, but which can be improved. In other words, we don't just sit and hope that things will work out; we have a role to play to make that come about. That seems to me to be the reason for the existence of the writer.

WACHTEL You have distanced yourself from your parents' Christianity, but in your essays especially and even in talking to you, I feel that you assign to literature and the imagination almost the same kind of spiritual or even religious value, that fiction is a kind of salvation, or can be a salvation.

ACHEBE Yes. And so one hasn't really moved all that far away. We have a proverb which says that the little bird that flies off the ground and lands on an anthill may think it's left the ground, but it hasn't.

WACHTEL How do you convince people of the redemptive powers of fiction?

ACHEBE I don't think it needs a lot of heavy work. I think good stories attract us and good stories are also moral stories. I've never seen a really good story that is immoral, and I think there is something in us which impels us towards good stories. If we have people who produce them, we are lucky. I can't make a very large claim for what I do, I just make a modest claim because we really don't know.

I feel that there has to be a purpose to what we do. If there was no hope at all, we should just sleep or drink and wait for death. But we don't want to do that. And why? I think something tells us that we should struggle. We don't really know why we should struggle, but we do, because we think it's better than sitting down and waiting for calamity. So that's my sense of the meaning of life. That's really how I would put it, that we struggle, and because we struggle, that struggle has to be told, the story of that struggle has to be conveyed to another generation. You have struggle and story, and these two are quite enough for me.

WACHTEL You're giving me a variation of a story that's told in the novel *Anthills of the Savannah*, about a leopard and a tortoise, and it's a story that's told twice, first in a village and then to university students. It's about what you're saying, the meaningfulness of the struggle itself, that to have struggled is important, so your children will know that you struggled. Can you tell that story, the story of the leopard and the tortoise?

ACHEBE It's a very short one. The leopard had been looking for the tortoise and hadn't found him for a long time. On this day, on a lonely road, he suddenly chanced upon Tortoise, and so he said, "Aha! at last, I've caught you. Now get ready to die." Tortoise of course knew that the game was up and so he said, "Okay, but can I ask you a favour?" and Leopard said, "Well, why not?" Tortoise said, "Before you kill me, could you give me a few moments just to reflect on things?" Leopard thought about it — he wasn't very bright — and he said, "Well, I don't see anything wrong with that. You can have a little time." And so Tortoise, instead of standing still and thinking, began to do something very strange: he began to scratch the soil all around him and throw sand around in all directions. Leopard was mystified by this. He said, "What are you doing? Why are you doing that?" Tortoise said: "I'm doing this because when I'm dead, I want anybody who passes by this place to stop and say, 'Two people struggled here. A man met his match here.'"

WACHTEL You've been living in the United States on and off over the last twenty years or so. Do you think of yourself as living in exile?

ACHEBE No, I don't. I spare myself that luxury and, as a matter of fact, I'm constantly planning for my return. I've been here now three years, since my accident, and it's partly medical, but I'm making arrangements to get back home. It's very important to me that I get back home. People at home also expect me back.

WACHTEL Despite the recent coup?

ACHEBE Perhaps *because* of the recent coup. The situation is so bad —

WACHTEL The fact that it's so bad means you feel a greater compulsion to be there?

ACHEBE Yes. People in fact do call or write me and say, when are you coming? I am very much involved in what's going on in Nigeria and I'd like to keep it that way.

WACHTEL Do you need to go back to Nigeria in order to write more about it?

ACHEBE I think so, though that's not an immediate problem. I have enough knowledge about the place to write the kind of fiction I want to write. I may not know what's happening politically this week, but that's never been my need; I've never really needed that kind of topical knowledge. I have enough residual information and knowledge to keep working for a time. What I need is the spiritual sense of connectedness one gets by being there.

WACHTEL I understand the way in which you are hopeful about the possibilities of literature, but are you also hopeful about Nigeria?

ACHEBE That's a tough question. I have said, and more than once, that always, even in my reincarnation, I would like to be a Nigerian. But as more and more bizarre situations occur, you sometimes wonder whether you haven't spoken too positively. I still think that we *might* just make it. We have squandered so much time and money and people, but I still hope. Here it's hope rather than belief. Even if we don't make it, then we'll have other arrangements. A country is simply an area or territory defined and called one thing, and if the people there don't really want to live together in that definition, then they can make other arrangements. I think we should give Nigeria at least one more chance to see if we can make it as a country.

January 1994
*interview initially prepared in collaboration
with Larry Scanlan*

REYNOLDS PRICE

In the tradition of Southern writers — after William Faulkner, Flannery O'Connor, Carson McCullers and Eudora Welty — comes Reynolds Price. In fact, it was Eudora Welty who encouraged Price to publish his first short story, while he was still in school. And Reynolds Price has gone on to teach other Southern writers, such as Josephine Humphreys and Anne Tyler.

Reynolds Price was born in Macon, North Carolina in 1933. Although he's travelled a lot, and was at Oxford on a Rhodes Scholarship, Price has stayed fairly close to home all his life. He was an undergraduate at Duke University in Durham, North Carolina, and that's where he got his first teaching job more than thirty years ago. He is now James B. Duke Professor of English.

Price is best known for two award-winning novels: his very first, published in 1962, *A Long and Happy Life*, won the Faulkner Award and has never been out of print; *Kate Vaiden* (1986) won the National Book Critics Circle Award. Both are set in the rural south and both feature restless, yearning and powerful women. In fact, Price has said that one of the things he likes about his work is that "it presents a rich...gallery of strong women."

Grace is not the first word that comes to mind when I think about modern fiction, but I do associate it with Reynolds Price. There is a generosity of spirit, and surprisingly profound connections made, and bestowed, by strangers. Grace, or something like it, also came to mind as I was reading Reynolds Price's memoir, *A Whole New Life* (1994), recounting how ten years earlier he had been diagnosed with spinal cancer. A physician told his brother that Price had "six months to paraplegia, six months to quadriplegia, six months to death." With candor and courage, Price describes the pain and fear, but ultimately the hope, as his condition stabilized. He subtitles his autobiography "An Illness and a Healing" and now refers to his "new existence as a seated man."

Reynolds Price is not only a novelist, but also a short story writer, poet, playwright, essayist and teacher. He's published almost thirty books, including *The Promise of Rest* (1995), which completes — with *The Surface of Earth* (1975) and *The Source of Light* (1981) — a trilogy of novels entitled *A Great Circle* which is concerned with nine decades in a family's life.

When we spoke, Reynolds Price was in the CBC's New York studio. He arrived there early and, as we were setting up, I could hear how he was chatting with and charming the various people who came by.

WACHTEL You've written about your very first memory and it's an unusually precocious one; it's a scene that takes place while you're still just a few months old, an infant. Can you describe that for me?

PRICE I was roughly six months old and I'm lying out in the sun; presumably it's summer in North Carolina, and I'm wearing only a diaper. I'm sunbathing, which was looked upon as a very good thing to do with children in the 1930s. We lived in the country and the family we rented rooms from had a goat and the goat suddenly grazes his way over to me and then begins to nibble on the corner of my diaper. I can hear the goat bell and feel the sun and smell the grass, and that's literally the memory. I don't remember being frightened of the experience at all and apparently I wasn't. My mother saw the goat coming and ran out and rescued me.

WACHTEL What is it about this particular memory that resonates for you?

PRICE I really don't know why, of all things, that particular one has survived. In those years my parents were travelling a great deal, living in small rented rooms because my father, like so many other Americans, had awful trouble keeping employment in the years of the Great Depression.

WACHTEL Am I right that you give that early memory of being on a blanket to Kate in your novel *Kate Vaiden*?

PRICE She has a version of it, exactly. For years, when I taught freshman English at Duke University, the first composition I would give the students would be to describe, as accurately and truthfully as they possibly could, their earliest memory, even if it were only in ten words. Almost always that memory would come from when the students were three or four years old. The only student who ever had an earlier memory than my own was a sixteen-year-old woman called Anne Tyler, who went on to become a very famous novelist. Her memory was of being in her crib, I think, when she was about three or four months old.

WACHTEL You work a lot through memory in your writing, memories and dreams. Are they a gift, a great resource?

PRICE I've often felt that they were. I have as many nonsensical dreams as most people, or dreams that seem tattered and disordered and third-class surrealism, but I have had a number of dreams, especially in the last fifteen years or so, which did seem to me to be communications at the very least from my own unconscious mind to myself, dreams that seemed to advise me on things, to warn me of things. I take dreams perhaps not quite as seriously as Joseph does in the Book of Genesis but I tend to take those particular kinds of dreams very seriously.

WACHTEL I'd like to go back to your early years, and maybe a little past the six-month mark. Your childhood in rural North Carolina has been such fertile ground for your writing. Can you describe the world that you grew up in?

PRICE I was born in 1933, which was not quite seventy years after the end of the catastrophic Civil War. It's hard to remember that 600,000 citizens of the United States died in that action, and my part of the South, the upper South, suffered a great deal from the last days of the war. When I was born it was still a relatively poor part of the United States. The particular county in North Carolina where I was born was heavily agricultural — cotton and tobacco. The population was about seventy per cent African American; almost all of those people were employed either in domestic jobs or in farming. If I look back to records of the South before the Civil War and to the post-bellum South, I can really see that in so many ways it was both good and horrendous. My part of the South in the early 1930s was very much the South of the old days. Black people in my childhood were technically free American citizens, but in many ways they lived in a world which treated them as though they were still chattel slaves.

WACHTEL You said that you were born "an avid observer and witness," and this was something you got from your parents, who were tremendous watchers of the world

PRICE Yes. Both my parents, and each of them in a very different way, were very committed and almost unceasing observers of the world, witnesses, visual spies on the world. My father did it in a more cautious way, because he was an anxious man; he always thought that the world was just about to do something awful to him. My mother had a much more sanguine view, athough both her parents had died when she was very young and all her life she thought of herself as an orphan. But she had a much more delighted sense that the world was this great spectacle of comedy, and certainly of tragedy. The part of it that interested her most and caught her eye was the part we call Vanity Fair, the place of fools and bumpkins, and although she was a very kindly person, I think she saw what was innately comic in a great deal of human behaviour.

WACHTEL In writing about your parents you've referred to a three-way marriage among you because you were an only child for about eight years. It's a very strong image.

PRICE It is a strong image and I'm absolutely certain that this is not an adult conclusion that I've foisted back or retrojected onto my childhood. When I was four or five years old, it was beginning to dawn on me that we were this indissoluble triangle and that my relation to them seemed to be the same as their relation to one another. Obviously I knew nothing about sexual attraction and didn't perceive that that aspect of their relations was omitted from my relations to them — thank goodness it was — but I had this tremendous sense that we were in a kind of life raft together and that our duties to one another were extremely strong. I think my parents felt it as well, not because I turned out to be a particular kind of child but simply because I was a child at all. My arrival drastically changed their lives. My father had been a fairly desperate alcoholic; he was thirty-three years old when I was born, and he was in terrible trouble. When I was being born and my mother was having great difficulties in childbirth and it looked as though I or my mother or both of us might not survive the labour, my father went out and made this deal with God that if I survived and my mother survived, he would stop drinking. We survived, and he did stop drinking for the rest of his life.

WACHTEL To feel such a tight bond with your parents must have been profoundly reassuring, especially to someone who — as you have described yourself — was quite a lonely child. But what happens when that breaks up? How do you separate, or when do you move out of that circle?

PRICE I didn't have great difficulties moving away from my family and from home when the time came to do so, and I think my parents had a kind of natural grace. Certainly they were not in

any sense psychologically or psychiatrically sophisticated people
— they hardly knew that such disciplines existed — I think they
had such deep decency and such innate human skills that they
never leaned on me or my brother, who was born when I was
eight; they never leaned on us in the way that so many parents
do, in an attempt to turn the child into virtually another organ of
the parental body. So though I felt very much involved in the
marriage with my parents, when the time came to leave home
and go off to college, I had very little trouble doing that. I don't
remember ever feeling homesick or having to make desperate
late-night calls just to hear a familiar voice. My parents did live
only twenty-five miles away from where I was in university, but
very frequently I didn't see them for weeks or months at a time
and that didn't cause me great difficulties.

WACHTEL Your parents were also avid storytellers. How did that
shape your view of the world?

PRICE First of all, it delighted me and in some ways it rather
spoiled me because it led me to expect that all other human beings
were going to be as amusing and as narratively gifted as both my
parents. That is definitely not the case, as I found later; lots of
people in the world are crashing bores. But I think it had to have
huge effects — I can't necessarily specify what they were — on
my genuine sense that human life is a narrative, a story, that each
of us generates with every move he makes, and that that story is
partly controlled by the individual who's living the life, but also
it's ultimately of course controlled by something else, whether you
want to call that God or fate, or metabolic destiny, genetic destiny. I grew up convinced that not only my own life but the life
of the planet and the life of the universe was a story, and that it
was a story being told by someone that I feel uncomfortable calling anything except the Creator. My sense of the world as being
a creation is very basic to my view of the world.

WACHTEL That's the Big Story told by the Big Storyteller.

PRICE The Big Story told by the Big Storyteller — presumably
to itself, to himself or herself, whichever gender, if any, the Creator
observes at any given moment.

WACHTEL When you thought about yourself becoming a story-teller, or the people around you as telling stories, was that in some way a reflection or an echo of something bigger?

PRICE I was very aware that in our family circle and in our outer circle of friends a good storyteller was a very popular, much-loved person. Like most normal children, I had a strong appetite for love and approval, and I realized that if my father could gather a crowd any time he turned up and started telling stories, and it was a laughing and affectionate crowd, then that would be a good skill to be able to learn from him. And I think I did.

WACHTEL When did you take that storytelling a stage further and decide to become a writer?

PRICE I first began seriously thinking of a lifetime's commit-ment to writing when I was about thirteen years old, in the eighth grade in North Carolina public school. I didn't really fix that idea in concrete until I was in high school, which meant that I was about seventeen years old. I had a particularly wonderful English teacher, who encouraged the small amount of writing that I'd done up to that point and gave me the sense that I might go on and spend a life doing it.

WACHTEL Your novel *Kate Vaiden* is written in the first person and you've called it "an emotional autobiography of my mother." What did you mean by that?

PRICE I mentioned that my mother's parents died when she was very young — her mother died when she was five and her father died when she was about twelve — and she was reared, very luck-ily, by an older sister of hers, who was eighteen years older than my mother and was married and had children. The sister moved back into my mother's family home and simply reared my mother and a slightly older sister of my mother's after their parents had died. Even so, and in spite of the fact that she had virtually no sense of self-pity whatever, I think my mother defined herself very early as an orphan, as someone who had been abandoned, not willingly, but who had indeed been abandoned by her parents much too early in her life. I was always fascinated with this as a child, because children have a kind of love-hate relationship with the idea that your parents can vanish. Some days I would come home from school and my mother would be lying on the sofa looking rather melancholy and I would semi-already know what was wrong and I would say, "What's wrong?" and she would say something like, this is the anniversary of my mother's death, or of my father's death. It was rather Victorian of her to feel that way but it was a very genuine and deep sense of loss. So I found myself in the early 1980s suddenly thinking in a voice, a feminine voice, which had many resemblances to that voice of my mother's, and I found that I wanted to let that particular voice tell an entire life story. And so with very little sense of what the destination of the book would be, what the whole plot would be, I dived in and extrapolated this woman whom I call Kate Vaiden and let her begin talking. The story that she invented, which is the body of the book, doesn't at all resemble my mother's life story, but I think Kate's mind, Kate's psyche, her feelings, her resourcefulness, and that slight emotional skittishness in her, very much come to me from my mother.

WACHTEL When I hear you talk about your mother being an orphan, I'm reminded of how much loss and abandonment, or fear of loss and abandonment there is in your fiction, from the idea of a child left alone and afraid in the dark to actually being left behind. What is it about that fear of absence that draws you?

PRICE The first thing I would say is that I assume it's a universal human feeling. For all of us as children, our darkest fear is that our parents will disappear in some way or other. Our absolutely darkest fear is that our parents will wilfully abandon us because they do not love us enough. In my own case, I was partly shaped by my close contact with my mother's own fear. I was perhaps even more deeply affected when I was twenty-one years old, by having to be the caretaker of my father as he was dying of lung cancer. It was a very short death; he was only aware that he'd had lung cancer for the last two weeks of his life. But for that two weeks I had an incredibly intense, pent-up-in-a-small-hospital-room relationship with him. Much as he loved my mother, he seemed to want me around him more than he wanted anyone else. And it gave me — earlier in life than many citizens of Western

Europe and the American continent know now — a great sense
of the fragility of human life and our absolute inability to predict
good luck or the continuance of anything that we're at present
enjoying or valuing.

WACHTEL You've remarked that it was very significant for you
that both your parents died when you were relatively young. As
you've just said, your father died when you were twenty-one;
your mother died when you were thirty-two. Did that give you
a certain perspective and perhaps even a certain freedom in writing about them?

PRICE Yes, it did. Obviously I don't mean that I'm glad my parents died young or that they died early in my life, but I'm saying
that given the fact that they did — and incidentally I think they
both died of the effects of smoking a great many cigarettes over
their lives — they got out of my path. I was left a person who
didn't have the melancholy chores that so many others have, of
watching a parent move slowly into old age and feebleness, and
often a very sad mental dissolution as well. My parents died in
virtually the prime of their lives and my memories of them are of
two strong and loving people to whom I felt an enormous debt
of gratitude.

WACHTEL Relationships between children and parents, and the
role that memory plays, is something that you explore in your
fiction. There's a recent story called "His Final Mother," in which
a boy sees a vision, a ghost of his mother, who's just died. But his
vision of her is set in the time before he was born, so he has to
find a memory of her from his own experience to hang on to.

PRICE I don't know quite where that might have come from in
my own imagination. I do know that when I was very young,
before I started going to school at the age of six, I was fascinated
by looking through the little boxes of snapshots that my mother
and father had taken of one another and of a lot of members of
the family, from the time that they first met, when they were
barely out of their teenage years. I love the way that both my parents looked when they were even younger than when I'd known
them. Maybe that's where that notion in the story came from, of

the boy's suddenly perceiving his mother in her own youth before his birth. I've always had this powerful sense of how my parents looked and what they must have been like before I was born.

WACHTEL I'm thinking about how present the dead are in your fiction. There's another story, "The Golden Child," in which a little girl died before the narrator was born, and she becomes a very real presence for him.

PRICE She was a first cousin of mine, the daughter of one of my mother's brothers, and she was always called Little Frances, she was never called Frances in our family, and she never got to live to be older than that. She contracted osteomyelitis in the early 1930s, when there were no antibiotics to treat it, and she died this horrendous death because it went into meningitis. My parents didn't resist talking about the awfulness of that death in my presence when I was growing up. It's been only in the last thirty or forty years that people in the Western world have managed to segregate their children from the very older members of the family. I grew up with aunts and uncles of all ages. The students whom I teach now at Duke University very seldom have had much experience of anyone older than their own parents, but I knew people in my childhood who were born in the 1840s.

WACHTEL But in this particular story it's someone you *didn't* know in your own childhood who had such a grip on you.

PRICE She was a very haunting figure. Sooner or later every child has to learn that human beings are not eternal, and I think I learned that largely from hearing my parents talk about Little Frances' awful last ordeal and death. I learned that life was a very fragile commodity and that we must love it the best we can because we're not guaranteed it beyond this moment. I can't remember the first family funeral I ever attended but I suspect that it was the death of my father's mother, who had been born in 1861; she died when I was about four years old. I have very vague memories of attending her funeral. That's probably my first actual encounter with death, and I remember being lifted up to see her body lying in the coffin. It didn't frighten me, it just seemed like one more thing that I was learning about.

WACHTEL This might be the place to talk about ghosts. There is this other-worldly element in your fiction, this other dimension.
PRICE I myself have never had an experience of seeing anything that I would call ghostly. My mother did not know that she was going to die on a certain afternoon in May of 1965, but that morning, before she had her sudden cerebral hemorrhage and died, she told her next-door neighbour that the previous night, when she had been alone in our house — my father had been dead for eleven years at that point — she had lain down on the couch to watch "The Johnny Carson Show" before she went to sleep. She actually went to sleep watching the show. She woke up some hours later and sat up on the couch. She was suddenly aware that my father was sitting on the easy chair which was immediately next to the couch. In telling this story to her neighbour, my mother said something about the fact that she'd woken and got up and walked through the living-room and the dining-room and was in the downstairs bathroom when she realized that my father had been sitting in his chair. She told her neighbour that she felt very calm and walked all the way back to see him again and that when she got there he was gone. About five o'clock the next afternoon she was talking on the telephone and this massive artery burst in her brain; she immediately became unconscious and was dead by the middle of the night. And that turns out, as I found years later looking into it, to be one of the most common forms of encounters with ghosts: the departed loved one returns to summon the living loved one on into death. I was very struck by that story which her neighbour told me, and in fact I made it the conclusion of a novel that I wrote shortly thereafter, called *Love and Work*.

But do I believe that human personalities return in that form? I would certainly have to say that I don't disbelieve that they do; I think it would be impossible to prove that negative proposition. I've known two or three other sane people in my life who are absolutely convinced that they have had quite real, palpable encounters with people who couldn't have been there, who were either dead or projecting their presence from a very great distance. So I would say that that's a form of human mystery that I tend to look at very seriously, though I certainly don't think I have any explanation of the complexity that must lie behind it.

WACHTEL You've talked about having very intense relations with the unknown and certainly things you describe as visions have had a very powerful effect on you.

PRICE Yes they have. I think I've only had one experience that I would call a vision, which I describe in a recent book about my own experience with cancer. But from early childhood, from about the age of five, I remember intense emotional experiences, almost always when I was alone, and those experiences slowly came to seem like perceptions of sudden shafts of insight into the reality of the unknown, the reality of the Creator who put this entire immensely beautiful, immensely horrible universe together and placed us in it. My first such experience was when I was about five and I was out-of-doors and I stuck a knife into a pine tree and I bit down on the blade of the knife, which I'd seen Indians do in movies, and I suddenly had this sense of the whole of creation, the whole of nature, and me in it as being one huge, completely related organism. It's the kind of vision that years later I discovered Wordsworth had as a child. Wordsworth said that the sense of the unreality, the unphysicality of the world, was so great that sometimes as he was going to school he would run ahead and literally embrace a tree trunk to prove to himself that it was not an insubstantial vision.

WACHTEL Even in your stories that are firmly rooted in this reality there's still some element of the extraordinary — often through a powerful, unexpected connection between strangers.

PRICE I've never been that much of a wanderer. Apart from four years when I attended graduate school in England and lived in Oxford, I've never lived for long periods of time outside my part of North Carolina. But I am fascinated by the experience of the pilgrim who's alone and afraid in a hostile world or even a benign world, and it does seem to have recurred very frequently in my work. I tend not to examine those traits very closely for fear they'll go away.

WACHTEL One could even argue that, in your fiction, sometimes the connections between strangers may be easier than between friends or lovers.

PRICE I think they frequently are. We've all had the experience of being on a bus or a train or an airplane and having a stranger sit eight inches away from us, and suddenly a rather idle question on our part triggers some great confessional outburst. They'll tell us about how miserable their marriage is or how their daughter has just died of leukemia, or how they've just cheated on their wife or husband for the first time. Sometimes one gets trapped by a bore, especially now that I live in a wheelchair I can get trapped by bores, but very often I've learned absolutely fascinating and sometimes useable things from total strangers who chose to confide in me in an anonymous environment like that of, say, an airplane over the southwest desert of America.

WACHTEL You're often described as a Southern writer and I know it's a label you resist if it suggests anything reductive, but you do write out of a strong sense of place. You've said of your home in North Carolina that "it's the place about which I have perfect pitch."

PRICE I think that's true, and I'm very glad I've been rooted all my life in a particular place. I don't understand what kind of human being is going to be constructed out of a life that is as rootless as the ones that so many young people live in the United States today. I'm deeply concerned about that, and it has a ramification, as I mentioned earlier, of their simply never getting to know people older than their parents. But I was given the great gift of a stable childhood. I've mentioned that we moved around a great deal but in a very small radius, and we always lived within a hundred miles of my parents' home towns, so we always had close access to our extended family. I myself, when I came back from graduate school and took my first job teaching at Duke University in 1958, chose to rent a little house on one side of a small pond in the country outside Durham, North Carolina. I lived in that little house for about six years and then some people came along and built a house on the other side of the pond and

I bought it in 1965. So now I'm almost thirty years under the same roof and I find that an ideal way to live, for me as a writer in any case.

WACHTEL Earlier, when you mentioned the Civil War and how it's not so very long since the Civil War ended, I was thinking it's always Southern writers who remember that.

PRICE It's always Southern writers who mention it because we lost the war. I suppose the victors forget much more quickly than the losers, because the losers suffer so much. The South is now being invaded by people who have grown up in other parts of the United States. Even in my own childhood, a Yankee was simply someone who wasn't born and bred in the South, and a Yankee was looked upon as not necessarily anyone hostile but as someone who was rather amusingly different, who talked funny. It's still entirely possible to find a great many Southerners in villages and small towns who take that view. I happen to live in a sizable metropolitan area, with one of the highest concentrations of Ph.D.s in the world, so my particular part of the world isn't as intensely Southern as the one I grew up in; but out in the country where I live, I can still walk to my next-door neighbour, and literally find him and his wife talking and thinking like the oldest people I can remember from my childhood. You can tap in to that old Southern tradition at very short notice, if anyone is interested in getting off the interstate highway and talking to the real natives.

WACHTEL How would you characterize Southern writing?

PRICE I would say it's been the best writing in American literature, quite simply. If we look only at a previous generation, the generation of William Faulkner, Katherine Anne Porter, Robert Penn Warren, Eudora Welty, Tennessee Williams and Carson McCullers, it may have looked, twenty years ago, as if that tradition had played itself out. But rather amazingly and wonderfully, in the last fifteen to twenty years, we've seen a renewal of Southern writing, with the rise of a number of very fine young novelists and poets and dramatists who very much think of themselves as being Southern.

WACHTEL Is there anything in terms of the concerns or preoccupations of Southern writers that creates a commonality, or is it just that they're all really good?

PRICE We remain one of the two or three major strands of American literature which is obsessed with the whole idea of family: African American writing; American Jewish fiction; and Southern literature. If you look at metropolitan American literature, such as the New York novel or the L.A. novel, you're likely to find that family doesn't signify in the book as deeply because these are people who live on interstate highways, in automobiles. So I would say first that a Southerner is someone who's obsessed with family and, secondly, a Southerner has something that absolutely nobody else has, on the North American continent anyway. And that is an emotionally intense and intimate contact with African Americans throughout his or her early life — and that's an experience and a blessing which literally no one else in the United States has shared with us.

WACHTEL How do you think that's influenced your writing?

PRICE I write about African Americans because it's my conviction that black people revealed themselves honestly to me in my childhood; I mean, no one can fool a child about affection or love, and I know that in my childhood I was loved and cared for very intensely and very genuinely by a number of black women and a few black men. I felt that gave me certain angles of insight that other people might not have. As complicated and as horrific in some of its aspects as the relationship of blacks to whites has been in the American South, in the states of the old confederacy, the fact remains that we are the only people, again on the North American continent, who have never ceased to have on a day-to-day basis an intimate relationship, in all senses of the word *intimate*, with African Americans who are the descendants, the heirs, of people who were brought to this continent in chains.

WACHTEL Your memoir, *A Whole New Life*, is an account of the terrible illness that struck you ten years ago and has left you in a wheelchair. Can you describe what happened?

PRICE It's exactly ten years ago. I was walking across the university campus with a colleague of mine and he said, "Why are you slapping your foot down on the ground, your right foot?" And I said, "I'm not," and he said, "Yes, you are. Listen!" And I suddenly realized that I was putting my right foot down awkwardly, rather not putting it down, but sort of abandoning it and letting it fall down as I walked. Over the next few weeks, as I began to notice myself, I was having a harder time walking a straight line and in many other ways my walking was becoming compromised. I tried to deny it and told myself that I was simply a fifty-one-year-old man who didn't get enough exercise. But in about a month I had to confess that I was in some sort of serious trouble and I took myself to Duke University Hospital, which is one of the world's great medical research centres, and in a couple of days they discovered that I had imbedded in the centre of my spinal cord an enormous malignant tumour, a tumour that was about ten inches long and about the thickness of a pencil, laid down so intricately amongst the nerves of my spinal cord that at the time of that first surgery, in 1984, they were completely unable to remove it. They managed to remove only about ten per cent of it because it was so implicated in the crucial nerves of my cord that I would have died had they attempted to remove more. They let that wound heal for about a month and then they gave me the maximum amount of radiation, which was then the only other available therapy. In the course of that treatment my legs were rapidly paralyzed, almost certainly as a result of the therapy itself.

The therapy arrested the growth of the tumour for nearly two years, until the tumour recurred in an even more vicious form and I began having hallucinations and other awful symptoms. But by that time an ultrasonic laser scalpel had been perfected and in 1986 it was possible for my original surgeon to go back in and remove the tumour. Since then I've had annual MRI scans, which have shown no recurrence of cancer. As we all know, cancer survivors never claim cure, we claim that we are recovered at this particular moment, and that's certainly the way I feel. But it has been an extraordinary gift of time, certainly considering that the original prognosis was that I might have a year to a year and a half to live.

WACHTEL The story of your life in the last ten years is in some ways full of the themes that run through your fiction — family and friendship, pain and loss, memory and dream, extraordinary connections between people, even moments of grace — but what you had to live through is real. Near the end of your book *A Whole New Life* you say that the last few years have been better than the fifty-odd years that preceded them. How have they been better?

PRICE It's been better in some very large ways and in some small particulars, and some of the ways are obviously so intimate that they're not really discussable. But I think some of the very big ways are simply that, like anyone who becomes paralyzed and is suddenly physically extremely circumscribed, I found that I developed a far greater sense of patience and tolerance in my daily life. I'd never been exactly an "A-type" personality, highly driven, but I have become considerably more serene, and that has been very good for my writing. It's made me a better witness of the world and a better transcriber of the reality of the world that I think I see.

It's also brought me huge advantages in terms of my having had proved to me what every human being hopes for, which is that he or she is loved, and as the young woman says in Yeats' famous poem, we all want to be loved for ourselves alone and not our yellow hair. My hair was black and is now white, but I of course always wanted to know I was loved for myself alone. It's been proven to me by extraordinarily selfless friends, ranging from the age of my students in the university to people even older than myself. I was also the beneficiary of the marvellous medical skill of some of the technicians who worked on me, though, as I make clear in the book, I have no words of praise, in fact words of deep regret and almost excoriation for a very small number of the doctors with whom I had to deal.

WACHTEL One thing for sure is that the last ten years has been a period of great productivity for you.

PRICE I'm working in about double, sometimes triple, speed apparently.

WACHTEL And as you say, the books are different from what came before "in more ways than age." How so?

PRICE I think they are probably freer books. They come out of a mind that's perhaps less hedged in with qualifications and uncertainties; they come out of a certain state of mental confidence, of calm, and I think it's been good for the work, it's been good, literally, for the prose itself.

WACHTEL I guess your saying your life is better, I mean, given all the pain and agony you describe in your book, it's hard to understand —

PRICE Perhaps I've become a little Oriental, perhaps a little Hindu, in the sense of realizing that an enormous number of the things that looked so precious to me, certain physical skills and physical abilities and capacities, were in fact hindrances to my life. St. John of the Cross says that only when we have put away from ourselves the desire for created things can we begin to look upon the face of eternity. I'm not saying I've achieved some sort of beatific vision, but I am saying that I've learned how to surrender a great many things that I had thought were very important and ultimately turned out to be utterly meaningless and completely unnecessary in my life.

I'm aware that it sounds like a slightly idiot claim but it's one that's true for me; I wouldn't ask anyone else to believe it about him or herself, but if you handed me a choice that I could go back and reverse the traumatic challenge which I faced ten years ago, I think I'd choose to live through the extremely complicated and very difficult but also very productive and winning decade that I've had.

May 1994
interview initially prepared in collaboration
with Sandra Rabinovitch

JEANETTE WINTERSON

Years ago, when I opened Jeanette Winterson's first novel, *Oranges Are Not the Only Fruit* (1985), I laughed out loud. It was the witty deadpan style combined with unconventional content: a coming-of-age story about a foundling raised in an evangelical household: "My father liked to watch the wrestling, my mother liked to wrestle; it didn't matter what." The narrator's mother expects her to become a missionary, a saint and a model of purity. She does, in fact, become a preacher with her mother's group, Society for the Lost. But then she falls in love with another church member, a girl, and her life takes a new direction.

The central character of *Oranges Are Not the Only Fruit* is named Jeanette, and there are obvious parallels with Winterson's own life. She grew up in Lancashire, the adopted daughter and only child of Pentecostal evangelists. She wrote sermons at eight and has said she can't remember a time when she *wasn't* preaching. At fifteen, after getting involved with another girl, she left home. Later, she took a degree in English at Oxford.

Jeanette Winterson was only twenty-six when *Oranges Are Not the Only Fruit* was published. It won England's Whitbread Award for best first novel, and it was made into a television drama and feature film. Winterson wrote the award-winning screenplay. Her next novel, *The Passion* (1987), won the John Llewellyn Rhys Memorial Prize. It's about a cook in Napoleon's army who falls in love with a beautiful woman, a Venetian bisexual cross-dresser born with webbed feet. Then came *Sexing the Cherry* (1989), a historical fantasy set in seventeenth-century England, featuring a grotesque giantess named Dog Woman and twelve dancing princesses. It won the E.M. Forster Award from the American Academy and Institute of Arts and Letters.

But it was Jeanette Winterson's 1992 novel, *Written on the Body*, which brought her not only fame but notoriety in England. A love story set in modern London, Winterson included an homage to Monique Wittig's *Le Corps Lesbien*, in which the lover obsessively tracks the inside of the body of the beloved. *Written on the Body* has been translated into sixteen languages.

In 1993, the literary magazine, *Granta*, included Winterson in its Best of Young British Novelists. Winterson concurred in the *Sunday Times* when she was invited to nominate the greatest living writer. She wrote, "No one working in the English language now comes close to my exuberance, my passion, my fidelity to words." Winterson was dubbed one of England's most outstanding, "least modest great authors." When her next novel, *Art and Lies* (1994), appeared — bringing together three voices, named Handel, Picasso and Sappho — the critics were eager to pounce. "For an experimenter these are hard times," she's written. "The challenge is exhilarating and enviable. The struggle is vertical." Winterson's next volley was a book of essays, *Art Objects: Essays on Ecstasy and Effrontery* (1995).

Jeanette Winterson was born in 1959. She's always been an ambitious, subversive and imaginative writer. "It's a problem in some ways having been told that you can change the world," she's said. "If they say it to you young enough you

believe it for the rest of your life." She spoke to me from the
CBC's London studio.

WACHTEL There's a line in your novel, *Art and Lies:* "There's no
such thing as autobiography, there's only art and lies." What do
you mean by that?

WINTERSON I mean that there is far too much emphasis put on
the life of a writer rather than on a writer's work. Anybody can
lead an interesting, a difficult, a traumatic, a fantastic life, but those
lives don't translate themselves into books that speak to many
people all over the world. What makes the translation is art itself,
the skill and ingenuity and work of the writer. The only way into
a piece of literature is through the front door: you open the book
and you read it.

WACHTEL I want to talk to you mostly about art, but also a bit
about the life. You were raised in Lancashire as the only child, as
the adopted child, of Pentecostal evangelists, and at one point you
yourself became a preacher. Can you talk about that environment?

WINTERSON I've really decided that I won't talk about that any
more because it seems to me that my own life is entirely insig-
nificant. I will die, I will be forgotten. Perhaps my books will last,
perhaps they won't.

WACHTEL I'm interested, though, in the way in which certain
aspects of the way you lived in your childhood, for instance the
idea of being a preacher, of having a sense of mission, of a rever-
ence for language and the power of language, later affected your
approach to art.

WINTERSON Of course it was extremely useful training to be
brought up in an environment where you must attract other people to your way of thinking, you must win them over; it's the art
of persuasion, it's rhetoric in the old-fashioned sense. I learned
how to handle language and the spoken word and the written
word, and I learned how to persuade. That's what preachers do,
that's what preachers are, and the most successful preachers are the
ones who are able to convince their audience that the audience

themselves have got it wrong and the preacher's got it right. And the artist tries to do this too — there are close parallels — except the artist does it in its own right, for its own sake, not for some higher purpose, not for God. You can see from the look on somebody's face whether or not you're persuading, and that does translate itself to the way you then write. It's not that you have an audience in mind, it's simply that you can imagine what will perhaps tilt the balance in your favour, how to get underneath the barriers and the defences which people normally put up to protect themselves from intrusion.

WACHTEL You seem to have a particular passion for language and it comes out very forcefully in *Art and Lies*. There are phrases such as "by my words will you know me," and you talk about "the winged word," "the mercurial word" — image after image about the power of language. Why does language inspire you in this way? Do you know where this passion comes from?

WINTERSON I suppose it comes from the Bible. I was raised on the Bible. I dare say I know it better than anybody else, certainly most modern people, and it is a wonderfully written book. It contains in it ways of speaking, parables and stories, fictions, which are very potent and very personal. For me, language is a freedom. As soon as you have found the words with which to express something, you are no longer incoherent, you are no longer trapped by your own emotions, by your own experiences; you can describe them, you can tell them, you can bring them out of yourself and give them to somebody else. That is an enormously liberating experience, and it worries me that more and more people are learning not to use language; they're giving in to the banalities of the television media and shrinking their vocabulary, shrinking their own way of using this fabulous tool that human beings have refined over so many centuries into this extremely sensitive instrument. I don't want to make it crude, I don't want to make it into shopping-list language, I don't want to make it into simply an exchange of information: I want to make it into the subtle, emotional, intellectual, freeing thing that it is and that it can be.

WACHTEL One of the things that I like about the way you celebrate language is that you're also fully aware of not only its powers but its limitations. I was reminded of the T.S. Eliot line, "I have
to use words when I talk to you." You have lines such as, "What
can be known about me? What I say? What I do? What I have
written? And which is true?" You're very conscious of the artifice
of language and its limitations.

WINTERSON Yes, it is artificial, but it is, as yet, the best way human
beings have found to communicate to one another their deepest,
their most difficult, feelings. And that is the preserve of poetry and
of true fiction, to put roots down through the surface into the
subsoil of the human heart and to draw up those elements that
would otherwise lie locked there, unheard, unspoken, perhaps un-
regarded. Language can do that, and I think that it is the duty of
the writer to go on pushing language forward because if it's not
developing, if it's not growing, if people aren't using it in unique
and different ways while at the same time regarding its tradition,
then that language is going to start atrophying.

WACHTEL Is the emphasis on language itself traditionally thought
to have been the domain of poetry more than prose? Is that something you feel you have to counter?

WINTERSON I feel that things are changing. Art forms must always
change. Until the nineteenth century the dominant art form in
English was the epic poem; and then in the nineteenth century,
particularly from the 1840s on, we find that the novel is becoming much more important. The novel is essentially a nineteenth-
century product, which was again challenged in the early twentieth
century by the modernists. We know about this. We know Oscar
Wilde starts it off, trying to pull away all that terrible Victorian
realism and get back to something which is highly wrought and
artificial and strange and self-conscious, and the modernists of
course take this up. But the modernist experiment stops horribly
with the Second World War, and I feel that there was so much
dreariness in literature in the late forties, fifties and sixties, until
we get to a writer like Angela Carter, for instance, in 1967, who
is prepared again to use words magically, inventively, to use them

as more than vehicles for something else but to use them in their own right. It seems to me that the modernist experiment has to be picked up again.

WACHTEL Some critics have observed that there's something old-fashioned about your writing in the sense that it is going back to what you're calling the modernist experiment.

WINTERSON I think it's very odd when critics talk about the nineteenth-century novel as something which is alive and trendy and important when it was a construct for the nineteenth century and was thoroughly kicked over, and quite right, too. I think we should be going on with that experiment. You cannot stop in art, you cannot fossilize art in a redundant form, and you cannot take a point in history and favour it above any other point and say, ah yes, this is the way to do it. If you want to read nineteenth-century novels, there are plenty for you to read, and you may as well read the real thing and not go out and buy a reproduction. Personally, I loathe reproduction furniture; I'd rather have something made by a living designer, just as I'd rather have something made by a writer now who, whilst recognizing patterns and traditions, is prepared to go on pushing the experiment forward.

WACHTEL From your first novel to your most recent, your work is becoming less tied to narrative, to story, in the conventional sense. Why is that?

WINTERSON It's a particular experiment that I am pursuing. I don't say that it's the only experiment by any means, I don't say it's the experiment for everybody, but this is my contribution, this is what I can do, and so I'm doing it to the best of my ability. For me the challenge is to fuse the densities, the exactness, the precision of poetry with the scope and the emotional possibility of the larger canvas of a novel, where you can use character and situation and place — however you use it, however bizarrely — to bring in more than you can perhaps say, particularly in a shorter poem. I think it's important to try to bring those disciplines together and to see if we can produce quite a different kind of art form, quite a different kind of fiction.

WACHTEL And then what happens to story?

WINTERSON Obviously there must be a way of bringing the book satisfyingly to the readers. But readers, I think, are more sophisticated on the whole than critics. They can make the jumps, they can make imaginative leaps. If your structure is firm and solid enough, however strange, however unusual, they will be able to follow it. They will climb with you to the most unlikely places if they trust you, if the words give them the right footholds, the right handholds. That's what I want my readers to do: I want them to come with me when we're going mountain-climbing. This isn't a walk through a theme park. This is some dangerous place that neither of us has been before, and I hope that by travelling there first, I can encourage the reader to come with me and that we will make the trip again together, and safely.

WACHTEL You've talked about two things that distinguish us from other animals and that's the possibility of language and an interest in the past. I want to talk a bit more about your own interest in the past because you've made such vivid use of history in some of your fiction. *The Passion* takes place in part during the Napoleonic campaigns, and *Sexing the Cherry* is a fantastical story that's set in part in the seventeenth century, in Cromwellian England.

WINTERSON I can see no reason to be bound by chronological time. As far as we know, the universe is not bound by it; as far as we know, it is yet another construct of ours, this worship of the clock and the idea that there is a past and a present and a future which trot along obediently in line and never swap places. In our own lives we know that that's not true because human beings seem capable of moving imaginatively, backwards and forwards, of pushing out of the body. I think of it really as an out-of-the-body experience — that's not something that only shamans and New Age hippies have. It's something that we all have quite often in our lives. And I wanted to bring that into fiction because it seems to me to be a more honest reality than the rather dull reality of the clock.

WACHTEL The epigraph to *Art and Lies* invites us to enter the world of your novel. It's a quote that says that "The nature of a work of art is to be not a part, nor yet a copy of the real world, but a world in itself." What is the world you want us to enter in this novel?

WINTERSON *Art and Lies* is a journey into deep inner space, and the characters in the book are not characters in the physical sense that we know them on the street or perhaps even in our own lives. They are consciousnesses. They are ways of talking about ourselves, writ large, as we might be, more than we are. I know that the world of *Art and Lies* is a strange one, but it is a deeply emotional one and it is one which probes and peels away at the complacencies and habits that we take for granted and drag behind us as so much baggage in our lives. The worlds that I create are always worlds where it's possible to find new space, not to be cluttered any more, to leave behind things which perhaps drag you down, things that you don't need. In the book there is this freedom from gravity that we've been talking about. It is a sanctified space. And when you come out of it, what you do is up to you; but for a while it puts away the clutter and the jangle of modern life and gives time, infinite time. It may take four hours to read the book but actually it takes an entire life. The journey that you make is not one of the clock: it's an interior one, and in it you travel through time, through space, through place.

WACHTEL Why a sanctified space?

WINTERSON Because it's a space that has been cleansed of other associations. It is itself, it's coherent, it's self-realized, it exists in its own right. Every work of art must be that; it must be a closed world. That is, you must be able to enter it and find it coherent and orderly, and be able to return to it to discover things you hadn't found at first. But there is something cathedral-like about it: it's a place where you can rest, contemplate, refuel and go out again knowing that it remains there for you. All art presents a sanctified space.

WACHTEL I wouldn't think of rest in relation to your work. I would think of it as perhaps soaring or provocative or disturbing, but rest is not the first word that comes to mind.

WINTERSON It depends what you want from your cathedral. In mine there are choirs and orchestras, but there is also the peace of otherness, the peace of difference, the peace that you feel any time you get out of your own environment. That in itself is often a release for us. People need to take their vacations, need to get out of the house — anything that releases the moment of unbearable tension. I hope that my books do release those moments of unbearable tension and that the reader is relieved in some way, literally, of things that perhaps they didn't even notice they were carrying.

WACHTEL *Art and Lies* features three interwoven monologues by characters whom you call Handel, Picasso and Sappho. Why have you chosen to name your characters for these particular artists? What resonance do these names have for you?

WINTERSON Naming is important to me, and we do find as we go along in the book that of course these names are not the real names of anybody, which is a game I like to play, because what *is* your identity? Is it the name you were given? Is it the name that you choose for yourself? All of these characters have to think about that. I think a writer is allowed a certain leeway. I wanted to call my Catholic priest, my cancer surgeon, Handel because Handel is the composer who means the most to me and it is his formality, his mathematical precision and his quiet beauty which I wanted to give to my character. Also, the sense of loss that I find in his music. But then, ultimately, his sense of triumph. And I like the effrontery of calling a young, unknown woman Picasso; I thought that was suitable. She wants to paint. Let her! Let her be a genius. Why not?

WACHTEL And Sappho?

WINTERSON Sappho may or may not exist. She is both a long-dead poet and she is a person in her own right, and we never quite find out about her mysterious agency. She holds the book together through her commentary and her reasoning and also her emotional power, which is eventually what brings the book to a proper close, finishes it. I wanted to talk about Sappho the poet, and I wanted to challenge ideas that we have about sexuality and about sexuality and writers and, even now, she's more famous as the number-one lesbian than she is as a great poet.

WACHTEL But part of what she represents in your book is, as you put it, the number-one lesbian.

WINTERSON Yes, it is. She offers a dangerous and different sexual identity. And obviously I want to do that. You know, I'm never going to write jolly straight romps. There has to be in my books that kind of glorious perversion.

WACHTEL Handel, the first voice in the book, is a very compelling character. He is, as you say, a former priest; he's now a celebrated cancer surgeon, a breast-cancer surgeon, who has been subjected, as we eventually learn, to unusual surgery himself. Can you talk a bit about the tradition, the practice of being a *castrato* within the Catholic church? Why did this interest you?

WINTERSON It's a wonderful story. Until the nineteenth century, there was really much less anxiety about sexual difference and about sexual propriety. For instance, in opera, until the nineteenth century, cross-dressing roles were usual: men sang as women, women sang as men. The composer — Handel in particular — simply chose the voice that he wanted; he would usually write for a celebrated singer and use that singer regardless, in whatever role he liked. So the opera audience was quite used to seeing people on stage pretending to be what they weren't, just as we in Shakespeare are used to seeing boys dressed as girls and girls dressed as boys. It's really not a modern thing; it was only in the nineteenth century that people suddenly thought, my God, we can't do this, it's disgusting! And of course you don't get it again until Strauss's *Rosenkavalier* in 1911, where he uses cross-dressing roles. But the nineteenth century: no. What you can have in the nineteenth century is music hall, even music hall camp, and you can have pantomime, but it's all got to be clear that what we're seeing is a girl dressed up as a boy or a boy dressed up as a girl. We're not supposed to believe in it, we're not supposed to be troubled by it, it's supposed to be a joke. I wanted to put back the troubling aspect of finding in yourself desires that you are not supposed to feel. There's a wonderful piece in Casanova's diary where he says, "Whenever he saw a *castrato* on the stage, he and lots of other lusty heterosexual men would fall head over heels in love with this fascinating, compromised creature." Of course that is creating emotion around the forbidden, which is also what art does, to go into those forbidden places and say, well, what do you really feel? Not what you're supposed to feel. It's very disturbing. Our queer culture is working now in the same direction: lesbians are no longer afraid of saying, well, I think that man's really sexy. And this is a good thing. It's breaking down rigid notions of sexual identity, whether homosexual or heterosexual. But of course we haven't got there first, we're just returning to something which the nineteenth century very kindly stamped on for us. I'm not fond of the nineteenth century.

WACHTEL I noticed. If I had to say what features really distinguish your work, one would be this fascination with language, and the other would be the blurring of the boundaries between the sexes.

WINTERSON I think it's necessary to be more than your sexual identity. It's necessary to free yourself up. That's the process I'm interested in. I want to see how much emotion we can pack into a life, how much emotion we can pack into a work. It's about feeling. To limit your feeling seems to me to be dangerous and pointless. So I would like my readers to feel things that they have not felt before and to explore emotional territory that is otherwise closed to them. That's the aspect that fascinates me. But as for language, you know, if I wasn't in love with language, what right have I to be here talking to you? What right have I to put pen to paper? It's more than a job: it's a life, it's a vocation, it's everything to me, and I must fulfill myself in that way and by fulfilling myself, I hope that I can give the best possible work to my readers.

WACHTEL I understand you read for about five hours a day. What do you read?

WINTERSON My reading is very wide and it's rather obscure, I suppose. At the moment I'm reading Chaucer, at the same time as reading Virginia Woolf again and Robert Graves. I feel part of those people, those friends who are dead, who are gone. Their work influences my work. Of course it *must,* it's a connection. Unless I have a thorough soaking in all writers who have written in English then I cannot call myself an English writer. It's a fantastic language, and to be ignorant of it as a writer is a sin that must exact the ultimate penalty, I think. If hell exists, that's why one would go there, for calling oneself a writer and not knowing anything about English literature. So I feel that I have to continue to immerse myself; and also, I solve technical problems that way, and if I'm troubled, I can usually find someone who can help me. Of course they are dead, but that doesn't matter because their books are still alive.

WACHTEL You seem to dislike not only the nineteenth century but in *Art and Lies* the late twentieth century. Contemporary London in particular comes across as a very bleak, grim landscape.

WINTERSON Well, it is, and I think we have to fight against that. We have to fight against the disintegration of society, which is happening not just here but in many places in the world, and unless we fight against it, it will certainly happen, and then all the forces of reaction and of money and of power will take over. I don't want to live like that. I think that art can make a difference because it pulls people up short. It says, don't accept things for their face value; you don't have to go along with any of this; you can think for yourself. It gives you a kind of self-reliance. We all feel powerless and we can't really manage to do anything because there's just so much. I want to try and cut through those feelings of apathy and powerlessness and be a kind of rallying point, offer a rallying cry, to people who would otherwise feel dispossessed.

WACHTEL Handel, the doctor in the novel, is weary and disillusioned. At one point he refers to himself as "a chessboard knight," and a question that haunts him — and to varying degrees haunts us all — is this question: how shall I live? Is there an answer to that question?

WINTERSON It's an individual answer, and it's certainly not an answer that can be got easily. It's the answer of a lifetime. It seems to me to be the work that we are here to do, to answer that question — first of all in our own lives and then as a community. I don't answer the question in the book — I wouldn't be so gross as that — but I do think it has to be asked, and if people then begin to ponder on it and ask it of themselves, then that is a good thing. I do believe that when you start asking these questions, you find the answers that you need, if you'll put in the effort, even if it takes a lifetime. And there's a lot of effort in these books. They're not simple, they don't offer easy solutions.

WACHTEL The nature of art and its relationship to truth are vexing questions in *Art and Lies*. At one point Handel asks, what should he trust, actual life or imagined life? You talk about the meaning of the word "invent," and say that originally it meant *to come upon*, not *to devise* or *contrive* or *fabricate*, but *to find that which already exists*.

WINTERSON Yes, because it's from the Latin *invenire*, which means *to come upon*. This takes us back to Plato's idea that we are in a continual state of remembering, that the human life span is to remember, to remember the things that we are, that we can be, that we've left behind — to remember the glories of the soul, as Plato would have seen it.

WACHTEL How does that apply to you as an artist or a writer? Do you see yourself as having to uncover what's already there? I think of your books as inventions.

WINTERSON It is a question of always going back and uncovering what is already there because the artist is something of a dredger: you have to let down your net and pull up things from the mud, from the silt, that are unrecognizable, that have been forgotten, that have lain disused and ignored for a long time. You bring them up and you clean them off and you look at them and you bring them back into the present where they can speak, where they have a place. I think it's a dual role of dredging and of cleaning, but then also of re-creating so that you are always offering something that is right for your own time, that is new in itself.

WACHTEL You were saying something about offering a beacon of hope in *Art and Lies*. But there's a lot of anguish in that book, and not just in Handel or Picasso, who's a young woman struggling to overcome a childhood of abuse. In large measure it seems fairly relentlessly pessimistic, at least until quite close to the end.

WINTERSON I don't think it's pessimistic at all because everyone in the book finds a particular redemption which is right for them, and Picasso in her own story leaves behind a loveless, violent, privileged childhood and cuts loose and learns how to heal herself. To learn how to heal yourself seems to me to be the most important thing that you can do because at that moment you are genuinely self-reliant, and if other people hurt you — as they will — it won't matter because you have now in your own hands the tools of healing. And Picasso achieves that, which is very significant. Both Handel and Sappho arrive at a resolution for their own lives, not a trite one, but one that takes them much further than they were when the book begins. I am not interested in what I think the Americans call "closure." I don't want to tie things up nicely; I want to leave them open and ambiguous, and perhaps with a sense of things going on outside of the last page. All my books end like that. There's always another journey which is beginning at the end of the book. It's the same in *Written on the Body,* the last paragraph begins, "This is where the story starts. . . ."

WACHTEL *Art and Lies* ends with "It was not too late," which is a very hopeful kind of statement. Where does the hope come from?

WINTERSON I am irrepressibly hopeful. Also irrepressibly happy, in spite of it all, which doesn't mean to say that I'm either complacent or indifferent. I *have* to believe that in the end what is good, what is honourable, what is exceptional about human beings will triumph over what is simply small and mean and devious. If I didn't believe that, I might as well slit my own throat now and certainly stop work, because writers have to believe that their words will carry on speaking to people and that there is a people worth speaking to. You have to believe in a kind of continuity, and you do especially because you look back at the past and you were glad that those books have been written, that they exist, that they are there for you now, and you want to go on adding to that.

September 1994
*interview initially prepared in collaboration
with Sandra Rabinovitch*

ALICE WALKER

Novelist, essayist and poet, Alice Walker is one of the most popular African American women writers. She was born in Eatonton, Georgia on February 9, 1944 — the eighth child of sharecroppers. As a result of a childhood injury, she lost the sight in her right eye, a calamity which enabled her to attend an elite black women's college in Atlanta on a scholarship for the disabled. After two years, she transferred to an elite white women's college, Sarah Lawrence, in New England. It was at Sarah Lawrence that she started to write publishable poetry and short stories.

In the late 1960s, Walker was active in the civil rights movement in Mississippi. In fact, she married a white civil rights lawyer and they had a daughter. In the 1970s, she established her reputation as a fiction writer with two novels, *The Third Life of Grange Copeland* (1970) and *Meridian* (1976), and with two books of stories, *In Love and Trouble* (1973) and, later, *You Can't Keep a Good Woman Down* (1981). Her candid, searing writing about the lives of black women was acclaimed as a breakthrough. "One of the most important, grieving, graceful and honest writers ever to come into print," is how the African American poet, June Jordan put it.

But her big breakthrough came in 1983 when Alice Walker's novel, *The Color Purple* (1982), won both the Pulitzer Prize and the American Book Award. An epistolary novel about Celie, a poor, beaten-down Southern woman, *The Color Purple* was a surprise bestseller and then a major motion picture, directed by Steven Spielberg and starring Whoopi Goldberg. In 1996, Walker published her screenplay of that novel and her reflections on the film in a book called *The Same River Twice: Honoring the Difficult.*

The letters in *The Color Purple* are written by Celie to God, and also by her sister Nettie, who's a missionary in Africa. This connection to Africa led to Alice Walker's next two novels. *The Temple of My Familiar* (1989) was described by the South African writer, J. M. Coetzee, as "a mixture of mythic fantasy, revisionary history, exemplary biography and sermon." And in 1992, *Possessing the Secret of Joy* was Walker's indictment of ritual female genital mutilation.

Alice Walker not only *writes* about resilient, heroic women, but through her own bold fiction and activist politics, she has become one for many readers. For the last fifteen years, Walker has lived in northern California. She spoke to me from San Francisco.

WACHTEL You've said of your background, growing up poor, black and in the American South, that no one, no writer, could wish for a more advantageous heritage. What do you mean by that?

WALKER I wasn't speaking of the poverty; I was speaking of the richness of the landscape, the people, the community, and my sense of having very interesting and solid parents, who of course had their difficulties and problems, too, but on the whole were quite admirable.

WACHTEL Can you give me a picture of the environment that you were raised in?

WALKER I was raised in the country until I was thirteen and we moved to town, and the town itself was country — it was very small. I am thinking now of all the various little houses we lived in, and in each one we saw no one else. We could look out any window and only see trees and the sky and hear various running streams, and this is what I really long for, often.

WACHTEL Your parents and grandparents were sharecroppers; you were the youngest of eight children. Do you remember the feel of the place?

WALKER It was very much in the South, in Georgia, and quite isolated in many ways. Of course there was absolute apartheid and, as in South Africa, this did not simply mean a separation of the races. It meant that white people got all of the best of everything and that people of colour got very little of anything — very little if any health care, very little dental care, all the way down the line. It was about the white people taking the lion's share of what would sustain life and leaving the barest of everything for people of colour to survive on.

WACHTEL You've written about your father, a relationship that was complex and at times difficult. He was one of the first black men to vote in Eatonton, Georgia, in the 1930s. Can you tell me more about him?

WALKER My father had eight children and for the first four of those children he was still in the prime of life — he was healthy, he was strong, he was optimistic. He believed that if he got the vote, for instance, things would absolutely change forever, for him and for his children. So he was a very different kind of man then. He was actually a community activist and was responsible for organizing the first schools in my community and hiring the first teachers, including my first teacher. But by the time I became, oh, I guess six or seven, it was very clear that he had become very disillusioned and also his health had begun to fail, so he was a quite different kind of father for me than he was for my older sisters and brothers.

WACHTEL In what way?

WALKER Oh, shorter of temper and much less willing to believe in anything. He was disillusioned, because he had worked all of his life and had very little to show for it, and he had become rather bitter.

WACHTEL In one of your short stories a character is moved by reading about Richard Wright's father, who becomes for this character almost a symbol of a door that refused to open and that was always closed like a fist. I know this is a fiction but it seemed to me that it was very heartfelt.

WALKER It is, and not just for me; this is something that happens to so many people. Often parents don't realize that when in their disillusionment they close themselves off from their children, they really are hurting them very deeply.

WACHTEL In your essay about your father you say that you share many of his characteristics, not just physical but others as well. How is that?

WALKER I have my father's love of good food and cooking. I have my father's love of nurturing. I think of him, especially in the years before I was born, as being the primary nurturer in the family rather than my mother. He had a much higher level of comfort with taking care of the children and cooking than she did. He also loved music as I do. He was not someone who was all that selective about the kind of music; he just loved music itself.

WACHTEL You've written: "What I regret most about my relationship with my father is that it did not improve until after his death." What happened?

WALKER I had reached a period in my own life of great despair and an understanding of how difficult it is to change a social and political system just by sheer will and putting your body and mind on the line. At the time I was also having difficulty with my marriage. It was one of those difficult passages of life when you as the child can begin to understand the passages of your parents, and you begin to know some of the troubles they've seen, and I was able to feel a greater empathy with him. This was wonderful because all along I had loved him, but we had had so many struggles and he was also very sexist — of course for me that meant a constant battle. But through everything I had really loved him and admired him. I always thought he was very beautiful as well, so I came to enfold him in my own spirit.

WACHTEL You say that your father taught you something very important: not to bother telling lies because the listener might be delighted with the truth.

WALKER I don't think he told me in those words because that's an adult way of dealing with the subject of truth-telling. What happened was that when I was three or four, I broke a jar, and given that I had siblings I could have said that they had broken it, or I could have said that it had slipped. I remember that he asked me if I had done it, and I looked at him and I thought, gee, this is a person I really love and he would be happy if I hadn't broken this thing. On the other hand he was looking at me with such expectancy that I found myself coming up to meet his expectancy with a real need to express the truth, because that's the most wonderful feeling there is. So I said, "Yes, I broke the jar." His response was not to fuss and not to spank me or anything but rather to beam this incredible love in my direction, and that was his way of teaching me about telling the truth and what is possible. It is possible that if you tell the truth not only will you be delivered yourself from the prison of untruth, but the person who hears the truth will also be opened and can be delighted, as he was.

WACHTEL You also talk about your mother as an important influence but more with respect to the stories that she told you.

WALKER No, more in respect to her being an earth goddess actually. She was an amazingly creative gardener and someone who was wholly connected to earth life, and this is partly because she grew up on a farm and lived her entire life on a farm. There was very little about growing plants and animals that my mother didn't know, and I was mesmerized, enchanted, by this knowledge and wisdom and the ease that is possible living on the earth. It seems to me that the gift of being shown how to live on the earth is incredibly great and the gift of story is just about as great but maybe comes just a tiny bit after that.

WACHTEL I'm thinking about the gift of learning how to live on the earth. Is that something that took a while to really take in, though? It would seem to me that's something that would take almost a lifetime to learn.

WALKER Yes, I think you take forever to learn that. Some people will never learn it. Obviously — look at the earth! But there are people who actually do know how to live on the earth and have done so without harming it, and that is what she was able to show me.

WACHTEL You lost the sight in one eye through an accident when you were eight years old, and when I read that it reminded me of another writer, Jim Harrison, who also lost an eye at around that age (he was seven). He said that it left him with a sense of uncertainty about the world, that at any moment you might fall through the earth where the crust is thin. How did it affect you?

WALKER First of all, it wasn't entirely an accident. One of my brothers shot me with a BB gun. But I think we will all fall through the earth whether the crust is thin or not — that is the end for each of us and it's not a bad thing. I think it has connected me to people who are injured and it has made me much more patient and much more empathic with people with injuries, and it has helped me to see how much of the world is injured and how the earth itself is injured. There are a lot of lessons in every bit of adversity, and sometimes they can be almost overwhelming, but if you can stick around to learn them, they're very useful.

WACHTEL I'd like to talk about how you came to writing because you seem to have developed a very powerful sense of mission as a writer. How or when did you realize that writing could be not just an outlet but a tool?

WALKER When you say "tool" I think about a pen and a typewriter, those things as tools. I think of the act of writing as creative as if I were making a basket. That is in fact how I see what I do, that it is the creation of something in the world that hasn't existed before in just this form and that while I am engaged in it, I am at a very high level of concentration, absorption and joy, and this is something that I hope to pass on to the person who receives this thing that I have created.

WACHTEL I was thinking of tool not as something mechanical necessarily but more as a tool for change. I think at one point you said you were brought up to look at things that are out of joint or out of balance and then try to bring them into balance.

WALKER That is what storytelling does. So any story in that sense is a tool because no matter how bleak it may seem, and how deep the myth, what it is doing is bringing you into balance when you hear it and when you connect with it.

WACHTEL You wrote something quite startling in an essay where you said that "writing saved me from the sin and inconvenience of violence."

WALKER I think it's true that there is an awful lot of anger in the world, and in me, and that there is a real need to be creative with it rather than destructive. I think of violence as basically useless; it doesn't solve anything. The more violence you create the more violence you have. So it really is an inconvenience. It's like lying; if you lie, you're constantly trying to remember what you lied about and how you lied. With violence, if you create it, you're always trying to figure out why you did it or how to deal with the messiness of it or, later on, how to absolve yourself. Much better to create something, much better to talk.

WACHTEL I was thinking of that when I read about how the first story that you ever wrote, but didn't publish, was called "The Suicide of an American Girl," and then the second story, which you did publish, was called "To Hell with Dying." This was when you were just twenty or twenty-one. I don't want to put too much weight on the titles, but what happened to get you from "The Suicide of an American Girl" to "To Hell with Dying"?

WALKER Well, just life itself. After a while, the thought of suicide as the remedy, which takes you out of the picture but leaves this wonderful earth that you would be missing, started to pall and my love of life won over. I realized I would miss the smallest things in life. I just had a friend visiting me in the country over the weekend and she brought some oranges — she put them in a bowl and every time I passed by I would smell these oranges and I finally stopped in my tracks and stuck my whole head in the bowl, smelling these oranges, and I said to her, "You know, when I'm dead, this is what I'll miss." They reminded me of the oranges of my childhood, when one orange would perfume the whole room and it was the most amazing thing. It was like having a very small sun that had a scent in the room with you. And it's as basic as that. The scent of an orange, the feel of the breeze, how water feels when you get in it when it's really cold in a creek. Whatever madness is going on in the world that seems impossible, there's also the orange and the stream and the breeze.

WACHTEL In your novels and stories, you've created a portrait of the black woman as one of America's greatest heroes. Why did you make it your purpose to celebrate her?

WALKER Oh, absolute love. From my mother to my first-grade teacher to all of the teachers that I had — I had wonderful teachers — I could see that these women were great human beings and it amazed me that they were not only unsung but were put down daily, consistently, and this was not at all what was in my heart when I saw them. I always saw the person who was struggling to take care of the family and keep the community going. I remember how my mother used to keep the whole church going. With the little money that she made from being a maid, she would buy this cheap carpeting and put it in the pulpit in the church and she would reupholster the chairs in the church and she would wash the curtains, and she did all of this and nobody ever asked her whether she wanted to speak to the congregation.

WACHTEL Lissie, a character in one of your recent novels, *The Temple of My Familiar*, recalls her past lives and says, "In lifetime after lifetime I have known oppression," and she enumerates all the origins of that oppression. Then she says, "but I've always been a black woman" — although we discover in the story that's not always the case — and she says, "this was just luck." Why luck?

WALKER Because she obviously loved being what she was. The great joy of life is to be happy with what you are and who you are. There's no greater joy. It's like being born as a rose, knowing you're a rose, and being delighted that you're a rose and not a tulip, and this is what she's expressing. However, since we've all been on this planet for such a long time, we've all been everything, and this is what she has to admit. She has to admit that as much as she doesn't like white people, or white men, this is also part of who she is, so that is what she's talking about eventually, though not during that passage.

WACHTEL One of your most compelling portraits of a poor black Southern woman is in your best-known work, *The Color Purple*, in the voice and character of Celie. Can you tell me how her voice came to you?

WALKER From a lot of black women, older black women, but especially my step-grandmother, Rachel, who had this laconic, vibrant way of speaking. She spoke so much like who she was that if she were behind a curtain and you heard her speaking and you'd never met her, I think you could see her. She was very true to her voice. And this was always intriguing to me, because she was also someone who had been much abused and beaten down but who remained a generous person. I could see the generosity and the kindness when I was growing up. And I could also see that the people who were oppressing her — not just her husband but the white people in the larger society — I could see that they didn't see her at all.

WACHTEL How did you go from the voice of Celie to the story of *The Color Purple*?

WALKER The story came to me while I was swimming in the river. It came to me while I was walking in the meadow. It came like things do come; they're there. What you need to do is be receptive and what is there for you to bring into the world will find you.

WACHTEL *The Color Purple* has been your greatest critical and popular success and it's taught not only in literature courses but sociology and history classes. Do you have a sense of why that is?

WALKER I think it makes people laugh, and it also makes them think about God. I think of it of course as a theological work, and I think many people are able to connect with that. It poses questions from someone that you never hear asking the questions. Most people think they've never heard a person like Celie asking: Well, why are we here? What is going on? Who are you? If there is a God, what is it?

WACHTEL You say *The Color Purple* makes people laugh, but certainly initially it's a very harsh, grim portrait when Celie is talking about her life and how she's been abused by men, starting with her father. In fact, it's been criticized for its unsympathetic portrayal of men, particularly how black men treat black women.

WALKER I have had very poor critics. It has been hard to connect with some of the criticism because it seems to be about something that's not there. Many critics have said that they didn't bother to read the book, and therefore they're just talking, and there's not much I can do about that. I find the men in *The Color Purple*, as in most of my work, to be people who change and grow, develop, become better lovers, and these are big things.

WACHTEL At that time — we're talking a little over ten years ago — you seemed to be breaking a taboo by speaking out — not only through your fiction but also in interviews — about the cruelty of black men towards their wives and families as one of the greatest American tragedies, how black men came to recognize their own oppression but were ignorant of how they oppressed black women.

WALKER To phrase it like that is reductive because as a feminist I am able to perceive sexist oppression all over the world, and I write about it in the black community because that is where I am. But it's not to isolate black men as being more abusive or more destructive or more hurtful. It's true that you would hope that African American men, Native American men, you know, Chinese American men, Japanese American men, that all of these men, because they have suffered under racism, would be more sensitive about sexism in their own communities, but this isn't the case.

WACHTEL I wasn't suggesting that you were singling them out; I thought it must have taken a certain amount of guts to break those taboos because it wasn't something that was being talked about in the community.

WALKER Love really means that you have to talk, and that's where this is coming from. I have seen a lot of violence and I know that unless we do address it, it is not going to go away, it's just going to grow. And in fact that's what has happened.

WACHTEL In spite of its awards and popularity, there were attempts to ban *The Color Purple*, and you say even your mother objected to the opening of the novel because she found the language offensive. Did you anticipate that when you were writing the book?

WALKER I didn't care. I was totally happy writing it, and every day I felt so much joy being with the characters. I was hopeful that people could feel the way I did about them and would be able to see that even the worst people manage to reach a different plateau in life. I always thought of it as a gift, and like with any gift, you hope that people will enjoy it. But I didn't spend much time thinking about its reception.

WACHTEL *The Temple of My Familiar* is an adventurous and unconventional novel and you described it once as "the story about the last five hundred thousand years." What was your intention here?

WALKER It was to relate history or "herstory" in a way that included me and included people that I care about. The way history is written and what most people learn, especially before the last twenty years, was something that left out almost everyone. I wanted to show that there has always been a different way of relating to what one thinks of as God, there have always been many different ways of relating to animals on earth, many different ways of relating to people who are different from you, and there have always been people who've had an opinion different from yours. And so I needed that scope, all of those years, so that I could go back and look at some beginnings, go back and look at Africa, for instance, at a time when it was not so impoverished and beaten down and exploited, but when the people were still in possession of it as their continent. And I wanted to explore colonial history, especially the British colonial history, and its exploits in Africa and on other continents.

WACHTEL Lissie is an important character and she has many different lives in this novel. Can you tell me about her?

WALKER She is someone who has lived forever and reincarnates when she wants to, but she always reincarnates with someone whose spirit she recognizes as this person Hal, and they have been together for such a long time that they are practically interchangeable, and this is something that interests me. Men and women, male and female, often feel that they are completely separate, when in fact my sense of people is that we are one. We really *are* one, and it is society that forces us into roles that give us the appearance of being absolutely different from each other. We're not. And this is what you see in the relationship between Lissie and Hal.

WACHTEL As a modern black man, what does Suelo learn from Lissie?

WALKER He learns from Lissie and Hal how to endure, how to put love first and struggle to retain it, but he also learns how to relax and to cook, eat and enjoy life, to walk and to see what you're walking on, and to know that you are alive to do that. He's also learning how to value the woman that he's lucky enough to have in his life.

WACHTEL I'd like to talk for a moment about your short stories. In many ways, as you point out, they chart your own experience and the phases of your life. How does it feel to re-encounter them in a collected edition now?

WALKER I still like them and I'm very glad that I wrote them, even the ones that scared me at the time of writing, because I think that they document an emotional time, a psychic time, in the struggle of black people, women mostly, in this country. Re-reading I find it's almost like seeing the seeds of a lot that has unfolded in society today.

WACHTEL You talk about the excitement of writing of the forbidden in relation to these stories. What were you thinking of?

WALKER So much of my work has been about encountering what is absolutely taboo, not just wife-beating and child molestation, but genital mutilation, inter-racial love, all of that. It has been very exciting to write what hasn't been written and to understand that by doing that, you are making a mirror for people. Art gives you a mirror to look into, but it's not a mirror that's hostile; you don't feel it's judging you.

WACHTEL You point out that the women in your first collection of short stories barely realize that they have a place in the world, while your second collection is filled with women who are finding or have found where they belong. What kind of progress have these women made? If you were to pick up their lives now, where would you place them?

WALKER I think most of the women in the second book would still be those women. They would be irrepressible. You know, they would be like most of us fighting different kinds of illnesses — I have friends who have had mastectomies and I have friends who have died of AIDS; I have friends who have lost their children to crack and even so, with all of this horror that we live with now, these are women who continue to be who they are. They don't back down. They don't say, I'm not whatever; they say, oh yes, I am that, and I intend to enjoy this sandwich.

WACHTEL It reminds me of the traditional Southern greeting that you mention in *The Temple of My Familiar*: "All those at the banquet."

WALKER It's great because life really is that: We are all at the banquet, and it's a shame that many people are kept from knowing they're at the banquet because they are enslaved in poverty and oppression. But if you can connect with the sunlight and the earth, it's easy to know, if only for a moment, that you are at the banquet, too, and it's for you, life is for you.

March 1995
interview initially prepared in collaboration
with Sandra Rabinovitch

AMITAV GHOSH

One of the great pleasures of my job is the sense of discovery that occurs now and then when I come across someone I've only heard of, and find myself in the company of an eloquent, literate, compassionate voice. That's what happened to me with *In an Antique Land* (1992) by Amitav Ghosh.

It's not an easy book to describe. Even the publisher's dust-jacket blurb acknowledges this: "*In an Antique Land* is a brilliant hybrid, a subversive history in the guise of a traveller's tale." It's also an account of Amitav Ghosh's field work as a social anthropologist in a village near Alexandria, Egypt. At the time, Ghosh was in his early twenties, a scholarship student at Oxford. He was tantalized, not only by village life in *modern* Egypt, but also by some notes in the margins of letters written in the twelfth century. They told of an Indian slave who had worked for a Jewish trader in Mangalore, a port on the southwest coast of India. Ghosh decided to find out whatever he could about this twelfth-century Indian.

Amitav Ghosh tells the remarkable story of his cultural and historical investigations in parallel lines: one follows his own sojourns in Egypt; the other reconstructs the medieval trading world of the Indian slave. Both reflect Ghosh's preoccupation with rootlessness or exile as a norm in the Middle East and Asia, not only in the late twentieth century but throughout history.

Certainly those themes fit his own peripatetic life. Amitav Ghosh was born in Calcutta in 1956. His family came from Dacca, in East Pakistan, which is now Bangladesh. He grew up in India and Bangladesh, and also lived in Sri Lanka. He studied in New Delhi, Oxford and Alexandria. He's taught in India and in the United States and now lives in New York City.

There's a distinct and compelling humaneness in the way that Amitav Ghosh writes — whether it's in his nonfiction book, *In an Antique Land* or in a *New Yorker* account of the 1984 riots following the assassination of Indira Gandhi (1995), or in his novels, *The Circle of Reason* (1986), *The Shadow Lines* (1988) and *The Calcutta Chromosome* (1996). He writes with a respect for his characters, real or imaginary. As a *New York Times* critic wrote of him: "The author's voice, for all its power, is a modest one in the very best sense — it is always used in the service of his story, shining a luminous intelligence into the lives of the people he creates."

WACHTEL Borders, boundaries — whether real or imagined, natural or artificial, whether political or social — the boundaries and the borders that divide people and places figure very prominently in your work. Do you know why that is?

GHOSH I suppose it's because I've had to go back and forth across so many in my own life. But also because in our lives today borders are so binding, aren't they? They constrain one. They're almost an extension of the self, of a collective self. You get used to seeing maps of a country; it's drawn in a certain way on the wall. And you begin to identify with that map: that map begins to show you where you are or who you are, or where you live, what your place in the universe is. I remember many years ago when I first saw a map of India, which showed the line of division across Kashmir, what's called the Line of Actual Control, it was an extraordinary shock. It seemed almost like a redefinition of one's known world.

WACHTEL Can we talk about some of the borders you've had to cross? Although you were born in Calcutta, your family was from what was then East Pakistan and what became Bangladesh.

GHOSH Yes, my father's family, who are from the Bangladesh region, moved to India in the 1850s and settled in a certain part of eastern India called Bihár. My mother's family, who were from the Bangladesh region as well, moved to India much later. But in both instances there were very close connections and a constant movement back and forth between India and the region that is now Bangladesh. I suppose everyone from my kind of background — and that means probably about half the people in the whole of Calcutta — all grew up with that dispersed notion of where we belong. I went to school in north India, and one of the things that struck me very much was that a lot of my school friends were able to talk about home as the village or the old town that their family had always lived in, and their old family house. These were things I could never speak of because our village and our old family house were on the other side of the border. And it's a dislocation that I think many people in South Asia have experienced and that more and more are experiencing with every passing year. In part this dislocation was caused by the partition of the Indian subcontinent, but it's also been a continuous process for many thousands of people since the 1950s. A lot of dislocation has been caused by technology. Many people in South Asia have been forced to move because of dams or vast factories or whatever.

WACHTEL But you had a curious experience because you had an opportunity to go back, not exactly to your village, but to your ancestral city, to Dacca, when your father was part of the Indian diplomatic mission there.

GHOSH That's right, yes. In fact, that was a very curious thing. When I was about four or five years old, my parents moved to Dacca, but as Indian citizens. So we were brought up in a diplomatic community, but we were in this place which was actually our home; this was where all our ancestral memories were. But we were there as foreigners, as people who'd come across from India. That certainly produced a sense of dislocation.

WACHTEL An outsider's image of India has been so coloured by colonialism that even now it's sometimes hard to get a clear picture of life there, and you yourself have said that it is still puzzling to be from a culture that was re-created by colonialism. Can you talk about that?

GHOSH You have to remember that the impact of colonialism varies across India. The part that I came from, Bengal, and especially the city of Calcutta, was the most deeply affected by colonialism of any place. The colonial contacts go back more than three hundred years. The British really created the city of Calcutta — there was nothing there, except a couple of villages before the British arrived. So in Bengal it's almost impossible to think of what it would be like without the colonial impact of the last several hundred years. It would certainly be something completely different — if indeed we can imagine what that difference might be.

WACHTEL This sense of displacement occurs in your work. Your second novel, *The Shadow Lines*, is divided into two parts: the first part is called "Going Away" and the second is called "Coming Home." What did you want to explore in this book?

GHOSH In India we always say that every writer from Bengal and Punjab has to write a novel about partition and I suppose this was, in a sense, my partition novel. I always wanted to write a book about the division of India, which was a three-way division, not just a division of India and Pakistan, but also the division of India, Pakistan and England, because that's really the division it was. It was an imagined sundering of links. And these links weren't really sundered at all; they were just re-created in different ways. This was also for me very much a book about violence, about religious violence and political violence, and the ways in which religious violence occurs in civil society and, at the same time, the way in which that violence sometimes gets translated into war between states. So a large part of the book is about the difference between riots and war — riots between people and wars between states, and what these kinds of violence might mean for us.

WACHTEL It's interesting, because *The Shadow Lines* is about partition and about the connections between India and England, but it's also a book about using your imagination. The novel's narrator is a boy growing up in Calcutta but his imagination takes him all over the world.

GHOSH That's what it was really about for me, how you fill the world with what's inside your head and how you populate it for yourself and imagine it in different ways. But also it's about the ways in which you confront violence from other patterns of the imagination, from other ways of thinking about the world.

WACHTEL One of the things that the narrator, the little boy, seems to have to learn is that if you don't claim your imagination for yourself, other people will construct things for you. He talks about how a place doesn't merely exist, it has to be invented in your own mind, and that if you don't use your imagination, you'll be dependent on other people's inventions.

GHOSH That's something I certainly believe. A part of the book is also about writing, and one of the strange difficulties I had in writing this novel was not so much writing about India as writing about London. London is not a city I know terribly well — I was a student in England and I spent a couple of years there so I'd often go down to London. But suddenly, when I picked up the pen and started writing about London, I realized that the whole city comes to you imagined by the great weight of English literature; that whole tradition of writing about London or what London looks like, what its flavours are, really bears down on you. Especially in that circumstance, it's very, very hard to achieve precision about your own vision, about what *you* saw there. That was one of the interesting things for me about writing the novel, trying to shrug off the huge weight of imagination about the city that sat on my shoulders, whether I liked it or not.

WACHTEL There is a vivid scene in *The Shadow Lines* where the boy comes to realize the significance of imagination and how important it is to be very alive to the whole world. I had a sense that this was also a novelist in training, or a novelist reminding himself what is available. Although you're not necessarily the young narrator, was there something in the way you grew up that made you sensitive to this approach, this attention to detail, this very roomy imagination?

GHOSH I suppose it was just that I was a bookish child. I'd spend a lot of my time simply looking at things. I think that happens to children who move a lot; when they're taken from one place to another, they tend to live more and more in their own minds. That was the case with me.

WACHTEL Issues of nationalism arise in *The Shadow Lines*, and some of these are voiced by the boy's grandmother, who's another important influence in his life. The grandmother talks about the British identity as being forged in war; they know they're a nation, she says, "because they've drawn their borders with blood, war's their religion and that's what it takes to make a country." What do you make of her position?

GHOSH One thing that struck me very much when I first went to England was what a very military society it was in some sense. I remember how startled I was when I went into an Anglican cathedral for the first time and I saw regimental colours hanging inside. To an English person I imagine this is perfectly normal. To me it seemed shocking that these trophies of war should hang in a place of religion. I began to think about English society differently. I think war as an institution in England, in British society, has played a part that's basic to the formation of not only the British empire but also what it means to be English. And that's something that comes as a surprise because you don't read about war in Jane Austen or George Eliot. But it's really war that's omnipresent in nineteenth-century British history. This was a warrior society: they were fighting wars around the world. Wars everywhere! There was no period of five years or so that went by without the British fighting a war somewhere.

WACHTEL But the grandmother in your novel seems to be holding this up as a model, saying that it's a good thing, that a sense of national identity is necessarily embedded in war.

GHOSH That was certainly her view, and it's a view that I think a lot of people around the world hold. I'm sure you've heard how in America, people say the nation begins to feel like a family when there's a war on. It's certainly one of the things that makes nationalism so militaristic and so violent, I think.

WACHTEL The "Coming Home" section of *The Shadow Lines* is somewhat ironic in terms of coming home, because the book's climactic events, which are violent, take place in Dacca, rather than Calcutta. And you'd actually witnessed such riots yourself in 1964 when you were a child.

GHOSH Yes, but the novel was triggered for me by other riots — in 1984. I was actually finishing my first novel at the time, but in 1984, if you remember, Indira Gandhi was assassinated by her Sikh bodyguard, and there were terrible riots that engulfed cities such as Delhi and Kanpur, when mobs of people attacked Sikhs and killed many of them. I happened to be in Delhi at that time and, along with many other people in university circles, we formed relief parties and went on marches and did the usual things that groups like that do. I think the riots of 1984 were, for my whole generation of Indians, a catastrophic event. They had a shattering effect on me. It was one of those periods which you really can't forget. It suddenly put everything up in the air. Here we'd been living in the city, which seemed like such a solid city, and then one day we saw columns of smoke going up from the houses around us. We saw our landlords, who were Sikhs, cutting off their hair or changing their names. We were walking down a street that was a perfectly familiar street and suddenly it was barricaded or filled with people with swords and sticks. It was the most extraordinary sensation of seeing the world go into reverse, go into a

period where every kind of normalcy was in suspension. After
these riots I started thinking very much about what this kind of
violence meant. I realized that in fact I'd seen things like that all
my life, that I'd been in riots myself—when I was a child, I'd
been caught in riots—and that riots were something I'd lived
with all my life. Yet this one riot had caught me completely by
surprise and really assaulted my imagination in this way. Then I
felt that I really wanted to write about it. The only truly autobiographical element in that novel is about those riots in 1964.
It's one of the strongest memories I have — of being caught in a
house, being surrounded by a mob, my whole family inside the
house. I have this clear memory of it. After 1964, my family and
I never spoke about it, not once, until I finally started writing *The
Shadow Lines* and then I asked my father what had happened. That
was when he told me about the riots in Dacca in 1964.

When I started looking in old newspapers, I discovered that
what I remembered was actually just the tip of this huge iceberg
of violence that had somehow splintered all across the subcontinent. That was when I started writing this book. One of the
things that I was very determined to do, especially having been
in those riots myself in 1964 as well as in 1984, was to contend
very seriously with what it meant to write about religious violence. One of the things that I'd learned from reading Gandhi is
that when you talk about nonviolence, the whole challenge that
nonviolence presents is that one has to find ways of using nonviolence, if you like, as a technique not just in politics but in
science, in literature and so on. So the question for me when I
started writing this book was: how do I write about violence in
a nonviolent way? I felt that this was very important because if
when we write about the violence that we see in our everyday
lives in India, if we merely reproduce that violence on paper, that
seems to me like failure. You're just adding to the cycle of violence that creates these kinds of cataclysms. So I wanted to write
about this violence that I'd seen in a nonviolent way, in a voice
that was essentially a pacifist voice. And that was for me the technical excitement of the book.

WACHTEL *The Shadow Lines* is a fictional investigation into truth and into history, using memory and building on bits of information. As a social anthropologist, that seems to be your methodology. Your book, *In an Antique Land*, begins with a scrap of information and then creates a very rich story out of it. The scrap in that instance is a reference to a twelfth-century Indian you call "the Slave of Manuscript H.6." Why did this character capture your interest, almost to the point of obsession?

GHOSH It *was* a kind of obsession, really. It happened exactly as I describe in the book: I was standing in a library at Oxford, and I was thinking, well, what am I going to do about a dissertation, when I came across a letter about a medieval slave who went from India to Egypt. This seemed to create a connection between India and Egypt, and I wanted to discover more about it, to see what there was I could write about.

WACHTEL You've said that when you went to Egypt, you knew nothing about the slave except that "he had given me a right to be there, a sense of entitlement." How does that work?

GHOSH One of the things that struck me very much when I was a student at Oxford was the sense in which, for many of the people who were doing anthropology with me, the places they went to do their fieldwork or where they wanted to study, were really whims for them; somebody thought about Polynesia and said, "Oh well, let's go to Polynesia," and someone thought about Africa and said, "Let's go and study Africa." Somehow I couldn't do it in quite that way; I felt there had to be a reason for me to go there, some sort of connection that I wanted to investigate. And here it was, the connection, and after that I knew that I had to go to Egypt.

WACHTEL And the fact that in the twelfth century there had been an Indian who lived in Egypt as a slave to a trader was enough?

GHOSH It must sound very strange to you, but you have to remember that in India, as young students, even as students of history, we thought of Indian history as being completely localized within India, and we forgot about the links that joined India with the world around it. In fact, very little has been written about the sorts of relationships that existed between India and Egypt, very little has been written about the relationships between India and East Africa, and those are very long links, going back millennia. There's very little about India and Southeast Asia, except for art-historical kinds of things. So it was with a real sense of discovery, actually, that I started on this, and I think that's not just a personal sense of discovery. All these links between Asia and Africa are more or less unexplored territories still.

WACHTEL I sense that part of your attraction to the richness of the trade in those times before European colonization is because it was so fluid, because borders could be crossed so easily.

GHOSH That's right. I suppose at the back of one's mind is this romantic idea that people really live where they belong and that they have deep roots. Think of the metaphor of the root: it suggests a tree, it suggests being tied to the soil, being deeply anchored in the soil. Yet think how misleading that whole idea is. I was living in Egypt in the village I've described in *In an Antique Land*, and Egypt after all is such an ancient civilization, one always thinks that if anywhere people are rooted, it must surely be in Egypt, it must be here in this ancient soil. And yet, in this village, everybody claimed to have an ancestor somewhere outside Egypt — in Saudi Arabia or in Damascus or in the Sudan or somewhere. So it's something that permeates the whole world.

WACHTEL Were you satisfied with what you were able to find out about this twelfth-century Indian?

GHOSH I was very satisfied at the end of the day, even though all I really found were scraps. But you have to set it beside other parallels. The very possibility of actually discovering an individual person, an individual voice, over eight centuries, it's so rare, so unusual. If you think of historical works written about medieval Europe, they really date from almost three centuries after the Slave of MS H.6, as I call him — they're mainly from the fifteenth and sixteenth centuries. In the twelfth century it would be very hard to write any kind of biography of an ordinary European. In that sense, once you've set it in a comparative perspective, I think it is pretty remarkable that I was able to get as much as I did. Part of the excitement was in discovering that as long as eight centuries ago people were travelling regularly between Spain and western India; they were going back and forth every year; there were huge settlements of mixed populations of people from Spain, Persia, Egypt, even Indonesia, living in India. We think of cosmopolitanism as a modern invention, but in fact, historically, people have always lived with the idea of movement and migration.

WACHTEL Your book *In an Antique Land* is as much about your own experience living in a village in Egypt, in the Nile Delta, as it is about your research and your historical subject. Did you anticipate what it would be like to live as the foreign *other* in that world?

GHOSH No. I had no idea really. It's a very artificial situation to be living like that, to be living in a place where you're just looking around and writing down things that you see. Everybody in the village would laugh at me and say, "When's your holiday going to be over?" because they thought that I must be on holiday since I wasn't doing any work that they were accustomed to doing — I wasn't digging in the fields, I wasn't going to the market. And in a sense that expressed the kind of unreality of the circumstance where you're completely isolated in this tiny village, in an out-of-the-way place, where, at least in the beginning, you don't speak the language very well. It's an extraordinary experience when you have to grapple with that kind of loneliness, the loneliness that comes from not being able to understand anything that anyone's saying around you. I remember the long evenings: I had a little transistor radio and I'd fiddle with the knob trying to find someone speaking English or Hindi or some language that I could understand. Just coping with that loneliness is quite an education in its own right.

WACHTEL You emerge as quite a charming and often somewhat comic or naïve character in the story; your persona in the book is the innocent abroad.

GHOSH Yes, I suppose that's true; that's the persona in which I wrote the book.

WACHTEL There's even a cross-cultural running gag throughout the book in that people are always asking you, "Is it true that in your country people burn their dead and worship cows?" And generally you take their horror in good humour.

GHOSH I certainly tried to do that when I was writing the book. At the time it wasn't always easy. I had to face these two questions not just once or twice, but four or five times every single day. When people who knew exactly what I would say would ask me this question at least once a day, I just renewed their sense of amazement that there could actually be a place where people are cremated rather than buried.

WACHTEL At one point you find yourself embroiled in a situation you don't like, where you are boasting that India has guns and tanks and bombs that are as good or better than anything that they've got in Egypt. Can you describe what happened there?

GHOSH There was this local imam who didn't particularly like me, and we somehow got into this argument and by the time it was over and I went back to my room, I found I was absolutely shaking. He began telling me, "Oh, you should tell the people in your country not to burn their dead." And I said, "Well, I'll tell them but I don't know if they're going to do anything about it." So then he said, "You know, burning the dead is primitive. Developed people don't do that." So I said, "It's not a question of development. You know, in my country there's just as much development as there is in Egypt." And then suddenly there was this curious kind of segue where we ended up talking about development, when we had begun by talking about cremation.

WACHTEL You describe it as "two delegates from two superseded civilizations vying with each other to establish a prior claim to the technology of modern violence."

GHOSH That's what it became in the end. We began by talking about cremation and burial and we ended up talking about who had more tanks and guns and bombs. It seemed to me a sad commentary on the nature of relationships between cultures.

WACHTEL Your work is about straddling borders and, at the end of *In an Antique Land*, you describe how an Egyptian official doesn't quite know what to make of you because you're not a Muslim nor a Jew nor a Christian. You don't fit, as you put it, "the categories dictated by history," and you talk about the "enforcers of history."

GHOSH One of the things that was very exciting for me in writing *In an Antique Land* was that it provided a point of entry into the modern world from a very unexpected perspective. Here we have a world in which it's hard to distinguish between Jews and Arabs. We have here Jewish people who are speaking Arabic, who are writing a certain kind of Arabic, who are really culturally Arabs, if you like, even though the religion is different.

WACHTEL What threw me was when they said *"Inshal'la"* I thought, wait a minute; I thought this guy was Jewish, and now he's saying this!

GHOSH There you are! And it wasn't just that one time. Here you have these very devout Jews, and when they write their documents and when they have invocations to God, it's almost invariably as *Inshal'la,* or *Bismillah,* which are quintessentially Arabic terms. You have that whole world that we've come to know today in terms of confrontation between Arabs and Jews in the Middle East, and religious violence between Hindus and Muslims and other religious groups within the Indian subcontinent. Then suddenly we have a world where it's all turned around, where in fact every different kind of community has found some way of accommodating other people. And that was very exciting to me. I don't think in the Middle Ages anybody would have been surprised if a person from another religion had gone to visit a shrine that belonged in some sense to another religion. The shrine that I went to in Egypt was in some sense a Jewish shrine, but, historically, Muslims have gone there as well. When we go there today, after the history of the last thirty or forty years, we're all primed to respond in certain ways, and the people who are responsible for upholding those visions are often people in power, like policemen or military men or people who don't think about these things very much but who are just doing their job. And that was what was startling. I came to this shrine inside Egypt, which has historically been an ecumenical sort of shrine, and suddenly I have this policeman asking me, "What are you doing here?"

WACHTEL It's funny that you call it ecumenical because I was just thinking that if I had to describe your work, it really is fuelled by a pacifist, ecumenical spirit.

GHOSH I hope so. I certainly hope so.

WACHTEL You've said that all the movements and uprisings in India revolve around a single issue, the issue of identity, and that the rest of the world can learn from India because of its diversity and the diversity that India has had to deal with. Do you have a sense of what kinds of answers can be found there?

GHOSH I think India is a very important place in the sense that there's a significant political experiment underway there. With the breakup of Yugoslavia, with the breakup of the Soviet Union, India is today one of the few surviving multi-national, multi-ethnic, multi-religious kinds of states in the world. India, and possibly Indonesia and a couple of other places, are the last places where you actually have widely varying and different cultures trying to make their lives together. This is different from the North American situation, where it's a melting pot, where you have immigrants coming in from different places. In India you have deeply rooted, local civilizations and cultures trying to find some sort of political accommodation. I think a lot hinges on different cultures being able to find some means of accommodating each other within a common political framework.

January 1995
interview initially prepared in collaboration
with Sandra Rabinovitch

E.L. DOCTOROW

Edgar Lawrence Doctorow started off as a script reader for
Columbia Pictures and then as a literary editor in New York,
first with New American Library and later Dial Press. But for
thirty-five years now, he's dedicated himself to writing popular
and intensely readable novels — taking as his subject, as one
critic put it, "the making of the American people."

Ragtime (1975) takes place in early twentieth-century
America; *Loon Lake* (1980), *World's Fair* (1985) and *Billy Bathgate*
(1989) are located in the 1930s; and *The Book of Daniel* (1971)
in the 1950s and '60s. To put things in historical context and
lend a further air of actuality, Doctorow often intersperses real
people in his fiction. In *Ragtime*, for instance, Emma Goldman,
Theodore Dreiser, Sigmund Freud, Henry Ford and Harry
Houdini figure in the lives of Doctorow's fictional families. *The
Book of Daniel* is set against the spy trial and execution of Julius
and Ethel Rosenberg.

E. L. Doctorow was born in New York City in 1931, and
he's something of an "urban romantic." Not only are many of
his novels set in New York, but in *The Waterworks* (1994), the
city of 1871 is virtually the main character — dreamy, atmospheric, menacing, peopled by Civil War veterans, journalists and
sleazy politicians. As Doctorow says, "I realized I was writing
about everyone Edith Wharton had left out."

Doctorow can be playful and elusive. When asked once
where he gets the ideas for his novels, he said that *Ragtime* came
from staring at a wall in his house in New Rochelle and writing the sentence, "I live in a house built in 1906." He dropped
the line from the book, but it got him started.

An old hand when it comes to interviews, he has a relaxed,
friendly, avuncular demeanour. But what surprised me was his
spontaneity, his engagement. Twice in our conversation in the
Toronto studio, he started: First, at the connections I was
making between the conservative, text-based New Criticism
he had imbibed at Kenyon College and how that fit with his
socialist background. He acknowledged what an interesting
mix it yielded in him and clearly enjoyed unravelling it. Later,
when I observed a shift in his view of science and technology,
from the optimism of *World's Fair* to the darkness of *The
Waterworks*, he said, with bemusement, "I have to tell you at
this point that your perceptions are really making me very
uncomfortable."

One of my favourite stories of Doctorow's response to an
interviewer was when he was asked about the title of his novel,
Loon Lake. It's a rich, complex book, involving a failed, alcoholic
poet, gangsters, a rich industrialist and his aviatrix wife who live
in the Adirondacks and so on. Doctorow claims he got the idea
when he was driving one Sunday in upper New York state and
saw a sign that said Loon Lake. "You've got to let things happen
to you to write," he maintained. When asked, "What would
have happened if instead of passing a sign which said Loon
Lake, you passed a sign which said Lake Placid?"

"I did pass the sign," Doctorow said, "but I didn't notice it."

WACHTEL *Billy Bathgate* is the third in a trilogy of novels set in the 1930s, starting with *Loon Lake* and then *World's Fair*; did you have a kind of thirties project in mind?

DOCTOROW Not a project. That's not the way I work. An unintended trilogy is what those books are. The period appealed to me for all sorts of reasons that required writing the books to discover.

WACHTEL Can you tell me more about the 1930s and its appeal?

DOCTOROW It was the time when I was a child, and childhood is the age of indelible impressions. To a certain extent these books were acts of exorcism, the images of what I thought life was and always would be were attached to the thirties and to New York City. *World's Fair* and *Billy Bathgate* present themselves as boys' lives — one lived, however intensely, within a family, the other lawlessly with a surrogate family of gangsters. There's a great advantage to setting your book in the voice or from the point of view of a youth because you're allowed to recover all the wonderful, ordinary things that you don't express as an adult. Simple things that I don't think an adult would particularly dwell on, such as rhapsodizing about a water truck cleaning the streets and sending up a spray that creates a rainbow three or four feet above the sidewalk. But of course authors have always known the value of attaching their own sensibilities to a young voice — certainly Mark Twain knew that, and Dickens. It's a very workable strategy.

WACHTEL Tell me more about your own growing up in the Bronx.

DOCTOROW I think I'm probably most accurate and autobiographical talking about the Bronx in the first half of *World's Fair*. Much of the Bronx was a new neighbourhood, built largely because the subway had been extended from Manhattan, allowing people to commute cheaply and quickly. It was a place filled with parks and broad, sunny streets, and everything was quite clean. Everyone was poor, nobody had any money, but somehow it was all very liveable, and everything worked, and the schools and the teachers in the schools were first-rate. The teachers were probably overqualified. In the Depression, to have any sort of job was an achievement, so a lot of the best people found teaching jobs in grade school, and that was a great boon to little kids.

WACHTEL Was there a lot of music in your house? I understand that your father ran a music store and your mother was a pianist.
DOCTOROW My father owned a music store downtown, near Radio City Music Hall on Sixth Avenue, and he sold records — in those days they were 78 rpm's, shellac records, very breakable, as I was often told when I was allowed to play around the store — and sheet music, musical instruments and radios. There was no television then. It was a wonderful, exciting place to be. My brother and I used to go around hitting the drums and tooting the horns after the store was closed. My father was very genial and wasn't nervous at all about that. My mother was a very fine pianist. She loved Chopin and Schubert. So there was always a lot of music one way or another from both parents. And books of course — they were both serious readers. So while my father struggled to keep that store going during the Depression, and did for most of it, not losing it until the "little depression" came along in 1940, and while my mother fed us on something like a dollar a day, or perhaps even less, I was not aware of any of this. I wanted for nothing. It was a very full, rich life for me, though not without trauma. There was an uncle and a grandmother living with us. The bad times created extended families. And my poor old grandmother had "spells," as they were called, where she would run away and become very verbally hostile to those she loved. So that was odd. And there were strange people in the streets, of course — madness was not mitigated by drugs as it is today. In terms of the larger social context, you stayed out of certain bad neighbourhoods. And sometimes there were dangers to playing in the park. There would be raids, gang raids: boys from other neighbourhoods would come up from the eastern part of the Bronx, the Dutch Schultz regions, and you'd be playing ball and they'd come and hold a knife up to your chest and take your lunch money. Nevertheless, while there were these dangers, by and large it was a more liveable place than it is now.
WACHTEL What I get from these books is such a strong urban sensibility that I was wondering when you went to college in the Midwest, to Kenyon College in Ohio, was that a culture shock?

DOCTOROW Let me go back a little to answer your question. I went to a high school, the Bronx High School of Science, which was filled with children who were brilliant at math and science. You knew, they knew, they were going to win Nobel prizes in physics and chemistry — as many of them have. I don't know how I got into Bronx Science, but I gravitated to a corner office where the school literary magazine was published. *DYNAMO*, it was called. My first published story was in *DYNAMO*. So though I was greatly discomfited throughout my entire high school career, my literary life began there. I was encouraged in my writing by my English teachers. I had read a book by a very fine and, to me, mysterious poet named John Crowe Ransom, who was teaching at Kenyon College, and I decided that after I graduated from Science I would like to study there. To my astonishment I was admitted. My father took out a bank loan to pay the first year's tuition — and there I was, this Jewish kid from the Bronx marching out to Kenyon College in Ohio, which was one of the most beautiful idyllic campuses in the country, a classic storybook Oxonian sort of place — at least in its pretensions. Lots of ivy, the architecture a kind of western reserve Gothic. So yes, it was culture shock. But the administration was very enlightened in those days. Kenyon had been a polo-playing playboy school in the 1930s. Students had kept their own airplanes at the college airstrip, that kind of thing. They were very wealthy Midwestern preppies, for the most part. But the administration, and Ransom and some other great teachers, had decided to open the school up to roughnecks like me, poor kids, brains, upstarts from the eastern city public schools.

WACHTEL Was this a product of the Second World War? We're talking late forties.

DOCTOROW Yes. This was 1948. There were veterans there on the GI bill, and it became a very spirited place. It was organized around fraternities, and then all the people who would not join a fraternity or would not be allowed in a fraternity were *ipso facto* a fraternity of their own — that would mean, let's see, poets, Jews, Catholics, blacks, homosexuals, veterans, and a few boys with severe cases of acne. And we were of course the soul of that school. A great philosophy professor, Phillip Rice, told me it wouldn't have been worth teaching at Kenyon if not for its dissenting outcasts. So while I felt some cultural shock, I adjusted easily enough. I was not alone and I was getting the liberal education I'd hoped for after all.

WACHTEL One thing that struck me is that John Crowe Ransom is identified with something called the New Criticism, which is a focus on the text, a very close reading of a poem or whatever. The New Criticism has become associated with a kind of conservatism because, by focusing on the text as if it fell from heaven, you could disregard its social and its political context. Yet that's the very context you've come to champion in fiction. How did that come about?

DOCTOROW I value my experience at Kenyon. In fact I can't imagine my writing self, the composition of what I am as a writer, without that training and education, reading the poets and novelists, reading philosophy and doing criticism. We were very good at criticism, that was our sport. We did criticism at Kenyon the way they played football at Ohio State. And it taught me a lot: the tropes available to the writer, to the poet, the effects, for instance, of abutting a Latin word and an Anglo-Saxon word, or why one metaphor was ennobling, another not. I learned to hear the music in language. It allowed me to become a rather effective editor, which is the means by which I supported myself while I was writing my early novels. At the same time, the spirit of it was, as you indicate, conservative. In the 1930s, Ransom and another poet, Allen Tate, and a few others had been part of a political movement known as the Agrarians, which was extremely conservative. They were nostalgic for Southern society before the Civil War, when everything was gracious, with class clearly demarcated and slavery somehow not a moral consideration. But you see, it's possible to take what's good out of something and discard the rest. By the fifties Ransom had come a distance from that Agrarian nonsense. It was very useful to attend to the text and really learn how to deal with the construction of it, the nature of its imagery, and so on. Technically, the New Criticism was itself reacting to a very sloppy form of historical and biographical criticism that had been prevalent.

WACHTEL But where do you think your own commitment to being *engagé* came from? Do you attribute that to your Jewish inheritance?

DOCTOROW First let me define *engagé* or it may be misleading as applied to me. Fiction is a big kitchen-sink kind of art — no data is impermissible. I can take from science, religion, confession, history, myth, dreams and the mutterings of poor mad people in the street. I can give you facts and feelings, the outside, the inside, the personal, the poetical — the whole hog, as D.H. Lawrence called fiction, the whole hog. It would be odd, wouldn't it, to claim our lives, anyone's life, had no social or political character?

So, *engagé*: Yes, the family I came from was politically aware and thought a good deal about justice. My grandfather was a printer and had come to America in the 1880s as a very young man. Having made the decision that the problems on earth were to be solved on earth and not in heaven, he became a kind of a trade-union socialist in his thinking and in his sensibility. My father felt more or less the same way. So I grew up in this Jewish humanist, secular milieu of democratic socialists, though the women in the family tended to be more religious and more politically conservative. The fact of the matter is, when I write criticism now, I do pay attention to the authors as well as to the work, but perversely I also subscribe to the idea that it is possible to read a book, and get all the instruction you need to read it from the book itself, or from the poem itself. These days textual criticism has been reduced to absurdity by the deconstructionists — where the examination of the text has become so close it's burned a hole right through the page. It may be that deconstructionism is a form of book burning.

WACHTEL In an essay called "The Belief of Writers," you wrote that, compared to the 1930s, literary life today is decorous, that there's a timidity to serious fiction and a modesty of conception in language. Why do you think that is?

DOCTOROW That was an address to graduate writing students at the University of Michigan a few years ago. I was talking about how since World War II the university has become the great patron of writers — I'm not sure if that's quite as true in Canada as it is in the United States. This has been good for writers and some first-rate writers have emerged from that system. But what happens is that young writers come out of these programs probably technically more adept than writers were fifty years ago but somehow having academicized themselves. They come out with a Master of Fine Arts degree and go to another campus where they teach other young writers to get MFA degrees in order to teach. So there's this whole kind of shadow culture that has grown up of writing teachers teaching other writers to be writing teachers. This does have a constricting effect on the vision that writers come up with. You stay in the house, you close the door, and you pull down the shades — as if there's no street outside, as if there's no highway, no city, no country. Before the Second World War more of our novelists came out of the newspaper business. Hemingway was a newspaper man. Dreiser worked for years as a newspaperman before he wrote a novel.

So I think academia is one reason why contemporary writers have become rather timid about what they think fiction can do. And then of course you can blame television; television is very easy to blame just about anything on — the overpowering effect of the media, the dominance of film culture, and how it drives writers inward.

WACHTEL In that talk, by invoking writers such as Tolstoy or Stendhal, you argued for the big, socially conscious novel.

DOCTOROW I wasn't trying to tell anybody how to write — God forbid! But I was trying to suggest that writers have all sorts of ways of defeating themselves and of limiting themselves and of punishing themselves for the fact that they write.

There's one more thing to be said here. Perhaps it's too soon, but as yet there has been no work produced studying the effect of the Cold War on the American psyche. After all, it went on for nearly half a century. The Cold War circumscribed the lives of all but the oldest generation of writers working today. It certainly did mine. Only writers like Saul Bellow and Mailer, writers who are now past seventy, were at work before the Cold War. The rest of us, until very lately, have lived all our working lives under its conditions. And it had a pathology, like any war.

If we can talk about it for a minute, it basically had three phases. It began in fear — quite deliberately our politicians engendered fear in the American population; students were driven under their desks for nuclear drills, and people were encouraged to build bomb shelters in their backyards, stock canned food and so on. This was the period of McCarthyism and the Rosenberg trial, when people were signing loyalty oaths or losing their jobs because they'd put their names to some petition on behalf of the Spanish Loyalists in the 1930s. Everywhere there was retreat, intellectual and political conformism. The retreat was to personal life. In effect a kind of puritan civil religion was established.

Then there was the Great Reformation, as it were, the sixties — the counterculture of the anti-Vietnam War movement, and the growth of rock music and people growing their hair long and living poor as hippies. This was the second phase. Everyone young, it seemed — the civil rights movement, the anti-war movement — in revolt against the conformism of Cold War America, and no longer believing in the Cold War as a rationale for our presence in Vietnam. But that was short-lived — ten years out of fifty when the society was open, fractious, crackling with debate. Then the third phase — the reaction — a counter-reformation, as it were, with Ronald Reagan and the resurgence of conservatism. The sons and daughters of the sixties who had stopped the insane war were seen to be a generation that had betrayed America. This is a very rough sketch, of course. The Cold War after the sixties drove people — writers, intellectuals — away from public engagement into their own private lives. It certainly drove literary critics into the academy. They lost their public voice by and large, except of course for the apologists, the neo- and paleo-conservatives.

WACHTEL But you, meanwhile, were writing novels cutting big swaths through the decades. I think of *The Book of Daniel*. Unlike your colleagues in the Cold War, you were looking out rather than in.

DOCTOROW But I was not the only one. Generalizations are made valid by exceptions. During this time, one of the good things that happened in American culture was the flourishing of Afro-American women writers, and their finding a voice that of necessity creates novels of great social relevance. And there have been novels about the war in Vietnam and so on. But by and large, as a generalization, it is true that to write a novel, for instance, based on the idea of the Rosenberg case, would be seen by a critic as somehow adversarial to the United States. I remember a critic describing *The Book of Daniel*, and Joseph Heller's *Catch 22* as "adversarial." So you see the pathetic state of mind. The idea of the political novel still doesn't really have any currency in the critical community. People like political novels as long as they come out of other countries. Just as when President Reagan praised the Polish Solidarity movement. He liked trade unions as long as they were in Poland.

WACHTEL I'd like to talk about your most recent novel, *The Waterworks*. I understand you had the germ of it, but that it was twenty years before you came to write it. Why did it take so long — why did you have to write those other books first?

DOCTOROW Probably most writers have ideas for novels in their minds, some of which are on slow tracks and some on fast tracks. I think *The Waterworks* engaged something deep in my psychic structure, and it took a while to deal with it. In fact I started thinking about this book before I wrote *Ragtime*, and then after I wrote *Ragtime*, and then after I wrote *Loon Lake*, and then after I wrote *Billy Bathgate*. Somewhere along the line I wrote a short piece called "The Waterworks," and published it in a book, *Lives of the Poets*, in 1984. I couldn't get that piece out of my mind: Two men are on the embankment of a reservoir and see a child's model boat founder and capsize and sink in the water. When they rush into the adjoining waterworks building, they find the owner of the boat, a child, drowned. One of the men wraps up the body and rushes off leaving the other one to wonder what exactly has gone on here — as I did. The novel *Waterworks* in effect is an exegesis of the story. This is a dark tale that participates in nineteenth-century storytelling conventions staked out by Melville and Poe. It's a mystery of sorts, a scientific detective tale.

WACHTEL Poe is your namesake in fact. The "E" of your "E.L." is Edgar.

DOCTOROW Yes. But with all his dark tales of dungeons and maelstroms and people being sealed up alive, Poe found something in this happy democracy that no one had quite acknowledged before. This novel draws on all that, and somehow it took me a long time to come around to honouring that darkness in myself. For example, one of the themes of my novel is the relationships of generations — the attempt of the paternal generation to resist the natural order of succession. These are tough things to consider and find a way to express, I think. So it did take a while. And of course you discover things as you write. Water is generally understood ritually as a cleansing element having to do with absolution and redemption, personal salvation. In this book it doesn't work like that. On the contrary.

WACHTEL But there's a yearning for that.

DOCTOROW Oh yes, there is. But you see, in the 1870s the transporting of water to a city was a great technological achievement. So was putting a reservoir in the middle of a city, as New York did — actually, it wasn't in the middle, in those days Fifth Avenue and 42nd Street was the northern edge of town. Putting water under pressure allowed them to keep the city from burning down again and again, as it had numerous times. It was a great technological achievement. They were proud of their technology. The steam-driven rotary press could turn out tens of thousands of copies of newspapers in a couple of hours. They had telegraphy — they could send cables across the ocean; they had transcontinental railroads. They thought they were modern, as they were.

WACHTEL You're talking about a number of things I want to unravel. There's a tension here, because water is thought of as cleansing, and at one point your character refers to this remarkable reservoir as being like a baptismal font, or as needing to be like a "baptismal font, for the gigantic absolution that we require as a people." At the same time you begin with an image of this reservoir drowning a young boy. Death, not life. What kind of absolution is that?

DOCTOROW Exactly. Here's another apparent contradiction or paradox. McIlvaine is an old newspaper editor who's thinking back thirty years. He describes the newspaper business with some pride. At the same time, when all this news was collected and printed in such a dazzlingly short time, it was distributed by kids, impoverished newsboys, who ran around the streets waving the papers in their hands. So the culture created the technology, which was an act of social genius, which in turn created children running around the streets making a few pennies in order to survive. So first you create the culture and then the culture creates you.

WACHTEL *The Waterworks* is a book about wide-ranging corruption and excess, and it unavoidably prompts comparisons with our own times, and particularly the 1980s and the Reagan era. Was that intentional?

DOCTOROW Not intentional, only inevitable. Because whenever you write about the past you of course reflect the present. Even if you're a professional historian and you're writing history, you're serving the needs of your own time. That's why history has to be written and rewritten for every generation. You can't avoid that. Whenever I write a book I really stay in the lanes. I don't think about what it is supposed to mean, I don't think about its relevance, I don't think about what may or may not be referential, I don't think about how it's going to be published, or if people are going to read it. You really live in those sentences, and the only way out of them is through the end of the book.

WACHTEL The historian and critic Simon Schama, in a review of *The Waterworks*, remarked that the reflection of our own times here is "not a pretty picture," more than is usually the case in your books. Do you feel this is a darker vision?

DOCTOROW It is a dark tale. I think it has a certain kind of morbid tension and suspense. Certainly it's the most heavily plotted book I've ever done. It describes a process of discovery — people trying to find out what they would rather not know.

WACHTEL I was thinking more in terms of the atmosphere of corruption.

DOCTOROW Perhaps. But how different is it now? There's a larger corruption than the merely political. In one sense New York is radically changed from those days and in another it's quite the same. In those days there were vagrant children running in the streets. We don't see that any more. We have social policy now, but somehow we still have abandoned kids caught in the welfare system. In those days there was no Veterans' Administration: there were a lot of young men, maimed and terribly hurt, who had come back from the Civil War and couldn't get work; they begged on the streets, they stood in the remnants of their uniforms and begged in front of the department stores. We don't have that any more, but we have veterans of the Vietnam and Gulf Wars who are having terrible reactive traumas that the government doesn't seem to want to deal with. The skyline of the city is quite different: the skyscrapers, the World Trade Centre and so on. But I remember one evening I was looking out over lower Manhattan from my study window and a fog came down, covering the World Trade Centre, covering all the glass towers of lower Manhattan and covering the Woolworth building that had been built in the 1920s, and all that was left was the ground-level city, the nineteenth-century city. It's still here. The moral heedlessness is still here. Life given to the fittest. So everything's different and somehow the same.

WACHTEL By going back to nineteenth-century America, or nineteenth-century New York City, you're rewriting history, you're re-inventing it. What is the pull of history for you?

DOCTOROW I didn't think of rewriting history in this book at all; I think everything I say about the time is quite true.

WACHTEL But that's always the case. I remember reading how, when you wrote *Ragtime*, you said the way you researched it was to find some responsible source for the lie you were about to create.

DOCTOROW Well, that was one way of putting it — of saying the factual accuracy in *Ragtime* is far greater than most people think. In *The Waterworks* my representations of the state of government in 1871 are quite accurate. What we mean by the larger truth is the truth of fiction, the truth of metaphor, the envisioned truth of the moral character of society. You may not be able to find in the municipal records that Boss Tweed participated in a conspiracy to prolong the lives of rich old men by scientific means, but it seems to me that metaphorically speaking it's undeniable. His was a deadly way to run a city, and children did die all the time.

WACHTEL Along with the corruption that *The Waterworks* explores is the danger of this kind of unbridled, scientific or technological expansion — the manipulation of nature. Is that something that worries you?

DOCTOROW Apparently it does. Nevertheless, just to confuse things for you, the fact is that Dr. Sartorius uses procedures in this story that became acceptable medical practice generations later. So there's some ambiguity about him. He is not your run-of-the-mill mad scientist; he is represented, for instance, during the Civil War as having made great advances in surgery, and in discovering how to save limbs and save the lives of soldiers.

WACHTEL He's an innovative and inventive scientist, who in your story uses his science for very dark ends.

DOCTOROW Well he just keeps going, you see, it's a matter of irrepressible intellect. People in many professions will make a genuine contribution that brings them great repute and honour, but then they'll keep going and somehow plunge past the borders of moral consensus.

WACHTEL I was thinking that your vision of science and technology, as it comes through in *The Waterworks*, is quite different from the end of *World's Fair*, where there's a sense of real hopefulness in 1939 — the city of the future, the world of tomorrow.

DOCTOROW You may be right — though that book does view the world of tomorrow with some irony. On the other hand, if I consider the achievements of science and rationalism and the Enlightenment in contrast to the visions and the operations of the

solely religious mind, I would have to come down on the side of
enlightenment. It's not easy to break these things down into simple categories because it's a different kind of thinking that you do
in fiction. Everything is given its due — rationality, irrationality,
science, religion, poetic expression and daily, ordinary speech.

WACHTEL The hero of *The Waterworks*, both the romantic hero
and the narrative hero, and a number of other characters in the
book, are journalists, not fiction writers. I was thinking about
your own experience in a high school journalism project that
you've described, and about the difference between being a journalist and being a fiction writer, because in a sense you romanticize the life of the journalist in your novel.

DOCTOROW The narrator McIlvaine says at one point: a reporter
is a dog that comes back with the story and drops it at the publisher's feet. I've known a lot of journalists and that's exactly how
they are.

I couldn't have done this book if I hadn't found McIlvaine's
voice and realized he was a journalist. In an early draft he was one
of several characters — it was a multiple narration — and whenever it was his turn I got very happy, and then I realized he had
to tell the whole book. Suddenly that shifted everything. I began
looking at the front pages of newspapers of the time. On micro-
film. There were no illustrations, all the stories were single column,
six or seven of them going down the page in parallel descents.
There were no banner heads, no headlines that went across two,
three, four columns, let alone the whole page. And in his life, as
he searches for his missing young freelancer, Martin Pemberton,
McIlvaine is dealing with a number of disparate, mysterious
events that seem to have no connection with one another, just as
the stories going down the front page, separately ruled, seem to
have no connection. But everything on that front page finally
does connect, if you only take an objective view of your society;
it's all one story, always, just as all the mysterious events of the
book finally connect as one story, as if in a headline's flash across
the page. That was a very important image for me to have and it
was a gift of this particular narrative voice.

My own career in journalism lasted about five minutes when I was in high school. I took a course in journalism at the Bronx High School of Science, and at one point our task was to go out and do an interview with someone. I brought back an interview with the stage-doorman at Carnegie Hall. He was a prematurely aged Jewish refugee who'd lost his entire family in Europe during the war; and he was badly dressed — blue serge double-breasted jacket and brown pants. He'd come to work every evening and bring his lunch in a paper bag with a thermos of tea, and he would drink his tea in the old world way by putting a cube of sugar in his teeth and sipping the tea through the sugar. And all the great artists of the day, the recitalists — Paderewski and Horowitz and Rubenstein and Heifetz — loved him because he knew the classical repertoire, he was very well-informed — a sweet, good man. And they all called him by his first name, Karl. Karl the doorman. I handed that assignment in and the teacher said, "You know, this is a really terrific interview. It's so good I think we ought to run it in the school paper. So what I want to do is send one of the photography students down to take Karl's picture to go with the story and we'll get it in the paper." I said, "I don't think that's possible." And she said, "Why not?" I said, "Well, Karl is very shy." The teacher said, "What do you mean he's shy? He spoke to you, didn't he?" I said, "Well, not exactly. There is no Karl; I made him up." It seemed to me so much more sensible to make something up than go through the tedious business of actually interviewing someone. At that moment, you see —

WACHTEL Your career was set!

DOCTOROW I didn't realize that this was a portent at the time. I got an "F" for a grade and I felt really bad; I had transgressed. It was only later that I realized that transgression is the life and soul of fiction, that unless you are in touch, somehow, with the forbidden, you're not going to write anything worthwhile.

October 1994
interview initally prepared in collaboration
with Larry Scanlan

LOUISE ERDRICH

Louise Erdrich is French Chippewa on her mother's side and German American on her father's. Both her parents worked at the Bureau of Indian Affairs boarding school near the Turtle Mountain Reservation in North Dakota. This is how Erdrich describes it: "I grew up in a small North Dakota town, on land that once belonged to the Wahpeton-Sisseton Sioux but had long since been leased out and sold to non-Indian farmers. Our family of nine lived on the very edge of town. . . . I could walk for miles and still find nothing but fields, more fields and the same perfectly straight dirt township road. I often see this edge of town — the sky and its towering and shifting formation of clouds, that beautifully lighted emptiness — when I am writing."

Louise Erdrich has written a series of remarkable inter-related novels, set between 1912 and the present, revolving around the members of two families of the Turtle Mountain

Chippewas: *Love Medicine* (1984), *The Beet Queen* (1986), *Tracks* (1988) and *The Bingo Palace* (1994). The sweep of these interlocking stories has provoked comparisons with Balzac, Faulkner and García Márquez, because Erdrich has created, as one critic put it, "a North Dakota of the imagination," a world that "unites the archetypal and the arcane, heartland America and borderline schizophrenia." The stories are about love, death, ambition, history and magic. A dead person may reappear. A young man can lose his healing power. One story begins: "The first time she drowned in the cold and glassy waters of Lake Turcot, Fleur Pillager was only a girl."

Erdrich is married to another writer, Michael Dorris. They live in New Hampshire, where Dorris is the founder and head of Dartmouth College's Native American studies program. Between them, they've raised six children, three of them adopted. In 1995, Erdrich published her first work of nonfiction, *The Blue Jay's Dance*. Subtitled "A Birth Year," it's a journal of impressions and observations, a year in her life — from a winter pregnancy through a spring and summer of new motherhood. At the same time, it's a naturalist's view of growth and change. Her newest novel is *Tales of Burning Love* (1996).

WACHTEL Your four linked novels describe a very distinctive community in North Dakota. When did you become comfortable with using the Native American voice for your writing?

ERDRICH It took a long time for me because I'm of mixed background and I didn't really know what part of my French, Chippewa and German background I was comfortable with. Probably it happened after I'd worked with an urban Indian council and got to know the people there. My own ability to write the stories and voices came closer to what I wanted when I was about twenty-six, when Michael Dorris and I got married. He not only encouraged me but really lived it out with me, and that's when I started to concentrate on writing.

WACHTEL Michael Dorris is mixed blood as well?

ERDRICH Yes. A mixed-blood friend of mine once said, "You're psychically doomed," but he was laughing, because it gives a person an outsider's outlook on just about everything, and although it may be hard for one personally, as a human being, never to quite belong to anything, it's a great advantage to a writer.

WACHTEL When you were growing up, did you spend much time in the world of your maternal grandparents, who lived on a nearby reservation?

ERDRICH Oh yes, it's the treasure of your life to have time with your grandparents, and the time that I was able to spend with them is magnified, I think, in some profound way. As a child the days or weeks that you spend with your elders is very instructive and the relationship between a grandparent and a child is a very particular and special one.

WACHTEL Can you say what you learned? I know that's a very big question but when you look back now, can you remember the quality of the interactions?

ERDRICH I would say that a sense of peace is what stays with me. You don't get that from your peers; they haven't been around long enough. And one is close to one's parents in a very different way. But children are able to take instruction from grandparents and not feel threatened. Being in the presence of an elder is instructive in itself because even if someone isn't especially wise, they've lived a long time. My grandparents also happened to be wise, I think, and had sorted out a great many complexities in their lives, so that what I remember from my time with them is the kindness, the humour and the peacefulness.

WACHTEL You've written about the death of your maternal grandfather, whom you describe as once a "tribal chairman, pow-wow dancer." What kind of loss is his death for you?

ERDRICH In our families, our grandparents, even great-grandparents — I remember my great-grandmother — are the farthest reaches of our memory, the extensions of ourselves, and they live on through us somehow. I greatly miss having my grandfather's company; it's as though part of myself has gone too. He was a very intelligent, very funny man, and also grounded in his traditions.

So there's a mystery and a loss for me and for all of our family in that he was the most connected of all of us to his own background and tradition. Fortunately, his sons and daughters have a great sense of self and pride in their background, and I do as well, because of him.

WACHTEL In your writing, when you describe a confrontation between European and Aboriginal values, there's always some tension, particularly in the area of religion. You've described yourself as having had a gothic-Catholic childhood; tell me how that shaped you.

ERDRICH Probably the most dramatic part of my childhood was the education that was given to me by Franciscan sisters. I'm sure that children who are taught by sisters — and there aren't as many of us now — have a view of human relationships that's somewhat different from other people's because there's such power to the habit. The cloister is very mysterious and exerts a great pull over children. Within that education there were great extremes. I deeply loved one of the nuns who taught me, Sister Cecilia. But some of the sisters were so powerless and so frustrated that they had no understanding in dealing with children. All of this was pre-Vatican II, before the guitar masses. After Vatican II, I belonged to a "God squad," a group of teenagers who got together to talk about godliness and Catholicism and whatever was important in our lives.

WACHTEL How did you absorb Catholicism and native spirituality? Was it first one and then the other?

ERDRICH I'll return to my grandfather because I think that he gave the most powerful example of how those two worked together. He was not only a very devout Catholic but also a pipe bearer and he prayed in the woods; he used his own native religion in combination with Catholicism. I don't know how he quite worked out the inconsistencies between the two, but he did, and somehow they existed as one in him, and he was able to live them both out, incorporating native ceremony into his Catholicism in a way that I think enriched it. And for him there was no contradiction; he believed in spirituality.

WACHTEL How about for you?

ERDRICH For me there's a great contradiction. I can't reconcile the two. As a woman, I'd have to believe that I'm a lesser being if I were to accept Catholic dogma, and I don't believe that.

WACHTEL How would you describe yourself now in terms of belief?

ERDRICH The only way I can describe it is I'm still looking, still searching, and I think that's the way I'll be all my life. I believe in possibility and I believe we have to look, we have to search, we have to examine. I don't believe in any dogma; organized religion is something I can't adhere to, and yet it exerts a fascination, too. Native religion even more so, because I feel a very strong connection there. I think that returning to native religion and returning to tradition and spiritual ways is the great hope of tribal people today. And it's a great hope of mine that this become part of our lives. It's so important for our young people in particular. It has so much to do with holding values and holding culture and language, and I think that to be able to find a teacher and to get near a teacher is one of the most important things that can happen for a young person now, especially in a tribal setting.

WACHTEL You come from what you describe as a strong family, and you've been part of a strong family, a marriage with six children, but you don't often give us whole families in your writing. Why is that?

ERDRICH It may be that in my own inner life I still feel the fragmentation or I still see the characters as somehow not belonging to a completed world. And being from a mixed background, even though my family is central to me, there's still that outsider's sense of the rest of the world. The truth of it is that when you look at most families, there are not that many intact, perfect little units in the world. Most people have a jagged, complex family life that moves in and out of completion; there are only perfect moments, there is no perfect situation or life.

WACHTEL Certainly mothers are powerful figures in your writing. In one story called "The Leap," a mother is a trapeze artist who literally flies off to rescue her child. The mothers may be baffling or unconventional, but they're very dynamic women.

ERDRICH These works were written during those first years of having babies, when you just can't believe the power that being a parent exerts over you. I couldn't believe it. I began to understand my parents in an entirely different way. I totally forgave them — I couldn't believe what a good job they had done. That happens as soon as you have a child. You think: Oh, my parents were wonderful! How did they put up with me? My parents were very kind, and they were great examples as parents.

WACHTEL You write about magical power and about the presence of spirits: people who are dead sometimes hang around for a while. How much was that a part of your everyday life when you were growing up?

ERDRICH As I say, I was raised a Catholic, and Catholics believe that there's another world that's behind the screen of everyday life. I can't get that belief out of my head, and I can't get native belief out of my heart. There is something behind our everyday life and it doesn't matter what your background is. The dead haunt us, they live with us, that's the way they live, it's the only way we can keep contact with our loved ones. We have to keep them alive within our own spirits, within our own lives, and it's comforting, it helps us, *they* help us.

WACHTEL Spiritual power is a fragile thing in your writing; it's something you could lose. You don't romanticize native medicine or magic or the cultural values that have been in some ways embraced by New Age enthusiasts; you show us the betrayals and the disease and the failures as well. Do you see yourself in a sense as writing against the appropriation of native culture?

ERDRICH I don't have an agenda, but I do want to be honest about what it is to live on earth. I don't care what you are or what your background is, it's not easy if you're really open to what life is. You have to live the moments that come to you as gifts as best you can but there's no way we get out of this without feeling some anguish. We all do. To leave that out I think would be wrong, and it's no comfort to read about a perfect, happy world when a utopia isn't what we live in. We live in a problematic universe, but there are also moments of great joy and unity and harmony, and we encompass such extremes.

WACHTEL You've written about the actual appropriation of native land through taxes and seizure and racism that continues even today — for instance, in your story "The Bingo Van," a character can be beaten up by white thugs and have pretty well no recourse. How important is it for you to address these issues?

ERDRICH It is important. For instance, my own maternal background is of a tribe that has been terribly cheated. There's no tribe that hasn't been cheated. To grow up with the notion that you're from a cheated people gives you a particular outlook on life. When you grow up on tribal land you think, gee, there's not a lot of room here. Then you find out from your elders that the reservation, which was twenty times the size of the present reservation, was sold for ten cents an acre. You realize that the United States government really treated us like a bunch of dogs. You grow up with that; it's the truth of what people feel. What is so amazing about native people is their retention of those traditional values of kindness, and the toughness that enables people to continue to work through the judicial system to try for the return of lands and monies. It is an astonishing feat of survival. It is something that no one at the turn of the century expected, and to see cultures thriving, surviving, living with difficult times but continuing, it's a reviving lesson for anyone in the world.

WACHTEL How are your books received in the community you write about?

ERDRICH It's a mixture. There's always the reaction: why did you portray this person that way? that's going to make people think that there's drinking on reservations; or, why is this person so perfect? The response is as individual as people are. A lot of the reactions are intense, and that's even better. I'm glad people react, though I don't write to affect one person or another. My motive for writing really is pretty selfish: I love to write, that's the reason I do it.

WACHTEL You were saying earlier that you were surprised by the power of parenthood, the grip it has over you. You even wrote a

non-fiction book about it, *The Blue Jay's Dance: A Birth Year*. Why
was it so important for you to write about?

ERDRICH   I wrote the book in part because I felt as though I was
unprepared for the depth of the experience. The emotional
impact of what one feels as a parent is astonishing. Your greatest
instinct is to protect your child. You're so afraid in some ways; a
whole new level of fear is added to your life and a whole new
understanding of what it is to be loved by a parent. It comes into
your life because you identify so thoroughly with your child's
feelings, and that's the way it has to be. It's just genetic. I think in
the process of going through pregnancy and giving birth, you feel
a physical connection to your past, your future; you feel like you're
at the crux of something quite profound.

And I love to read something that makes sense of my own
emotions. While I was pregnant and raising small children, I
wanted something that talked about the emotional aspects, the
inner life of the parent.

WACHTEL   I was thinking that if parenthood is the abiding theme
in this book, then nature is the constant backdrop. How would
you describe your relationship to nature?

ERDRICH   Being part of nature is simply being human, and in my
case I was fortunate enough to be writing this book in a setting
where I could be much more part of a beautiful system of woods
and animals than I'd ever been before. We're all completely subject to nature. Whether we think about it constantly, whether
we're living in a city apartment and it's raining outside or whether
we're living in the country and out in the rain, we really *are* subject to nature, and it's something that, as a culture, we're becoming more aware of and gradually changing our definition of what
we mean by being human.

There's no way *not* to see yourself as part of nature — especially when you're pregnant and you're going into that very physical process. I like to think of myself as a more abstract sort of
person, a neurotic intellectualizer, but there was no way I could
deny my physical self. It was the first part of me to experience
becoming a parent, and there was no division between the intel-

lect and the body. There's no closer enmeshment than when you're involved intellectually and emotionally and physically in the process of raising a child.

The book was written in part for our daughters as well. I thought, when I try to explain this, I won't have the immediacy; it'll all be a blur when and if they become mothers. So I thought, I have to have something that tells them what I was thinking at the time.

WACHTEL The book moves along in a series of small and sometimes quite compact essays and observations and one of the sections is called "The Blue Jay's Dance." Was it your decision to make that the title of the book?

ERDRICH Yes, it seemed emblematic. There was an incident where I saw this very small, tough bird — a blue jay — do a type of hornpipe and drive off a huge, threatening hawk, and it did so because it had a sense of humour — or at least it seemed that way to me. I know that may not be true, but for me it was an extraordinary scene. I began to think about what it is about blue jays and all kinds of opportunistic animals, clever animals, that helps them to survive. And in some way that scene helped me. I had been going through what a lot of new parents experience — a combination of deep joy and sleeplessness that often produces sudden mood swings — you have all this at a time when you really want to focus on caring for a child. It's not an easy time to go through. And somehow this little scene helped me.

WACHTEL There's a line later in that section about the process of differentiating, about where you stop and the baby's needs begin, and this seems central to the book. Can you talk about that tension between yourself as a writer and as a mother?

ERDRICH I think part of the reason I wanted to get some of this down was because I didn't want to be a bad mother to be a good artist. I don't know what you do about the tension between the two because, being a writer, you do have to be selfish about your time and energy, and at the same time I'm completely drawn to and completely loving of our children. That's something I've been trying to figure out from other women's writing, women who are mothers and artists at the same time. I look to them for advice and hope, and in fact found quite a lot of hope in Toni Morrison's saying that she felt it was a great blessing and a boon to her to be a mother, it was something she could draw on that added to the depth of her experience. I think that's very true.

But of course if there's any reason to have children, it's because it's just inevitable and because one loves the process of being with a child and helping a child and growing up with a child. I felt that I was re-experiencing life in an entirely different way that I'd never expected. One forgets, for instance, that the sense of humour of a four-year-old is a certain kind of humour. It's very peculiar: there's an inability to tell a straight joke but doing everything backwards is extremely funny. Seeing something absolutely new through the eyes of a child was astounding for me; I really felt as though I was re-experiencing so much of the world. And I still do.

WACHTEL At one point you compare yourself to "a blue-eyed jumping spider." I wonder if you could elaborate on that metaphor.

ERDRICH It has to do with that tension between being someone who is warm and social and part of a family, and an artist who has to keep people at arm's length and preserve at least some form of solitude. I think that's very important, and it's something that we don't talk about a lot in our culture, the value of solitude; it's more the tragedy of loneliness. Perhaps it's because I'm one of seven children and have always been around great numbers of family members, but solitude seems to me increasingly something to be cherished.

WACHTEL You say that like the spider, if you don't hold mate or family at arm's length, you'll be devoured.

ERDRICH That's exactly right. To go back to the poor spider, it's usually the male who's devoured. But I was talking about the danger of being completely caught up in family. And devoured! It does feel like that. It does feel as though your personality goes out piecemeal to people you love, and sometimes it's difficult to gather yourself together for the work you love.

WACHTEL How did *you* manage? How did you organize the time to write with six children and a husband who's also a writer?

ERDRICH It was partly that we worked together very well. He's very organized and I'm very disorganized, and somehow we got things done because we're very different in our approaches. So for me it was having a partner, and that's the only way I could have done it. But it was also by being a little dogged and crazy about my writing time. You feel this compulsion, this obsession, that you have to do this, it's the most important thing in the world, and yet your baby is also the most important person in the world, and you have to do both somehow. I know a lot of people go through this.

WACHTEL In *The Blue Jay's Dance*, you create a list of women writers and when you enumerate them, you indicate those who've had children and those who haven't, those who've married and those who've stayed single. I know this is as impossible a question as, "Do women write differently from men?" but, "Do mothers write differently?"

ERDRICH I'm trying to figure that out too. I feel that Toni Morrison is someone who really has used motherhood in a very powerful way. For instance, her book *Beloved* talks about one of the most hideous possibilities in human terms, a mother killing her own child. She does it in a way that shows the depth of that love and attachment. The mother does it to save her child from slavery; she's keeping her child safe in a most terrible way. I think Toni Morrison used that to illustrate the real horror of what people were contending with.

I read other women and wonder what their own motherhood or their decision not to have children has meant for their work. Jane Smiley is someone else who's written about this, and I found that in *A Thousand Acres*, especially at the end, she universalized the savage instinct to protect, to preserve and keep, and I thought that it was the most astounding ending. I felt that being a mother somehow helped her do that because you become *so* protective, and it really does extend to the rest of the world in many ways. You want to protect not only your own children but also people in a more general way.

WACHTEL You speculate at one point that perhaps some of the most moving literature has been produced by men who didn't understand that they simply wanted to be women nursing babies. Could you elaborate on that? Clearly, you're not referring to the classic parallel that men make art, women make babies?

ERDRICH There's a great longing in literature for completion and for oneness. That's part of human art. Plato talks about it, and he thought of it as a sexual union — the two halves of one human wheel whirling around. The act of mothering a child, being so close to a child, and having a child so dependent upon you and yet giving to you so utterly, makes you feel a sense of completion, of being absolutely right. This isn't something that is experienced only in the mother-child relationship; it's experienced in many different ways, and that's one of them. My point is that art, literature, yearns for that completion.

WACHTEL You invoke someone I think of as the least likely to qualify as a maternal love writer, and that's Ernest Hemingway.

ERDRICH I was referring to his desire to prove his courage in the most quintessential macho way. But women prove their courage in different ways, and have not been valued for it in the way that men have. I think that's going to change, with more women writing. Women do survive and go through extremely difficult times, in labour; it's something we don't talk about much. It becomes this medical process that isn't really put into human terms; women aren't considered to have proved something. But I always find it astounding that women go into labour cheerfully, while being terrified on the inside. Women bear up so bravely under things that are extremely difficult, and we take it for granted. Labour is not just a medical experience, it's a religious experience, but it isn't recognized as such.

WACHTEL What were some of the fears that you had as you approached motherhood? You describe yourself as someone who once fainted when her hair was being cut, so I thought childbearing must have taken a lot of courage.

ERDRICH I really am a physical coward. As a child I wouldn't take vaccinations unless I was holding my mother's hand. So it was very frightening to me to be at the mercy of the medical system, but I was very fortunate because I had in my midwife a very good friend as well. She put me more at ease and made me feel more in control. But I was terrified, as many women are, of not being in control, of not knowing exactly what would happen. I kept trying to find out from other women how it was going to feel, how I was going to react, what I was going to do. It's very hard to describe anything so physical to another person, so I didn't have a clear picture of how it would be for me. And it's different for everyone. I used to go in just to talk to one woman who ran a lingerie shop because she'd had ten-minute labours, and I thought, if I talk to her and buy the right lingerie, that'll be my experience.

WACHTEL And you ask why no woman's labour is as famous as the death of Socrates. Why do you link those two events, a suicide and a birth?

ERDRICH A lot of *The Blue Jay's Dance* is about suicide and death, as well as birth. It was partly because a person who had lived in the house where I wrote the book had committed suicide, and partly because I kept feeling the full cycle of life. There are countless paintings of the death of Socrates. That was a heroic choice and it's something people draw many strands of courage from. But women don't talk about what it's like to be in labour, we take it as part of what every woman has to do, they just have to go through it. When you think of the birth of Caesar, the first person who had a Caesarian, it's all about Julius Caesar. It's not about his mother.

WACHTEL Why do you think birth *is* so little written about?

ERDRICH As I said, it's a religious experience, but it's been under the control of organized religion, and the process of birth itself has been considered unmentionable for centuries. You couldn't talk about it or describe it in a Catholic-controlled world. It was something that women died of constantly — there was a fifty-fifty chance of dying in labour around the turn of the century. I think it's part of our puritan background, that it's something we don't think about, write about, discuss. When women get together they do talk about it, but it's not something that is really part of a public dialogue. If women keep writing about it, it will become part of literature.

WACHTEL You write that meaningful pain can change your life. How?

ERDRICH I think the experience of pain bonds you to people who have experienced it. I was very fortunate in that I'd never had, before going into labour, a day of real physical pain. I'd had small things happen to me. But after I came back from the hospital, in addition to feeling the wonder of having a new life, I took pain a lot more seriously: I joined Amnesty International because I thought, this is something that's very deep, it's very instructive and it's very terrible for pain to be inflicted without this joyous purpose. I was a comparatively lucky person in birth, nothing happened that would be considered extraordinary, and yet for me it meant that I took a different look at the world.

WACHTEL You were saying that what flows through this book is not only birth but death, intimations of death. As you said, someone had committed suicide in the house you were living in. And three of your grandparents died around the time you were writing. How did you weave your way through that?

ERDRICH That was part of the attempt of the book. I had never written about myself personally before, and beginnings suggest endings. I kept thinking about this circle, especially as my grandparents — it seems to me, thinking back now — sort of walked off. They were my real connection and they are the real connection. My family is both very large and very close, and to have my grandparents leaving the world as these new children were entering it was a profound experience for me. I began to try to connect some of the threads and pull back some of those threads for our children as well. I was lucky because, as the oldest child, I was close to my grandparents; I was able to know them when they were relatively young. I spent a lot of time with them and I was close to them in emotional ways that I truly treasure. I wanted to bring that full circle and save it somehow for our children.

WACHTEL You call *The Blue Jay's Dance* "a personal search." What did you find by writing it? What do you know now that you didn't know before?

ERDRICH What I hadn't expected were the depths as well as the heights. I hadn't expected to go up and down so much in my reactions to things, or to be so emotional, or to be so overwhelmed with love. I hadn't experienced that kind of infant love. There's a kind of love that pours over one right after giving birth that just astounded me. I talk to other people now and I realize that it's part of human life and it frightens people sometimes. It's the kind of love that makes you go and check to see whether your child is breathing every five minutes, and it can be an annoying kind of love. But I became happier with things somehow.

Writing this book made me more cheerful. I hope reading it does the same for others who are admitting that they have some of these terrible feelings along with all of the joy. It frees one to experience the joy in itself.

June 1993/April 1995
interview initially prepared in collaboration
with Sandra Rabinovitch and Larry Scanlan

DAVID GROSSMAN

I first heard about the Israeli novelist and journalist, David Grossman, when his series of compassionate and troubling articles on the life of Jews and Palestinians in the West Bank was published in *The New Yorker* and, later, in a book called *The Yellow Wind* (1987; trans. 1988). It was twenty years after the Six Day War — that is, twenty years since the beginning of the Israeli occupation. This is how he described his experience: "In March 1987 . . . I went out to the West Bank and brought back this collection of essays, *The Yellow Wind*. The things I saw there were frightening, but even more frightening were the things that my interlocutors hinted at, in the spaces between their words. In their silences, between the teeth gritted in anger and hatred . . . were the seeds of disaster." Grossman had anticipated the Palestinian uprising, or Intifada, by six months.

A radio journalist who speaks fluent Arabic, David Grossman had already written *The Smile of the Lamb* (1983/1985), a novel set in the occupied West Bank, as well as *See Under: Love* (1986/1989), a complex fiction set in the late fifties in Israel, but also, in part, in a Nazi concentration camp during World War II. *See Under: Love* was a remarkable book, and it prompted comparisons with Günter Grass and Gabriel García Márquez.

Now, critics are calling David Grossman "Israel's finest novelist." In *The Book of Intimate Grammar* (1992/1994), he enters a boy's consciousness so persuasively as to evoke James Joyce or Henry Roth's classic, *Call It Sleep*. But David Grossman is starting to elude comparison altogether. His writing has a strangeness and a power all its own. *The Book of Intimate Grammar* is not only one of the most disturbing novels I've read in a long time, it is also one of the best.

David Grossman continues to write both fiction and reportage. *Sleeping on a Wire* (1992/1993) consists of conversations with Palestinians who chose to remain in Israel after 1948 when the state was created and its Arab neighbours declared war. Once again, Grossman's sympathies towards the Palestinians provoked controversy in Israel and abroad.

Born in Jerusalem in 1954, Grossman remains an articulate and thoughtful analyst of his country's political and social vicissitudes. When I spoke to him in the fall of 1994 (when he was in New York to promote *The Book of Intimate Grammar*), he was fairly optimistic about the peace process. Since then, with the assassination of Yitzhak Rabin in late 1995 and Hamas suicide bombers in early 1996, Grossman is less buoyant. When he appeared on CBC's "Newsworld" in March 1996, Grossman commented, "For most of us, Israelis and Palestinians, peace now is only a very nice word. . . .

"We are living in a situation of war, of fear. You relate to your children as if every moment might be — God forbid — the last. . . . Every step you take may be fatal, the wrong bus that you take or the lucky bus that you missed. This proximity of death is something that is burdening on the soul, on the psychology, on the language — it is everywhere until one starts to relate to life as a latent death. This is why we started the peace process to bring this to an end, to live with normality, with some hope, with a sense of future."

WACHTEL In an introduction to the paperback edition of your book *The Yellow Wind*, you said, "The writer's job is to put a finger on the wound, and do it in a language that the reader has not yet learned to insulate himself against." Why do you feel that's so much your job as a writer?

GROSSMAN I became a writer because I felt that urge, and I looked for a way to express it. I think this is the most important thing a writer can do because of the pain wounds cause; they can paralyze people. People learn to live with their wounds in a very distorted way. Sometimes you see how an entire personality is built around a wound or a flaw, and how this very cumbersome apparatus, which was meant to allow the person to live with their wound, becomes a prison. What writers should do is purify the words and try to remind us of the primal significance of words, to connect us with the sub-currents of our culture that have been forgotten over the years because modern life is so complicated and full of contradictions.

WACHTEL Do you know why your personality is drawn to these wounds, since you say that was your starting point?

GROSSMAN It's a very personal question and I'll answer frankly and openly. I think it has to do with a sense I have of being an eternal outsider to everything that I know, which forces me to create my reality through formulating what I see in my own words. It also has something to do with the way it's impossible for me to speak in words that other people have already spoken. I always feel that the writer is someone who is claustrophobic about words that other people have already used and therefore abused. I feel an almost physical urge to describe things in my own words. It's essential for me. That's why I wrote *The Yellow Wind*. I felt there was a battle between me and reality, because the words did not fit what I felt and what I knew, so I had to write about it. That's also what made me write *See Under: Love* about the *shoah*, the Holocaust, because I felt that most of the books I'd read did not really tell me the truth about how something like that could have happened to people like me — and I'm talking about both murderers and victims. They were ordinary people who were caught or fell into that situation. And finally, it's exactly why I wrote my novel, *The Book of Intimate Grammar*, because it describes the almost desperate need of Aron, my main character, to crystallize a language of his own, a language that will not be infected by the language of other people, of the outer world, of adults.

WACHTEL When you say that you have always felt yourself an outsider, I imagine you are speaking personally or psychologically, because you are an Israeli living in Israel, and would seem to be a part of a culture.

GROSSMAN Yes, there are always some dichotomies and contradictions that I cannot explain. I remember being a very social creature as a child and also being totally lonely — as most of us probably are. I feel very much an integral part of my society, and I want to be a part of it and to take part in this self-building society, especially now, with all the new developments that allow us suddenly to start to live a normal life with all its layers, and not only to survive, as we used to. And I take part in Israeli life, and I write and I want to influence it; I don't want to leave this stage for people who will try to manipulate me or tell me what to think and how to speak. But at the same time I feel an outsider, it's something very personal, I can't help it.

WACHTEL You are the first Israeli writer to cross the line into the occupied territories for your book of reportage, *The Yellow Wind*, which turned out to be a very provocative collection of interviews with Palestinians and Jews living in the West Bank and Gaza. Why did you want to make that journey?

GROSSMAN Three years before that I wrote my first novel, *The Smile of the Lamb*, and in both books I try to redeem the reality that was confiscated from me. We, the Israelis and the Palestinians, live in the utmost distortion possible. The situation of occupation is a highly abnormal one, as all of us know, but we don't know the minutiae, the small details of life, of harassment, of humiliation. What does it mean to occupy the other, not only from the political point of view — which is very narrow and abrupt and violent — but what does it mean to penetrate the other's privacy? To have dominion over the other's intimacy? To formulate reality for them every day? These are tough questions, and I wanted to deal with them because I felt that the newspapers and books I read did not give me those answers, and I started to feel almost suffocated in that situation. It was very much part of our life but we had no words for it. No words! And when you do not put some effort into imagining the reality that's in front of you, to try to see it in all its nuances, one day you might wake up into a reality that is unimaginable, as the leaders of Israel woke up to the Intifada. They were totally taken by surprise because they didn't know what was going on. When I published *The Yellow Wind*, six months before the Intifada, our prime minister, then Yitzhak Shamir, denounced me. He said, "Well, it's only a journalistic creation, it does not exist. I know, I have my men to tell me about what's going on in the field." And then he was surprised, like so many, again because of the contradictions of reality. People tend to shield themselves from what they don't want to see.

WACHTEL   *The Yellow Wind* explores very difficult issues for Israeli audiences, because the occupation calls into question Israel's sense of its own higher morality as a nation of sufferers and survivors. Amos Oz described Israelis as people who want the best country in the world, the purest, with the highest moral standards, or else they're totally disillusioned.

GROSSMAN   Well, I can share his wish, as everybody wants his place, his environment, to be the best. I think what we Israelis are now starting to understand — especially after peace is achieved — is that maybe it's better to have more pragmatic ideologies and not such lofty and divine ideas about our future. There is still much to do even when your dreams are not in the sky. On the ground there are still so many things that we can improve, and seek to understand for ourselves, because Israel has been in existence now for almost forty-seven years, and yet the basic questions have not been dealt with until now. For example: Who are we? Are we Jews or are we Israelis? To what extent do we, the new Israelis, take from Jewish history? Maybe there is a total difference, an unbridgeable river, that runs between these two, being a Jew and being an Israeli. What do we take from this Jewish history to bring up our children on? Is it only the catastrophes, the calamities, the suffering? Maybe there are other things, because now we have a chance for the first time to stand anew in front of our history. What about the Palestinian minority who live inside Israel? We have a minority of one-fifth of our population; they are Arabs, they are Muslims, but they live in a Jewish state. So is it their state? Can we really be democrats? Some other questions are: Are we a part of the Middle East? Do we internalize the fact that we live in the Middle East? Will the Middle East internalize us or forever see us as foreigners or strangers? You see, there are so many heavy questions. When one lives in Israel, one can write a whole book on each and every one of these questions.

WACHTEL Were you disillusioned? When you write such a compassionate book about Palestinians and are implicitly so critical of Israelis as occupiers and find there's a certain discomfort in seeing them that way, you're talking in some ways about the effect on the national psyche, but what about the effect on you?

GROSSMAN It was very difficult. I'm a product of Israel, of Israeli education, of so many of these slogans and clichés and of these truly authentic ideals, the way I want to see Israel. Suddenly most of these notions were broken and I had to find out what I thought, and what my part in it is, how I can protest. The weeks after I wrote *The Yellow Wind* I felt totally isolated. I finished writing it on the eve of the celebration of Israel's independence day, and this is an evening where we all gather with our friends and we sing melodies — this is an Israeli ceremony — singing songs that were composed after wars or during wars and they're all coloured with that, but we love them. This is the stuff that we are made of, in a way. And it was the first time that I was unable even to sing these songs, to sing with all the others, and I felt self-excommunicated, if one can say that. Right now the situation is totally different. Things that people were threatened or even cursed for saying seven or eight years ago, by the media or the government, those things are now said openly in the Knesset, to Rabin, our prime minister. Things that Amos Oz, Isaiah Leibowitz or other people used to say some years ago, Rabin is now

saying, and this is the official policy of Israel today. Israel is moving in a very positive direction, so we must remember that as well.
WACHTEL Listening to you talk about how troubling an experience it was to write *The Yellow Wind*, I'm thinking how you then
wrote *Sleeping on a Wire*, conversations with the Palestinians in
Israel rather than in the occupied territories. Why did you go back
to collect those stories?
GROSSMAN Because again I felt that this is a topic that nobody
speaks about and it is going to burst at some point or another, in
the near future. I believe that this is going to be the next explo-
sion, or the next threat in the Middle East, because once there is
a Palestinian state and the big Palestinian question has started to
be solved, then we shall have to face the problem of our large
Palestinian minority inside Israel. Who are they? Are they Israelis
in a state that declares itself to be Jewish, but they are not Jews?
Are they Palestinian, but living inside Israel? Maybe they shall ask
for autonomy inside Israel, which is a very difficult idea for
Israelis to accept. Maybe it's time for them to stop suspending
their decision. They have suspended their decision for forty-six,
forty-seven years. It's a very strange existence. I used the metaphor of an acrobat who walks on the wire, afraid to make a wrong
move, because if they walk towards Israel, then the Palestinians,
their brothers in the occupied territories, will shout against them.
If they make a move towards the Palestinians, then Israeli public
opinion will be very threatened. So they're fossilized on the wire.
They sleep on the wire all their life, so now it's time to wake up
and to decide. And you can imagine that this problem is rarely
dealt with in Israel because it's so threatening. It's much more
threatening than the question of the Palestinians in the occupied
territories, because we all know that the occupied territories can
be detached from Israel, it's almost a surgical operation, and I
think we should be detached. People will suffer very much from
that because many historic and religious sentiments are attached to
these territories, but it can be done and it probably will be done.
But the problem of the people who are our citizens and live inside
Israel, is a problem of identity. To what extent can we call ourselves

Israeli when they are also Israelis, and maybe they don't like to be called Israelis? So nobody spoke about it; there was not even a name for this minority. It was called "the problem of the minorities," or some other false term, and when you call something by a false name you deceive only yourself because reality has its own energy and dynamic. So I felt it was worth writing about.

WACHTEL Speaking of false names or metaphors, I can see how this might tantalize a novelist since these Palestinians in Israel are called "absent presences."

GROSSMAN Yes, in official Hebrew they are called "present absentees" or "absent presentees." I felt that this legal name manifests so much of their being here but being absent at the same time. And I felt it's time to redeem their absence and to start having a real dialogue because all the time we speak about co-existence, co-existence between us and the Israeli Palestinians. (When I say "us" I mean the Israeli Jews.) But there is no co-existence. There is only mutual ignorance that has continued for more than forty years. And again, you see, I started by talking about this wound. It is a wound. They did not choose to live with us, we did not choose to live with them; it was imposed on both sides by the War of Independence of 1948; and it was as if a bone were broken and then reconnected, but not in a healthy way. So the whole body teaches itself to move around this very fragile place in order not to break it again. Unfortunately what we have to do now is break this bone again in order to let it be reconnected in a healthier, more normal way, and this can be done only when you create a real dialogue that consists of authentic words.

WACHTEL One of the remarkable things about your non-fiction is the novelist's eye for detail. Your fiction is quite different in that it is much more dense and ambitious and disturbing in a different way. There's a very subjective voice inside your novels. I'm thinking here of both *See Under: Love* and *The Book of Intimate Grammar*. What takes you in this direction, into almost an internal stream of consciousness?

GROSSMAN Now I feel I can say that this is the only way for me to converse with life, with reality. I was reluctant to make such a lofty claim a couple of years ago, but now I just know it's true. For one year I tried not to write — it's impossible for me. So what started as the ultimate liberation has turned into a way to keep breathing. I know the depth I want to swim in, and that this is my place. Probably some people find it difficult to read, but I know what I want from a book that I read and because of that, from a book that I write. I have high expectations of a book; I'm not very fond of entertaining books. They're okay for when you take a flight or when you're at the seashore, but I'm a great admirer of Kafka. Kafka said, we don't need books to entertain us, we need books to be like an axe to the frozen sea in our souls. And I believe this is what I want from a book. When I read a book I want to emerge totally different from it, and really it is the only reason to write a book, in my opinion, so that the writer emerge different. I know what writing *The Book of Intimate Grammar* did to me, and it's sometimes quite destructive to your everyday life, but I think it's the only way for me to live in the world with all its contradictions. I want to explore all the nuances. I want to swim freely in all the depths. I need to create an environment of thinking for myself, of desires, of imagination, that is mine alone. I know it sounds very ambitious but this is the fuel that drives me. Now, after these books, I finally know what I want to achieve; I don't know if I will manage to do it but I do know that this is the direction I want to go in.

WACHTEL *See Under: Love* and *The Book of Intimate Grammar* are set in an earlier period in Israeli history, the period of your own childhood. Why did you want to evoke that time?

GROSSMAN Almost every writer I know tries to go back to the time of his childhood, which in my case coincided with the childhood of Israel. To have been a child at such an intense, significant era in the life of Israel, I think is worth writing about. So many things started to crystallize. There were so many lies, so many undercurrents, so many different dialogues and manipulations and stresses and heavy memories from the past mingled with this desire to build a new society, a society that would be like a baby that has no memory, that would be totally pure and clean. Well, it turned out that this baby was a very old baby, but I was there as a child and I wanted to go back to it. I think Rilke once said that our childhood is the great museum of memory. Sometimes I wonder why is it so difficult for me to go back to visit this museum — it's as if there is a very strong guard standing there trying to stop me from entering it again. I don't know why he's trying to prevent me from going back there and seeing the authentic me that I was as a child. Perhaps it's to protect the memories, to ensure that I will not abuse them.

WACHTEL *The Book of Intimate Grammar* is the story of a boy caught quite literally between childhood and adolescence. As one reviewer put it, "it's a coming-of-age story in which age never comes." He's stalled. Why focus on that?

GROSSMAN I think Aron's place, between being a child and being an adult, appeals to me very much, and in a strange way. It gives one a very rare and sometimes upsetting but also pleasurable opportunity to observe all the basic things of life, but you observe them from a somewhat distorted point of view. Questions of love, of sexuality, of being a sexual creature, of married life, and the fears and the anguish of being a child — all of these are questions that children have a desperate need to invoke, so that they can imagine their world out of a reality that is quite chaotic. The boredom of the everyday life of a child, the everlasting expectations of things that never come — since you are a child you have this alchemy of childhood, and you can create gold out of very boring things, especially my Aron in *The Book of Intimate Grammar*. He's a hypersensitive child and he looks at things as if through a magnifying glass and he re-creates every day and every thing in order — so he will be able to live in that reality, which is a very vulgar, violent, carnal reality. There is the reality of his home, his parents, and then the outer reality, the language of his friends who are maturing while he does not reach puberty for three long years — and all this exterior dialogue of the new country, the militarized country.

WACHTEL But he's so alienated from that reality; he's very imaginative, he's painfully self-conscious. One of his imaginative exercises is to play various kinds of spying games and then he sees himself, in a sense, as a spy in his own world, where he's only playing a part. "He's abandoned forever in enemy territory," I think is how you put it. As for the alchemy, it's not a golden world that he can create, even for himself.

GROSSMAN Yes, because we live in reality. But weren't you such a child yourself? When the novel was published, many people who had been kids in my class at school read it and they called or wrote or came to see me and they said, "Listen, we all were like that. It's exactly what we felt!" And of course as a child I felt that everyone else was glued together, and there was me, excommunicated, a little outsider. But I've come to think that there is an inherent solitude in the situation of being a child. Writing this book suddenly allowed me to talk about it and tell other people how I felt. And very quickly I understood that I was not alone. But maybe there are people who will never admit that they were so alone and so lacking in confidence and so thirsty to be absorbed into something bigger than them that would comfort them, that would give them a language, so that they wouldn't have to converse with themselves in this horrible language that is the language of an individual. My Aron deliberately tries to achieve all this with language, because the book is not only about childhood and not only about love and sexuality, it is first and foremost for me a book about the roots of an artist, a portrait of an artist as a young man, if I may say so, very humbly. I wanted to show where the origins of creativity come from, where there is a strong, almost physical need to create your own world and to legislate your own rules in that reality.

WACHTEL Language has exceptional power for Aron and one of the things he does, and the image of it was so very affecting, is that he has this notion of purifying words. There are certain words he likes the sound of, and he can purify them, he says, if he doesn't say them out loud for seven days.

GROSSMAN Yes, and then he has special prayers, he has to say them over again from the end to the beginning sometimes. He has a whole bureaucracy, you see, for purifying the words and then he is able to send them back into the world because he's entitled to speak them, they are his. This is something that I remember feeling very strongly myself as a child, that I could not say every word, but that in this alienated world some words had to be mine, words I could be deserving of and could say aloud. Aron took this from me in a cunning way.

WACHTEL And he spends a lot of time what you call "Aroning." It seems it's his means of internal escape. What happens?

GROSSMAN I hope I can explain this in English because English is the most difficult language to explain it in. When Aron and I were in sixth grade we started to study English at school, and we became acquainted with the present continuous: sleeping, going. We don't have that tense in Hebrew. In Hebrew we have enormous pasts, we have a very shaky future, and we have only one tense for the present. So suddenly a whole reality was revealed to my Aron: I am going. And because he observes reality with a magnifying glass, suddenly this go-ing goes on and on, and things happen in between, and the people who are outside you don't really understand what happens to you when you are go-ing. The book has been published in a dozen languages and in each language they manage to do it but not in English, because what can my translator, Betsy Rosenberg, say: I am going-ing-ing? So what we chose to do — it was her choice and I support it — is, whenever Aron starts to play with that, we wrote "He's Aroning." And I think it's very beautiful. In "Aroning" you see this slow meditation and the slow diving into himself, and I like the sound of it, this Aroning; it's like a little gloomy bell. Aroning, you know, it's going down, down.

WACHTEL Everything is difficult for Aron and everything is a betrayal; even his own body betrays him.

GROSSMAN Well, I think it's like that for all of us. Our body is the place through which we become acquainted with suffering, disease, ageing and death. The pleasures that our body gives us sometimes seem to me like very small and cheap bribes, and very brief ones. For Aron it's extremely important to settle those contradictions. What does it mean to live in two different dimensions —

the spiritual and the carnal? If we sat together and ate as Aron's family, we would eat potatoes, and one potato or part of a potato would eventually become father and the other would become part of mother and part of Aron's sister, Yochi. But what is it that comes from the outside and what is it that is me and will ever remain me, remain I, no matter what happens to me?

But I listen to myself in these headphones, talking about this to you, and I think, it's not a philosophical book, it is a book about the life of a child, and I wanted it to be that, I wanted it to be through the eyes of a child. All these questions that we are now talking about I hope emerge from the text of the book, but I didn't want to write a philosophical book. I don't like philosophical books as fiction; I want books to take me, not to teach me things.

WACHTEL Well, I think it's because the book is so powerful, it's philosophical or metaphysical in spite of yourself. But the way it hits the reader is much more visceral and in fact a lot of the book is very physical. When you talk about Aron, you make his world sound interesting and uncomfortable but manageable, but when you read the novel, the sensitive characters in it have a terrible time, not only Aron but also his neighbour. There's a neighbour in their housing development who just cracks. Reality is too hard to take.

GROSSMAN Do you know very many happy people? I think it's almost impossible to be really happy after the age of three, let's say. I don't deliberately try to write desperate books — not at all! Well, desperate, yes, but not depressing.

WACHTEL Now that's an important distinction.

GROSSMAN Yes. But I wanted to create a whole reality with all the dimensions that exist, and there is a lot of joy in the life of Aron. Maybe my Aron does not really understand what he is going through, but readers can suddenly be with him in that corridor of becoming an adolescent, they can remember their own childhood with all the nuances of that period. I think maybe this is happiness, that after all we are not alone. We are not alone: we all experience almost the same things, and if we just allow ourselves to tell this truth, then suddenly we are not alone. Every good thing that is said about this novel I immediately deliver to Aron. I feel he deserves it, you know. If, twenty-seven years ago, someone had come and told him, listen, one day a very intelligent journalist in Canada will ask you questions about your life, he wouldn't have believed it, he was so isolated then. So there's no justice. But there's some comfort.

WACHTEL But the acuteness of adolescent anguish or pain usually passes in life and in fiction; at least you become more aware that you're not alone, or conversely that everyone is alone and you derive some comfort from that, but here — and I won't give away the ending — it's very unsettling.

GROSSMAN Maybe it's because when we live through those things — when we are in the process — it is very efficient for us, for our survival, not to notice all those minor obstacles and anguishes, in order to keep going. And maybe when you come to write about something, you perform an act of self-cruelty and disarm yourself from your old defence mechanism, and you stand naked. Then you re-experience all these things and you realize to what extent you had to manipulate yourself then, as an adolescent, in order not to see these things, or what enormous strength it took to continue from day to day, sometimes from minute to minute. Maybe now, when we are all adults, it's time to go back and remember what it was like, and that we were not alone.

WACHTEL So when as a writer you put a finger on the wound you have some sense that there may be some healing. I'm putting optimism into your mouth, I don't know why.

GROSSMAN I'm a very optimistic character, by the way, I am. I think writing a book is a very optimistic thing to do. I don't think I can heal a wound: I just can describe it better. No more than that. I just want to re-map the wound, in a way, and to give it new names, and to say, yes, I also consist of that wound, it is mine, I'm part of it. That's the only thing I can aspire to.

September 1994
*interview initially prepared in collaboration
with Sandra Rabinovitch*

JANE SMILEY

Jane Smiley became famous with her 1991 bestseller, *A Thousand Acres*, which won a Pulitzer Prize and the National Book Critics Circle Award. A rich, satisfying and disturbing novel about families and farming in Iowa, *A Thousand Acres* is a brilliant re-working of Shakespeare's *King Lear*, though when I began the novel I didn't quite realize it. But soon the patriarch, Larry Cook, the owner of a thousand acres of rich soil in Iowa, decides to hand over his farm to his three daughters: Ginny, Rose and Caroline. Caroline, the youngest, the only one to have left the land to become a lawyer in the city, expresses some doubt. So Larry cuts her out. Gradually, everything disintegrates. The family is torn apart, Larry goes mad, a neighbour loses his sight, a storm rages. Finally, the farm is lost, the family broken and cast out.

But Jane Smiley's *King Lear* is told — not from the point of view of Lear, or Larry — but from the perspective of his elder daughter, Goneril, or Ginny. Goneril and Regan, or here Ginny and Rose, are devoted, troubled sisters — more victimized than treacherous. And the youngest, Cordelia, or Caroline, is not un-equivocally innocent. *A Thousand Acres* is a complicated and subtle novel that works on many levels — not least the sheer detail of domestic life on a farm.

Jane Smiley is known for — as one critic put it — her "unerring, unsettling ability to capture the rhythms of family life gone askew." She does this in her earlier short story collection, *The Age of Grief* (1987), and in a pair of novellas, *Ordinary Love* and *Good Will* (1989). Even her epic, *The Greenlanders* (1988) — a massive, grim, historical novel about a fourteenth-century polar colony, a European civilization that ultimately vanished — comes down to family sagas. Jane Smiley herself has been married three times and has three children.

Born in 1949, she teaches writing at Iowa State University in Ames. She followed *A Thousand Acres* with a campus novel called *Moo* (1995). I first met Smiley in 1989 and was struck by two things: how tall she is (6′ 2″) and how forthright. At the time, we spoke mostly about the families and relationships in her novels. The last line of *Ordinary Love* is: "I have given my children the two cruelest gifts I had to give — the experience of perfect family happiness, and the certain knowledge that it could not last." What I hadn't realized then was how deeply and sharply political Smiley is. This became evident not only in her recent novels, but also in a provocative piece published in *Harper's* (January, 1996): "Say It Ain't So, Huck: Second Thoughts on Mark Twain's 'Masterpiece'."

Jane Smiley spoke to me from a studio in Ames, Iowa.

WACHTEL Your novel *A Thousand Acres* has as its scaffolding Shakespeare's play *King Lear*. Can you remember the first time you encountered *King Lear*; did you see the play performed or read it at school?

SMILEY I think I read it at school. We read a Shakespeare play every year, so it must have been my senior year in high school. I don't remember if I liked it or not; mostly I was just scrambling to try to understand it and assimilate the teacher's opinion of it. But my response to the women, especially in the first two or three acts, was to be on their side and to think that they were being reasonable. Then the teacher would tell me that they were being unreasonable, so I would nod and agree. There was always something that stuck in my craw about the play, and by the time I was out of college, out of graduate school, and looking at literature more as an adult than as a student, I still had a residual feeling that the interpretation I'd been given over the years didn't accord with my own response to the play.

WACHTEL How was that?

SMILEY I always felt that the older daughters had a point, especially when they started discussing whether King Lear's followers should be accompanying him everywhere. In one instance, one of the daughters makes the claim that the retinue is causing lots of fights and that they're very obstreperous. I always thought, putting myself in her shoes, would I want that behaviour in my house? And that opened me to thinking, no, I wouldn't, and they *are* being reasonable. Of course, what the play posits is that their love for their father shouldn't be based on reason, it should be based on a deeper emotional attachment. It was hard for me to accept that too, that reason and emotional attachment should be so contradictory. Those were the seeds of my thoughts about the play as I got older.

WACHTEL How did those seeds come to flower? What drew you back to the play when you came to write *A Thousand Acres*?

SMILEY My thoughts would go back to the play when there was a production, and when I went to see the Kurosawa movie *Ran*, which was based on *King Lear*. My cousin is an actress and I would talk to her about what kind of production you could do that would give voice to this differing interpretation of the sisters. I realized that to do a production I would have to have a whole different career. But I could do that as a novel. Also, I saw *Rosenkrantz and Gildenstern Are Dead* and I realized that it was possible to rework the material, and that not only was it possible, it was a pretty honourable tradition. So I said, why not?

My husband, who hasn't really gotten enough credit over the last couple of years, said to me, why don't you set it on a wheat farm in Kansas? I dismissed that because I didn't know anything about wheat farming, but then one day we were driving down the highway in northern Iowa and I was looking out the window and I thought, I know plenty about corn and bean farms in Iowa so why not set it here?

WACHTEL What was your relationship with the play while you were writing the novel? To what degree did you feel constrained by the *Lear* framework or inspired by it?

SMILEY I felt that the only way to play the game was to adhere to the structure of the play as closely as possible — make it the ground rules for my novel. I saw *A Thousand Acres* as being in some sense a production or an interpretation of the play, and I didn't want to diverge from the material that was there. There were times when my editor urged me to depart from the play, especially when the older sister poisons the younger sister. My editor felt that it was a death blow to Ginny's existence as a sympathetic character to have her do this. I knew that I wanted the sisters to survive long enough to discuss what had gone before, so the poisoning couldn't succeed, but I did want Ginny to feel that urge, because to me in some ways that urge was very logical. I had to find the logic and present it in a compelling way so that the reader would be able to accept it and not lose too much sympathy for Ginny.

I have often found with writing that if you follow your instinct and then think about it and probe into it more, your instinct does turn out to be right for a lot of different reasons. So I worked on making the logic of Ginny's response clear. Then I realized that the way in which she could come to terms with her father's unthinkable act was to have committed an unthinkable act of her own. That's when I came up with the sentence, "She had to remember what she couldn't imagine." The idea is to have done something so unthinkable that you can't even imagine it and yet you did it, so you have to remember that you did it. I think people's passions often lead them into doing things that they can't imagine themselves doing. That was what I wanted to explore, and by having Ginny make the effort to poison Rose, she can explore this idea of being led by your passions into the unthinkable.

WACHTEL Once you commit yourself to a tragedy, though, there's a certain inexorable quality about it.

SMILEY In our time we've thrown out the old reasons for tragedy. We no longer believe in fate. We no longer believe in the judgments of the gods. We proclaim our belief in choice and agency and the ability to decide what you are going to make of circumstances, even if circumstances go against you. The old definition of tragedy has more to do with how you accept your fate or how you battle against your fate. I think that's one thing that separates my novel from the play, because the characters in the novel are all presumed to have been able to choose what they've done. So I'm not sure the novel is a tragedy; I think of it more as a novel in the tradition of realism rather than tragedy.

WACHTEL That's what I thought initially, but when certain things started to happen — the storm on the heath, the blinding of the neighbour, the disintegration of what starts out as an ordered world — then to me it felt as if tragedy *was* inexorable, that everything *would* ultimately fall apart.

SMILEY There is an inherent feeling of tragedy when people think that they are secure in their lives and then their lives begin to disintegrate. For a lot of people, if not all people, the things that make them feel secure have to do with what they own, the money they own, the land they own. Western culture is underpinned by this notion that you *can* own other living things: you can own land; in the old days you could own slaves; if you're a man you can approach the women in your family as possessions; you possess your children in a lot of ways. I do believe that relationships between living things, based on the idea of ownership, are inherently tragic because they're inherently an illusion. What appears to be stable is really unstable because, instead of an object being owned by an agent, there are two agents, one of which thinks the other one is an object. But the one who is supposedly an object can't help but be an agent, can't help but be autonomous, to some degree, and that goes for land and animals and people and children, all those relationships. I would say that the notion of the possessive relationship, which is very clearly a profound part of our culture, is inherently tragic. One of the things that the novel does is explore this idea of who owns what and if they can really own it, and what happens when the things that are owned assert autonomy and agency. Then everything does fall apart, from the point of view of the owners. But from the point of view of the people who are owned, it is an important shift, a rebuilding of the world in a new way. I think that that tragedy is at the heart of our cultural dilemma right now and so the novel explores that also.

WACHTEL Certainly it's troubling to encounter an ordered world that becomes a chaotic world, though I understand what you're saying in terms of shifts of power. But very early on there's a description about the signs of a good farm — "clean fields, neatly painted buildings, breakfast at six, no debts, no standing water." There's something very appealing about that ordered, assured world, and before very long it's all gone.

SMILEY When President Clinton was inaugurated, I was struck by a phrase in Maya Angelou's poem about the horror of history, can we ever throw off the horror of history? For many people in the United States, to look back on the history of this country in a positive way, to look back on that ordered world of neat farms and happy white families with their black servants and the open countryside, with just a few renegade Indians running off into the horizon, that kind of ordered history that we have been given images of and that we *long* for because we knew these images when we were children, that history is an illusion. One of the things that people in the United States or people in the Western hemisphere need to come to grips with is that it's morally problematic to long for those historical illusions, no matter how much we want them. In the first place, they had the facts wrong about what was happening, and in the second place they were perpetrated by a people who wanted to keep certain immoral and unethical systems in place. I think it's really important that we fight against that feeling of longing for that ordered world and that we embrace the breakdown of what we could call the horrible historical world, that we embrace its breakdown and the putting together of a new world that really *is* more just and more sustainable. Do you understand what I mean?

WACHTEL Absolutely. You're quite right. What I was referring to was this deep-seated yearning for order.

SMILEY But we don't long for it in the abstract, we long for it in terms of particular images — it may be an image of the 1950s or it may be an image of the 1910s, when life on the farm was pretty good actually. Or it may be an image of the 1940s, when it seemed as if the United States was the great saviour of the whole world. All of those images are lies in a lot of ways, and to embrace them, even though we long for them, is to do evil to people around us for whom those images are images of oppression or enslavement or tragedy.

I'll never forget, in the early 1980s, there was a speech in which Ronald Reagan asked in his completely vapid way: Why can't we go back to the 1920s when everything was wonderful? And the black community was astounded that he would assert a desire to return to a time when more black people were being lynched than in any other period since the Civil War. I think that's a lesson. Who knows if he ever learned that lesson, but at least the public did to some degree, judging from that outcry. I think it's a lesson that has to be taught and taught. My novel in a way is attempting to explore the same kind of lesson but in terms of other issues, not racism but land and family issues.

WACHTEL I'd like to talk about the setting of *A Thousand Acres*, which is your corn and bean farms in Iowa, the changing world of the American farm in the late twentieth century. Why did you decide to set this modern-day variation of *King Lear* on an Iowa farm?

SMILEY It struck me, as I was driving between Minneapolis and Ames, which is through southern Minnesota and northern Iowa, that first of all this part of the country is one of the most fertile areas in the whole world. It's also a part of the country where farms are essentially on their own. People have neighbours, but there are no large cities; people are pretty much left alone. The area was settled by mostly English, Scandinavian, German immigrants, who have a tradition of keeping to themselves. So here was a place where things could happen as they happen in *King Lear*, and do happen. Once I worked out that instinctive knowledge, I was astounded by how true it was. I read a book of case histories about how farms are passed on to the next generation, and every one of them was a variation on *King Lear*. And these are actual people's lives. Finally, the authors of the book said, there is no right number of children, there is no way that the farm can be passed on without precipitating a family crisis. That reassured me that this was an appropriate setting.

WACHTEL Your picture of farm life is completely convincing. An academic friend of mine said that this could be taken as ethnography; if we want to look back at farm life in America in the late seventies and eighties, *A Thousand Acres* could be the source.

SMILEY I did get a lot of mail from people who grew up on farms or who live on farms, who say that I have captured the flavour of farm life, and that's really flattering because that's what I was most anxious about when I was writing the novel.

WACHTEL How did you manage to do it since you didn't grow up on a farm?

SMILEY In general, it does seep in: I read the Des Moines *Register*; I read non-fiction books about farms; I used Richard Rhodes' book called *Farm* absolutely shamelessly; I read a lot of books about agriculture; and I also had people I called my "informants." One woman who lives down the street from me had lived on a farm with her husband and her two small daughters for about ten years. Another man in our community is a political organizer but he still farms and has been in charge of his family farm since he was thirteen (he's now about fifty-five). I went up to all these people and I said, "Read my manuscript," and they were happy to do so, and it's to those people that I owe a lot of the flavour.

WACHTEL What were the issues of farm life that you wanted to explore? You have talked about how you usually have a political idea in your books and that it gets embedded in a family saga. What about the politics of farming did you want to examine?

SMILEY It's all intertwined in my mind with the politics of family life. The family is completely penetrated by the notion of land ownership, and the farm and the ownership of the land become paramount — how long the farm has been in the family, whether the farm will be passed on to the next generation — and it's not clear whether the family owns the farm or the farm controls the family dynamic. The idea of the family staying on the farm generation after generation is a long-standing European and American tradition. But in modern American life there's the additional burden of technology. I think people are now beginning to question what sort of technology is appropriate to the land. Can you treat a piece of land as if it were an automobile factory and aim for efficiency of scale, for perfectly regularized input–output? In other words, if the ideal of modern American life is in some sense the machine, can you take this metaphor of the machine and apply it in a practical way to a piece of land, to nature, to cows, to dogs, to whatever it is that exists in the natural world?

WACHTEL I can tell from the way you're putting the question what your answer would be.

SMILEY Of course the answer is no, and we all — I think farmers, too — see more and more, as the years go by, that everything about their lives, from their bodies to their relationships to the family, to their relationships to the land, to their relationships to themselves, are destroyed by this image. There's an American writer named William Kittredge who's written wonderfully about this issue, and his family farmed thousands and thousands of acres in Oregon. He was in charge of the irrigation system on the farm at one point, and he said that by the time he had perfected the irrigation system, he had ended up destroying all of the wildlife habitat, all of his interest in farming, everything about his life outdoors that made it agreeable to live there. He was like any factory worker; even though he owned the place, he was totally alienated from his labour. He had to leave the farm. This experience, which I think culminated in the late 1950s, brought him to question the idea that technology, any technology, is appropriáte to farming, and that you can turn your land into a machine and know every year that if you put this much input of this kind into it, you will get this much output of that kind out of it.

WACHTEL You make connections between the treatment of the land and the treatment of women. At the beginning, the sisters, Ginny and Rose, are good farm wives, dutiful daughters, mindful of appearances — at least until things start to crack and fall apart around them. Do you see a direct link between the way land is treated and the way women are treated?

SMILEY My training is in literary history, and you don't have to look far in any piece of poetry or literature in the Western tradition to see the link that's made between women and nature, and usually the link is to the detriment of both. They're both to be conquered, they're both wild, they're both unfeeling — we can come up with any number of adjectives. The link that I make was handed to me by the literary tradition. I just make it in a new way by supposing that the link comes from the state of mind of the men who see the link, and that that state of mind causes damage to both the natural world and to women. That was about the smallest step I could possibly have made, given the literary tradition that we live in, that women can be identified with nature.

WACHTEL Of course it's also connected to your desire to rehabilitate Goneril and Regan, or see things from their point of view.

SMILEY They don't identify themselves with the farm, but Ginny and Rose see that their father's expectations and feelings of ownership and expectations about them are the same as they are about the farm — basically that he is in control and will be able to do things as he wishes. As their wishes come to contradict his, they see more and more clearly how they've been damaged by the assumption he's made that he's in control, and that all he has to do is desire something and there's no reason why he can't have it. As I get older, I often think that for many people, especially many powerful people, the only real reason that they do anything is that they want to, and that the justifications for doing it come after the desire. Ginny observes that all her father ever asserts as the reason for doing something is that he is who he is and this is what he wants to do. I think that many powerful people come to feel that that's enough.

WACHTEL You certainly question the premise of the Lear story by having the father sexually abuse his older daughters. That completely and radically changes the way we look at things. Some critics suggest that you're going too far, that incest is too much and that *Lear* is diminished as a result. What do you think?

SMILEY Certainly Lear the character is diminished as a result, but I asked myself: If we believe in our day that evil doesn't exist, we have to ask, why do the two women in the play act the way they do? The answer that our society gives to that question is that they're very, very angry. The women that I have met who are that angry are women who've been sexually abused in their families. So I was trying to make a logical link between the actions of the women and what might have caused them. That was one thing. Another thing that I always felt was that Lear's attitude towards his daughters — whether he was angry with them or whether he was pleased with them — was that their first duty was still to serve him. I felt this was rather narcissistic. It did not allow any autonomy on their part. That's a characteristic of abusers. They don't see the other person as an autonomous being; they see that person as someone who's going to go along with their desires, whatever they are. I felt that Lear, in his relationship to his daughters — not necessarily in his relationship to the other men — was an unchanging narcissist from beginning to end. That was another thing. The third one was that Lear walks on stage in the first scene and by the way he talks, it's as if history begins here, it's as if nothing has gone before. He's astounded when Cordelia is less enthusiastic about what she's going to say than the other daughters seem to be. I thought to myself, first of all, what could have gone before that would have created this kind of alienation in the family? Second, I thought, why would a man act as if today really was the first day of the rest of this life? Why would he be in a state of advanced denial about how his life had been before? An answer to that is that he has done things that he can't justify, so he just begins today.

WACHTEL In *A Thousand Acres* you use the Lear story as a frame-work, and in your epic saga *The Greenlanders*, you use old Norse and Norse sagas as *its* underpinning. You've written in a variety of forms about a whole range of subject matter, but mostly one way or another about relationships within a family. You obviously see connections between myths and families, or your approach to myth is through the family story.

SMILEY One thing that's happened to my generation of thought-ful people — I'm not going to call us "thinkers" or "intellectuals" or anything, but just my generation (I was born in 1949) — is that we've seen the end of the great social systems. We've seen the end of communism; we've seen the holes in capitalism. There's been a great debate about Christianity and about other forms of reli-gion, with the ensuing clinging to those things even as they are less and less a part of the mainstream. Unlike our parents' or grandparents' generation, it's much less likely that we'll put our faith into a social system or, for that matter, a systematic way of thinking about social life. It's then left to us, in some piecemeal way, to reconstruct a way of looking at the world now that the social systems have been proved wrong or not worked.

For me that's meant starting with the family and attempting to extrapolate from the family to the world, rather than starting with the world and attempting to extrapolate from some social system back to the family. I think American writers of my gen-eration are criticized sometimes for writing so much domestic fiction, but to me that's partly a sign that we're engaged in having families, and partly a sign that we're engaged in using our thoughts about families to try to understand the larger social world. If *we* can't come up with a way that integrates what we know with a larger system, maybe some younger people will. I think that's what's going on. That's certainly what's going on with me.

February 1993
interview initially prepared in collaboration
with Sandra Rabinovitch

HAROLD BLOOM

Before I read Harold Bloom, I was prepared to dislike him. Admire him perhaps, but not warm to him. His reputation is not only as a formidable critic, but also as a pugnacious reactionary, a conservative defender of the literary canon who dismisses — who contemptuously disdains — what he lumps together as the "School of Resentment." By this he means feminists, Afrocentrists and multiculturalists, New Historicists, and so on.

Then I read Harold Bloom — not about him, but his own words in *The Western Canon* (1994), and I found such an engaging, passionate mind, full of enthusiasms, and yes, strong opinions, that I felt immediately drawn to him. Here was good company. He made me want to read more — more of his own criticism and more of the books he so clearly loves.

Bloom says he's not an ally of the "left" or the "right" — aesthetically; reading the canon won't make you better morally, but neither is it the place to promote social or cultural goals. You read, he says, to confront greatness.

For the past quarter century, Harold Bloom has been, as *The New York Times* puts it, "one of the world's most influential critic-scholar-theorists." The breadth of his reading and his amazingly retentive memory are famous. He can recite Milton's *Paradise Lost* from beginning to end, most of Blake, Spenser's *The Faerie Queene*, Shakespeare, and on it goes. He's written more than twenty books and introductions for some five hundred volumes of literary criticism. "Everything about Harold Bloom is outsized," wrote one critic. Who more likely to survey *all* of Western literature, and decide what's important, what constitutes the canon?

My interview with Harold Bloom was the most surprising of any in this book. He was more emotional — at one point moved almost to tears — than any other writer. And this combination of emotion and intellect triggered an enormous response from listeners, who wrote and ordered tapes in record numbers. Bloom allowed himself to be moved and that touched us all.

Harold Bloom is Sterling Professor of the Humanities at Yale, where he has taught for forty years, and Berg Professor of English at New York University. He spoke to me from the CBC's New York studio.

WACHTEL You once said that there's no distinction between literature and life. I'd like to talk about that, about how literature became so much a part of your own life. Could we go back to your first discovery of English literature?
BLOOM I was raised in a Yiddish-speaking household in the East Bronx — I was born in 1930 — and lived in a neighbourhood where only Yiddish was spoken in the streets. To this day my English sounds a little odd, even though I was born in New York City, because I learned English by reading it and by guessing at

the pronunciation. So at times my language is very much my own in terms of pronunciation.

WACHTEL Why did you have to guess at the pronunciation? Is this because you learned English before you went to school?

BLOOM I started teaching myself English and some other languages, but primarily English, when I was about four years old. I was an obsessive reader as a young child, for reasons that I don't altogether understand, but an absolutely obsessive reader, and of course I was already reading Yiddish and I was studying Hebrew, but I did not study any English or hear any English spoken until I went to kindergarten when I was five and a half — but by then I'd pretty much taught myself to read English.

WACHTEL Have you speculated about those obsessive reasons?

BLOOM I was the last of five children in a loving but very poor family. We lived in a confined space, though we lived I think amicably enough, my siblings and myself. I was much the smallest. I was also clearly the cleverest — none of the others, I believe, went beyond high school. Had I been born into an affluent household and been the kind of person that I clearly was from the beginning, I suppose I would still have been an incessant reader. My parents were proletarian and their parents were proletarian; my father was a garment worker, my mother a housewife, and my grandfather was a carpenter, I believe, in Russia-Poland — he was murdered by the Nazis. I eventually found out from talking to all the surviving relatives that there had been great-great uncles who had been both Talmud scholars and Kabbalists, so there must be something that is inherited in this kind of an interest. When I was a very small child, for instance, any language that I learned to read — and this has been true throughout my life — I could read at a simply shocking speed. I don't read as quickly now, at the age of sixty-five, as I could when I was, say, twenty-five. Unless I force myself to slow down, and if I'm reading for information rather than aesthetic pleasure, I still read pretty much by turning the pages and taking in the whole page at once. And I have a scandalous memory, a frightening memory. Anything that has really moved me in prose or verse, I remember. I remember the poetry pretty much by heart and I can give a pretty accurate paraphrase, including a lot of quotations, of the prose. I guess I was a kind of freak.

WACHTEL I understand you can read five hundred pages an hour.

BLOOM I can still do that but I don't like to. I find various ways of slowing myself down, and obviously when I reread *Paradise Lost*, I read as slowly as possible. Even though I know it by heart, I still like to reread it.

WACHTEL Going back to pre-kindergarten or thereabouts, you learned English by sounding out the words of Blake's "Prophecies"?

BLOOM When I was a little boy I fell madly in love with Blake. I was rather like Northrop Frye before me, and eventually he became something of a mentor figure for me, though we didn't meet until I was teaching at Yale. I fell in love with Blake's poems, especially the long poems, when I did not understand them. How could I possibly have understood them at the age of four and a half or five? But I memorized them; I used to read them night and day — in library editions. I didn't own an edition of my own until a few years later when I asked one of my sisters to get me the Nonesuch Blake, which was an extraordinary expense for her, but she kindly did it. So that was the second book I owned. The first book I ever owned — I still remember this — I saved my money and I got *The Collected Poems of Hart Crane*, and that must have been when I was about six. To this day I'm madly in love with Hart Crane's poetry. I couldn't possibly have understood it then, just as I couldn't possibly have understood the Blake. I was just in love with the incantatory quality and the strangeness and the sound and the feel of it.

WACHTEL You were able to fall in love with great poetry which could move you before you could comprehend it?

BLOOM Who knows on what level one comprehends? The difference between canonical poetry — between, say, Shakespeare, Milton, Wordsworth, Spenser, Dante, Yeats — and inadequate poetry or less adequate poetry, or verse pretending to be poetry, or these days, God knows, the sorry stuff which is neither prose nor verse but pretending to be verse — all of this multiculturalist stuff here in the United States — the great difference in the end is that there are so many levels at which one could understand that perhaps one understands long before one can begin to understand. Probably one is understanding more than one knows at the beginning and then, at a later time, one can practise a kind of exegesis upon it. I certainly found it very strange. When I was still quite young, when I was about thirty-one years old, I wrote the commentary for David Erdman's edition of Blake. I haven't looked at the commentary in thirty years, but I remember that it was lucid enough. Probably it was based very soundly upon apprehensions that went all the way back. It had become as familiar as scripture to me, just as Shakespeare now is as familiar to me as either the Hebrew Bible in the original or the King James version.

WACHTEL Do you know what is the pull of poetry? I know that as a child you read lots of prose as you worked your way through all the shelves of the local library, but do you understand the particular pull of the poetry you still favour?

BLOOM It's the sense of crossing — it's why I myself could never write a line of verse and never tried. It's crossing a threshold that seems guarded by demons. It's entering that realm that I think children through the ages have entered: a sense of a magical world, a world of heightened perceptions, a world where everything is wonder and speculation. I think the hieratic language, the metrical element in that, the deeper and darker rhythms that wind their way in and out of the metric, I think the whole extraordinary question of the deep relation between sound and sense has a profound enchantment. There is of course visionary prose, right down to *Finnegans Wake*, which in a deep sense, I suppose, could be regarded as prose poetry, which has very much the same effect. And there is also that miraculous translation, if it can be called a translation since it's so much a re-creation in its own right, the King James version of the Bible, ultimately founded on the genius of two translators, Tyndale and Coverdale, both of whom were extraordinary writers of evocative prose.

WACHTEL For you literary criticism seems to have been a kind of calling; you say that you came to it very early and you've been utterly unswerving.

BLOOM I think that is the case. I remember when I was a small boy, I had a very nice uncle by marriage, a man named Sam Feldman, who owned a candy story out on Coney Island in Brooklyn. I was out there with him one day and he gave me some candy, and he said to me — I don't think I was more than eight at the time — "What are you going to be when you grow up, Harry?" and I said to him — we were speaking in Yiddish of course — "I'm going to be a professor of poetry when I grow up." I had no idea, really, what that meant at all, though I had heard already that there were places called Harvard and Yale.

I thought of this in a strange and sad way many years later, in 1987 and '88, when I was simultaneously Charles Eliot Norton professor of poetry at Harvard and still at my home base as professor of humanities at Yale. I was suddenly struck by Freud's great warning, "Beware of wanting anything too much."

WACHTEL Because you'll get it. But you recollected this with sadness?

BLOOM The sadness has to do with the fact that at Yale and at NYU, when my best students come to me, both women and men, and say, "Professor Bloom, we wish to be recommended to graduate school," I find myself terribly torn. Frequently, though I don't try to talk them out of it, I urge them to think very carefully about the situation that they're getting into because they are not ideologues and they're going to be forced to dissimulate, to pretend to adopt ideologies.

I do not exaggerate. I don't know what the Canadian situation is, whether it is as bad as the situation in American universities, but I have a rather profound, and admittedly polemical, despair about the condition of *most* of the teaching of literature in American universities and colleges at this time. I was born in 1930 and will be sixty-five next summer; if I had been born in 1970 and was getting out of graduate school now, I would not get a job teaching in the United States of America. I would have been no less gifted and no less learned, with no less a passion for poetry and the imagination than forty years before, but these ideologues would exclude me. I would not be able to secure a university teaching position.

I was talking to one young man the other day, who was wondering about the future, and I said — since I'm not the stuff of which lawyers and so on are made — if I'd been born forty years later I suppose I would have thought it through and decided to pursue my aesthetic interests and my critical interests on my own. I probably would have tried to become a graduate student in the history of religion — Gnosticism is one of my major interests — because the history of religion in the United States is still an academic subject. Though it is of course always subject to various theological pressures from this in-group or that in-group, nevertheless, compared to the study of what used to be called literature, it's a paradise.

Much as I on the one hand loathe, despise and abominate Newt Gingrich and the Age of Gingrich, which is now upon us, I have no more use for the wretches who have helped bring Gingrich into harness, the so-called New Left and the so-called counterculture — what I call the School of Resentment, which does dominate the teaching of what used to be called literature and is now usually called "cultural criticism" in American universities and colleges. There are now ideological means tests for getting into most American graduate schools; there are ideological means tests for getting appointed to an assistant professorship *almost* everywhere. There are only a few exceptions to this. I wish I were exaggerating, I wish this were hyperbole, but it is not.

WACHTEL I want to leave the present and future for a moment and go back to the past. I want to go back to this: Did you have an awareness of what you have described as a scandalous memory and a certain freakishness, when you were young?

BLOOM No, no, I took it all absolutely for granted. After all, I led a very private existence; I was mostly with my siblings and my mother and father and a few school friends, and I didn't do particularly well in school, simply because our neighbourhood was so bad, one couldn't go to the public high school. I went by exam to the Bronx High School of Science, which was the worst possible place in the world for me because, then and now, I have no interest whatsoever in science and very little in mathematics. So I did rather poorly; I didn't finish quite at the rock bottom of the class but I finished rather low. And I would never have gotten to be an undergraduate at Cornell or any other university, except that I took the New York State regents exam and finished first in the state. It was one of those multiple-choice tests that was based upon very wide reading and, having read everything and remembered everything, I was bound to get a perfect score in it. On that basis Cornell gave me a fellowship called the Phi Kappa Phi fellowship or something, even though I'd never even applied to Cornell, and they admitted me as a freshman. Once I was at Cornell, I met remarkable teachers, including M.H. Abrams, a very distinguished romanticist who's still alive. Abrams mentored me and, though I've tried to reciprocate by mentoring people, I don't think I've ever managed to do as much for anyone as Mike Abrams did for me. I owe Abrams a great deal.

I was a very shy and awkward person — I don't have many social graces now, but then I was painfully shy. I was so frightened at Cornell in my first year, I would keep very close to the wall when I walked down the hallways. It sounds almost morbid, though I don't think I was psychologically morbid. I felt so strange; it just seemed so bewildering to me. Then even more so, when four years later, in 1951, I became a graduate student at Yale, where I found the atmosphere very mixed. I managed to avoid most of the teachers of the New Critical, neo-Christian persuasion, which was the reigning orthodoxy then, except for one very remarkable man, William K. Wimsatt, and even though he and I fought like cats and dogs intellectually, he was someone with whom one could disagree. He was very Aristotelian and Roman Catholic. At Yale, as at Cornell, I found remarkable teachers.

WACHTEL Did you always realize that literary criticism was going to be your world? That you would be engaged not in writing novels or poems but always at the level of appreciating and analyzing?

BLOOM I started to read Dr. Johnson and Hazlitt when I was fairly young. I was reading them when I was a high school student and was absolutely enchanted by them, and I fell madly in love with Ruskin when I was about fifteen or sixteen, a year or two before I went up to Cornell. I knew that I didn't have a storytelling faculty in me. I tried it once; years later, in 1979, I wrote what I called "a Gnostic fantasy," *The Flight to Lucifer*. I wish I hadn't published it. It was all right to have composed it but I shouldn't have published it. The prose was pretty good but the story was totally dead; I haven't got an ability for prose fiction, and, as I say, verse for me is a threshold guarded by demons. I knew that I wanted to be some kind of a critical writer.

WACHTEL Is there a hierarchy? Do you feel at the very top is poetry and then fiction and then criticism? Do you conceive it that way at all?

BLOOM Well, I'm not quite sure how one establishes hierarchies. I do believe, and I've said this before, that literary criticism is either part of literature or it ought not to exist at all. Obviously, one is not and never will be Dr. Samuel Johnson or William Hazlitt, or Ruskin, or for that matter Northrop Frye, a very great writer; or G. Wilson Knight, whose work has always delighted me; or Sir William Empson; or Kenneth Burke, who became a kind of mentor to me. When I was breaking through into my own work in the late sixties and seventies, Kenneth befriended me and certainly wrote the only generous reviews I received of my books, starting with *The Anxiety of Influence*. Kenneth, alas, died last year, though at the very exalted age of ninety-seven.

It would be a very difficult question for me to answer. Quite clearly at their strongest, Johnson, Hazlitt, Ruskin, Walter Pater in the greatest essays and in *Appreciations*, Oscar Wilde in his extraordinary critical dialogues, Burke at his very best, Frye at his very best: these are aesthetic experiences. Johnson is certainly the best critic I have ever read in my life in any language I'm capable of reading. The greatest of *The Lives of the Poets* seem to me at least as extraordinary in their way as *Rasselas*, marvellous as it is, or as the great poem *The Vanity of Human Wishes*. I don't know about a hierarchy. I love poetry more than I love prose. I still, naturally, try to read every poem that reaches me. I guess it's an addiction.

WACHTEL The intensity of your personal response to particular works of literature seems to be the guiding principle for you in your critical assessment. Do your judgments always arise out of that intimate experience of reading?

BLOOM Yes, I'm afraid so. I know that this can be turned against me, and that I am much condemned for this in many circles. But it does seem to me that first comes the aesthetic experience, the overwhelming shock that something is indeed intensely beautiful and exalted and sublime, and then comes love. One falls in love, and out of that love, out of that deep affection, comes the psychic energy and, I hope, something of the skill to understand it better and help explain it to others. As I say, this can be turned against me because after all it could be said, well, if you don't think Alice Walker is a remarkable writer it's because you have failed to love her work; or if you don't think Sylvia Plath was capable of writing a poem, it's because you have failed to love her work. I would find it very difficult to have a response to that, except to say, these don't seem to me to be aesthetic artifacts, they seem to be something else.

WACHTEL You've talked about how the importance of reading deeply is to augment one's own growing inner self, to make a proper use of one's own solitude, which, as you describe it, is ultimately to confront your own mortality.

BLOOM Well, what else can it be? One reaches one's sixties, one's friends start to die of one disease or another or one accident or another; it's difficult to maintain old friendships, it's very difficult to make new friendships; one tries to be benign, one tries not to be self-aggrandizing; one tries to avoid relationships which might be self-aggrandizing. I mean, all human beings are like this. Sometimes one succeeds, sometimes one fails. But in the end, one is alone. We are all of us alone. I'm told these days we have to consider ourselves as beings in society. Well, I pay my taxes and I desperately hope the Democrats can make a comeback in our wretched country, and I try to contribute as much as I can to every possible charity and so on, but in the end one knows one is alone, that one lives at the heart of the solitude, that we all live at the heart of the solitude, that we all have the consciousness of mortality. Dr. Samuel Johnson was a much more fervent religious believer than I with my strange Gnostic Judaism can possibly be. I do have, I think, ultimate spiritual beliefs; like the Gnostics before me, I believe that there is divinity, there is a radiance, there is a transcendental, but that it is light universes away, we cannot reach it and it cannot reach us.

WACHTEL I get a sense that this relationship, the solace that reading provides, is not just a function or a characteristic of advancing years but has been your connection to reading from even a young age.

BLOOM It's not just a way of cheering oneself up; it's not, I hope, a way of aggrandizing one's own ego — and I'm perpetually accused of that. Why that is, I can't altogether understand. I once asked Norrie Frye that and he said, "Harold, you have a fierce personality and it gets into what you write. You're always going to be subject to that accusation." He added, "I've accused you of that myself." And he was right, he had accused me of that. It's pleasure in the end, but it's that intense kind of pleasure which has a painful element in it. Our solitude is a harsh thing. The Marxists tell me that the smallest human unit is two people. I think that's an idealism. I think we are in the end alone.

WACHTEL If reading isn't a solace, what is it?

BLOOM One is trapped in a perpetually growing inner self; it's a discipline for that growing inner self; it's an education for that growing inner self. It has a generous basis also, though I wouldn't want to put it on a societal basis necessarily. I don't know if it's a selfish activity in me. I've earned a perfectly good living. I cannot say that I was not also in it for the living and to support my children and my wife and myself. This is my fortieth consecutive year of teaching at Yale. I've taught tens of thousands of students; some of them occasionally come back or send me a letter and let me know that something was communicated to them, that something in their spirit is a touch less lonely. I don't want to be soupy about this in any way. I get a lot of letters about *The Western Canon*. I throw out the nasty ones immediately, whether right-wing or left-wing or those which accuse me of racism or sexism, or I don't know what kind of horror. But I get very touching letters from ordinary, common readers and some uncommon readers also, saying that I've helped send them back to a particular work, or I've helped send them back to reading, or that in some sense in some register I speak for them.

Gertrude Stein said so beautifully, and I'm never tired of quoting it, "One writes for oneself and for strangers." I think probably one reads for oneself and for strangers. Maybe in the end one even teaches for oneself and for strangers; certainly one is aware of the people in the room, certainly one gets to know their personalities, but there's a kind of despair in that also, because you can't ever really quite bridge that gap in teaching. Maybe there's an element of desperation in it, I don't know. Maybe there's some attempt to overcome one's personal limitations — which in my case are very thick indeed.

WACHTEL I'd like to talk about Shakespeare because he's such an important figure for you.

BLOOM Certainly. It'll be a great relief, instead of talking about the wretched old Bloom.

WACHTEL When you refer to "the wretched old Bloom," I'm reminded that you hold up Dr. Samuel Johnson as in some sense a model or a mentor, but he was also a man who carried a lot of melancholia.

BLOOM A great deal of melancholia, yes. Well, of Shakespeare's thirty-eight plays I think I'm madly in love with twenty-four, perhaps twenty-five of them, but what I love best is Sir John Falstaff, a figure beyond me, though in the realm of the imagination, as Dr. Johnson is beyond me in the realm of reality, and the greatest representation of wit in literature. I suppose I'd go further and say that Hamlet, Rosalind and Falstaff, are the three consciousnesses — I would have to call them that, against formalist criticism and against "resentment criticism," and historicist so-called criticism — they are the three human consciousnesses created by Shakespeare which are the most powerful and intellectually the most alive.

WACHTEL Can you talk about the consciousness that Shakespeare gives us?

BLOOM Take *Henry IV*, Part One, when you're first introduced to Falstaff and to Hal, at the opening of the play. I invariably find myself telling my students: Look, there used to be a purely formalist reading of Shakespeare when I was a young man, leading to L.C. Knight's famous rebuttal, "How Many Children Had Lady Macbeth?" in which we were reminded that these were not men and women but merely words; they did not exist before the opening line of the work and they did not exist after the closing line they spoke. Nowadays, with historicizing, we simply have another version of this kind of formalism, and we're told about bourgeois mystifications and class interests and gender distinctions and the struggle for power, et cetera. (That's why I'm purple in the face.)

I tell my students: Look, if you study those speeches of Hal right at the beginning, you have got to work your way back to the realization that you're at a very late, falling-apart stage of what had once been a very close and complex relationship, the full contours and dimensions of which we can never be sure of, but that there had been once something of the same affection and admiration on the part of Hal towards Falstaff that Falstaff still has for Hal. But something quite murderous, very angry, very rancid, very vicious has replaced it in Hal; a deep ambivalence now governs everything he says to Falstaff with the negative end of the ambivalence absolutely dominant. This cannot possibly be understood unless you intuit backwards, unless you induce by working out everything you know about the relationship as it's shown in the two plays or in Falstaff's death scene as it's recounted by the hostess, by Mistress Quickly, in *Henry V*. You can build up a very considerable foreground. Surely Shakespeare expects his audience, at least the keener elements in it, to intuit that foreground.

Shakespeare is always taking you beyond what could be called "realistic representation" of any kind. These figures are indeed larger than life, but the largeness comes directly out of life, and these are not just words on a page. These are, as Shelley says of his ideal forms in *Prometheus Unbound*, "bound forms more real than living man." But these are not visionary forms, these are something very close to living men and living women. That is now condemned as an A.C. Bradley or a Victorian approach. I always tell people that, though I have enormous admiration for A.C. Bradley's *Shakespearean Tragedy* and keep on learning a great deal from it, that no, my progenitor in Shakespeare criticism is Maurice Morgann, who wrote a book defending Sir John Falstaff, which caused Dr. Johnson to observe dryly to Boswell that next he'll be writing an essay proving the moral superiority of Iago. But Johnson knew what Morgann was up to. So did Hazlitt, in his *Characters of Shakespeare's Plays*, which is a most marvellous book. And actually, in the twentieth century an almost-forgotten Shakespeare critic, a man named Harold Goddard, whom I never knew — he was dead really before my time — wrote a marvellous book called *The Meaning of Shakespeare*. (He has no favour whatsoever with Shakespearean critics and academic scholars, but I find that the students I recommend it to are immensely illuminated by it.) He simply works at the supposition that Shakespeare's characters can be talked about in some ways, in spite of all this talk about Elizabethan conventions and historicist connections and so on, that they're to be talked about the way you talk about the characters in Dostoevsky, only more so. Of course we know from his *Writer's Journal* and other things how much Dostoevsky owes to the great Shakespearean nihilists, and you would not have Svidrigailov in *Crime and Punishment* if you did not have Iago in *Othello* and Edmund in *King Lear*. A British scholar, A.D. Nuttall, wrote a splendid book on Shakespeare called *A New Mimesis* arguing very strongly for quite an old-fashioned view of mimesis, and I find that Sir Frank Kermode, a most distinguished critic, quite frequently in what he writes about Shakespeare strikes a deep, answering chord in me. I think this older tradition is by no means played out.

Shakespeare matters in the end, aside from the extraordinary mastery of language, because he really seems to have done more towards inventing our psychology than anybody in the history of psychology, more in inventing how we think as well as representing how we think, than any philosopher in the history of philosophy. In a very deep sense it seems to me he has invented us, that after Shakespeare we become something much more ourselves. The thing that I always emphasize in teaching and in my chapter on Shakespeare in *The Western Canon* is something that obsesses me and fascinates me. Before Shakespeare — except for certain hints in Chaucer, in *The Pardoner* and *The Wife of Bath*, that I'm pretty sure Shakespeare used as hints and starting points — you don't have the phenomena of characters in literature who overhear themselves or who are suddenly struck by something that they have overheard themselves saying. And on the basis of that overhearing, whether they are speaking to themselves in a soliloquy or aside or speaking to others, they begin some extraordinary process of mutability and change. We do it all the time — we speak to ourselves or we speak to others and we are suddenly struck by how odd what we are saying sounds, or we are shocked by what we are saying, or we're made unhappy or we're ashamed of what we're saying. I don't find that that exists in Western literature before Shakespeare, except for a few hints in Chaucer, and after Shakespeare it is utterly commonplace. I take that as a clue or index to the extraordinary way in which Shakespeare changed us and which, indeed, to go back to an earlier matter we were discussing, Shakespeare invented this phenomenon of the perpetually growing inner self, in every one of us.

WACHTEL You give an example of this with Edmund from *King Lear*.

BLOOM That's the one which has always particularly engaged me. I could give hundreds of other examples, but that fascinates me the most because that's what first brought this to my attention. Edmund is lying on the ground; he has been given his death wound by his half-brother Edgar, though he doesn't know at first that it was Edgar, who's been fighting as a concealed knight without insignia. When he learns that it was Edgar, he's relieved, snob that he is, that at least he hasn't received his death wound from somebody inferior to himself in social rank. He is simply quiet and begins to brood to himself. He also listens to the recital by Edgar of the death of their mutual father, Gloucester, a death which Shakespeare — giving up the chance for an enormous scene — puts off-stage. It's rendered just as narration. Edmund claims that he's moved by this, but he doesn't seem to be quite sure what's happening. Then they bring in the corpses of the two queens, Goneril and Regan, neither of whom he loved — because he loves no one, not even himself, he's absolutely cold — but he had been the lover of both, and as he says, shockingly, "I was contracted to them both; all three/Now marry in an instant," because the two of them are dead. He is speaking out loud to himself, not to anyone else.

Then he says four extraordinary words that I can never get out of my mind. Remember, Edmund is the most brilliant, cold-hearted and deadly of all Shakespearean hero-villains, he is the deadliest figure in Western literature, really; he's quite frightening, though very strangely glamorous and appealing, if only because, as Hazlitt said, he is no hypocrite, unlike Goneril and Regan. And he says: "Yet Edmund was belov'd!" He overhears himself saying that and he is so struck by it that he cries out, "I pant for life. Some good I mean to do,/Despite of mine own nature." He's carried out to die off-stage, which means that we do not know who he is as he is dying. He doesn't know either; he dies without knowing whether he's taken back some of the evil that he's done. But it's an astonishing representation of change. It's a new kind of dramatic inwardness and it's dependent upon the externalization that is involved in overhearing oneself. It is an originality one cannot get over, an extraordinary breakthrough.

It's much more radical in the case of Hamlet, actually, than it is in the case of Edmund because Hamlet overhears himself and changes with every speech. The soliloquy scarcely exists before Shakespeare. He in any case transforms it out of recognition by making it radically inward. That radical inwardness in

Shakespeare, that radical commitment to the representation of change, and especially to willed change, is something we cannot grow tired of. It's something that will perpetually refresh us and teach us anew.

WACHTEL You credit Shakespeare with having a greater understanding of psychology and certainly a greater value than psychoanalysis in understanding ourselves, and in fact you advocate a kind of Shakespearean reading of Freud.

BLOOM Oh yes. I am convinced that it's no accident, as I say in the chapter called "Freud: A Shakespearean Reading," it cannot be an accident that Sigmund Freud, quite possibly the major mind, culturally speaking, humanistically speaking, of the twentieth century, joined of all things the crazy Oxfordians and persuaded himself that the Earl of Oxford had written all of Shakespeare rather than, as he put it in his dreadful Oxonian parlance, "the man from Stratford." I think it is because he could not bear to owe as much as he did to that mere *parvenu*, to that lower-class person as it were, that not-that-educated person. It had to be a great nobleman from whom he had derived so much. I believe he derived not less than everything. I think that the Freudian account of narcissism, of ambivalence, of schism in the self, the entire Freudian map of the mind, is Shakespeare's creation.

WACHTEL You tell a funny story about your own experience in analysis where your therapist observed that you were paying him to give him lectures several times a week on the proper way to read Freud.

BLOOM It was many years ago when I was going through a middle-of-a-life crisis and very nearly broke down when I was thirty-five. I was in analysis with a very distinguished analyst in New Haven for about a year and then for a while when I came back from some time abroad. He finally said, "Let's give it up, Harold, because we're meeting twice or three times a week and you're paying me to give me these endless lectures on the proper interpretation of Freud." For five or six years I taught a graduate course at Yale, and I gave it up because of what I began to call half-heartedly "Uncle Siggy's Revenge." Extra students used to gather for the three or four closing seminars of a sequence of twenty-eight or thirty because he got his revenge all right. The parapraxes, the psychopathology of everyday life, simply overcame me, and in the last seminars I could not say anything which was not a howler, an unintended double meaning. It was quite astonishing, and obviously showed some deep struggle on my part against Freud.

For years I was at work on a huge book which was to be called *Freud*, and then the subtitle was to be called *Transference and Authority*. That's the only book I ever set out to write that I had to abandon. It's now a yellowing manuscript up in my attic in New Haven. I gave it up because I became increasingly ambivalent in my reaction to Freud and I finally decided what I now firmly believe: that it's of no value whatsoever as science, makes no contribution to biology or even to the serious study of psychology, that as a therapy it is a disaster beyond belief — it's an outrage, a shamanism, and an ineffective shamanism — but that in fact Freud is one of the great writers of the twentieth century. He is the Montaigne of the twentieth century — that is to say, he joins hands with the greatest of all Western essayists. Freud is not quite Montaigne but he's as close to Montaigne as we have. He's a cultural thinker of a very extraordinary kind, and his influence is of course immense. But therapy? No thanks. Better the psychopharmacologist than Freud when it comes to questions of therapy.

WACHTEL I want to talk about your book, *The Western Canon* — I know we've been talking about it already, but more directly and even more simply back to basics, what is the canon? Why do we need it?

BLOOM There is no mystery about canons. A canon is a list. That's all. We need it because we *have* to read Shakespeare; we *have* to study Dante; we *have* to read Chaucer, Cervantes, the Bible, at least the King James Bible; we *have* to read certain authors; we *have* to read Proust, Tolstoy, Dickens, George Eliot and Jane Austen. It is absolutely inescapable that we have to read Joyce and Samuel Beckett. These are absolutely crucial writers. They provide an intellectual, I dare say a spiritual, value which has nothing to do with organized religion or the history of institutional belief. They remind us in every sense of re-minding us. They not only tell us things that we have forgotten but they tell us things we couldn't possibly know without them. And they reform our minds. They make our minds stronger; they make us more vital. They make us alive! You know, five years ago I was much condemned for providing my own interpretation of the blessing in *The Book of J*. I said that when somebody blesses someone else in what is called the Old Testament, the Hebrew Bible, it always means one thing: it means *more life*. Cervantes and Chaucer and Shakespeare and Dante — Shakespeare above all — provide one with the blessing of more life.

There is no set canon. There cannot be and there shouldn't be. I tried to make this very clear. But there are certain inescapable books that I really do feel we all of us should read as early as possible. What does education mean if it does not expose children and young people to Shakespeare and Cervantes and Dante? If Dante is too difficult, Shakespeare is universal. Shakespeare is the true multicultural author. He exists in all languages, he is put on the stage everywhere, everyone feels that they are represented by him on the stage. Cervantes is an absolutely universal author. My favourite sentence in my book is: "If multiculturalism meant Cervantes, then who could possibly protest?" But unfortunately, what is called multiculturalism in the United States *never* means Cervantes. It doesn't mean replacing a writer in English by Cervantes, which I would be delighted by. If the multiculturalists said to me, "No more Shakespeare! We will have Cervantes," I would say, "That's very sad, but still, if we have Cervantes, we have almost everything we need." Cervantes is an almost Shakespearean writer in his power. But it doesn't mean that with these people; it means fifth-rate work by people full of resentment, who *happen* to be women, or who *happen* to be Chicano or Puerto Rican, or who *happen* to be African American. They're by no means the best writers who are African American or women or so on: they are simply quite frequently the most resentful and the most ideological. The function of an education is not to make people feel good about themselves, it's not to confirm their sense of division of being out of one group rather than another.

WACHTEL Why do you think *The Western Canon* is under attack, not only from, as you put it, the School of Resentment and the left, but from the right?

BLOOM I'm certainly under attack from the right. I haven't read all the reviews, but I'm fascinated by what I knew would happen, that all the neoconservative journals — such as *Commentary*, and *The American Mercury*, *The New Criterion* and *The National Review* — have published harsh, angry reviews, denouncing me as a believer in art for art's sake and as somebody who doesn't believe that literature has a moral and religious basis. I'm condemned for saying that one does not read Shakespeare or even Dante for the moral or religious value of it. They have been just as savage in their way as the journalists and reviewers of the School of Resentment, the so-called left, have been on the other side. I have been very happy at getting it from both sides. It is as much vindication, I believe, as this book can hope to have.

WACHTEL Why is the canon the venue for this kind of debate, or battle?

BLOOM I suppose it is because we are a rapidly collapsing society. It's the emancipation of selfishness. In testimony before either a Senate or a House committee, one of these Gingrichites actually said, not only should we cut off money for all illegitimate children whatsoever, but we should again have a social stigma on illegitimacy! The function of the canon is to read Shakespeare and look at Edmund, the bastard in *King Lear*, look at the great bastard Faulconbridge — most magnificent creature — in *King John*. You wouldn't have these hideous moral imbeciles if they really could read Shakespeare, if they really had studied Shakespeare. I am firmly convinced of that.

WACHTEL Was it difficult for you to come up with a list of modern canonical writers?

BLOOM It was immensely difficult. I wondered if I should do it; I'm not sure I should have done it. Cultural prophecy is a mug's game and I did feel like a mug doing it, but everybody said, you can't just cut it off when you reach the twentieth century or when you reach 1950. Fifty years from now the latter part of that list is going to be full of howlers. It has to be. All one can do with that list is try to guard against one's idiosyncratic nature — and I'm fiercely idiosyncratic.

The function of the list is not to tell people what to study in schools. We all know what we should be studying in schools. We should be studying Shakespeare, Cervantes, Chaucer, for heaven's sake; we should be reading Dickens and George Eliot; we should be reading the books that we *know* educate human beings to be human beings and expand their vision in every way. It makes them larger and more intelligent and more humane and caring people, rather than the shoddy stuff we are so frequently offered now in the supposed name of social justice. All it brings about is boredom, hideous boredom; it discredits social justice and helps bring on the Gingriches of this world. I don't even know that one should study literature past Proust and Joyce, though I teach John Ashbery and others whom I feel very certain of — James Merrill and Thomas Pynchon and so on.

The purpose of the latter part of the list is to suggest books and authors that people may not have encountered, which I have had a great deal of reward from. Everybody should make their own list, really, particularly for the last fifty years or so. The canon that matters, the reading list that matters, truly we all do know what it is, even if we lie about it. Shakespeare is the Western canon, or Shakespeare and Dante are the Western canon, or Shakespeare and Dante and Cervantes are the Western canon. The greatest writers. The book deliberately confines itself to Dante to the present. Obviously Homer and Sophocles and Plato and Virgil and others certainly join that list also. These are the writers that we should all of us read and reread. There's no mystery about that. There's no ideology about that.

WACHTEL In *The Western Canon*, you quote the French critic Sainte-Beuve, who taught us to ask a crucial question of any writer whom we read deeply, What would the author think of us?

BLOOM Yes, it's something that has haunted me since the first moment I encountered it on the page of Sainte-Beuve. I couldn't read any more that day. I remember going for a long walk because it shook me up so hard. It's a very brilliant kind of statement, and it's something I think about a great deal, you know. What would the author of this work think of me?

WACHTEL What would Shakespeare think of Bloom?

BLOOM Well, I don't know who Shakespeare was. He has hidden himself. As Borges says, "He is everyone and no one." He has hidden himself behind all of these extraordinary men and women. He would probably say, "This is a tired old fellow with a great passion for reading and a great passion for poetry, who sometimes says useful things about it and sometimes doesn't." And perhaps he would have said, "This is a person of good will." What else could I hope for?

WACHTEL Why is the question so important, what the author would think of us?

BLOOM In the end, that is what the canon is about: the search for wisdom. One cares about wisdom, and one wants to be judged by wisdom. If one hasn't got it, one has to ask the biblical question, "Where shall wisdom be found?" And I suppose for me the answer is, wisdom is to be found in Shakespeare, provided you get at it in the right way. Wisdom is to be found in Cervantes, provided you get at it in the right way. That is what imaginative literature is for. It is for wisdom, it is for the highest mode of aesthetic experience, it is for cognition at the most profound level. Most of all, I think, it's for training memory, in the deep sense, because you can't think, you can't read, you can't write without memory. That's the function of the great canonical works: they teach you what is worth remembering and how to remember it.

January 1995
*interview initially prepared in collaboration
with Sandra Rabinovitch*

JAYNE ANNE PHILLIPS

In the early eighties, when Jayne Anne Phillips was featured in a special issue of *Granta* magazine devoted to American "dirty realists," this is how she was described: "Jayne Anne Phillips was born in Buckhannon, West Virginia, in 1952. She grew up in the Appalachians, has worked in amusement parks and restaurants, and has travelled door-to-door in mining camps selling home improvements and bathroom appliances."

Then her literary prizes and publications were listed. This emphasis on the low-rent side of life is only part of the picture. Jayne Anne Phillips' father ran a concrete business; her mother was a schoolteacher. Phillips — the middle child, sandwiched between two brothers — attended West Virginia University and later the University of Iowa Writers' Workshop.

Phillips, as one critic has noted, is both "a rooted regional writer as well as a rootless minimalist." The minimalist became widely known through her first short story collection, *Black Tickets* (1979). Peopled by criminals and misfits, a serial killer and a teenage prostitute, the book won praise from Nadine Gordimer and Raymond Carver. Carver called it "a crooked beauty." The "rooted regional writer" emerged in Phillips' first novel, *Machine Dreams* (1984). Here the mode, she said, was one of "investigative sorrow." Covering three generations of a middle-class West Virginia family, *Machine Dreams* elevates character over edgy language and examines war, from World War II to the futility of Vietnam.

Jayne Anne Phillips' next novel is an atmospheric, elliptical story. Told from shifting points of view, *Shelter* (1994) takes place over a few days at a Girl Guide summer camp in Appalachia in 1963. There are two pairs of best friends: Lenny and Cap are fifteen-year-old girls; Lenny's younger sister and her best friend are eleven. Into this female adolescent world enter two boys and two men. Buddy, eight years old, is the son of the camp cook. He's sexually abused and tormented by his stepfather, Carmody. Phillips says she "wanted to think about evil, the idea of whether evil really exists or if it is just a function of damage."

Shelter has the kind of foreboding that provokes comparisons with *Lord of the Flies* and *Deliverance*. Written in rich, lyrical prose, Phillips says the book "needed to be very dense, almost subterranean." When I was thinking about how to describe it, the words that came to mind were "ominous," "dread," "menace." Then I looked at a review of Jayne Anne Phillips' last collection of short stories, *Fast Lanes* (1987) and there were those same words used to describe *it*.

When I spoke to Phillips in January, 1995, her thoughts were focussed on her most recent novel, *Shelter*. She also talked about how, in the decade since *Machine Dreams*, she married, had two sons, and both her parents died. She now lives in a suburb of Boston and teaches creative writing at Harvard.

WACHTEL You've said that your novel *Shelter* is a book that you wanted to write for a long time. Why?

PHILLIPS I wrote the epigraph seventeen years ago, and in my notebooks I had various scenes and jottings about the characters, although in those pieces the characters were grown up. Now I think of it, my pattern is that I have certain ideas, or not really ideas but more a sense of an atmosphere that has in it all the mystery that the book will hold, and I carry that around with me for a long time, until I get to a point where I'm ready to deal with the risks of writing the material. I wrote three other books in between, but I always had in mind to try to write about these children, whom I understood to be girls, in this very isolated place. And I think after having written two books of stories and *Machine Dreams,* it was time for me to do something very different. I think my books have certain connections in terms of obsession, but they tend to be different in terms of how they work and even in their timbre or tone.

WACHTEL Do you know why this one took so long to germinate?

PHILLIPS I write very slowly; I usually spend about five years on a book, and I spent longer this time because I had a couple of children and other things happened. Some of the crucial issues in the novel are abandonment and isolation and vulnerability, and I don't think I really understood vulnerability until I was older.

WACHTEL Why is that?

PHILLIPS I think when we're very young we have a kind of impermeable belief in our parents, in their sheer existence. We have a sense of infallibility about ourselves — that's part of youth, I think — and it's not until we experience a loss that really cuts into our own identities that we begin to understand what death is. But grief is something that's quite separate even from loss. Grief has to do with living with loss, with the kinds of paths it cuts through the way one thinks. It can be very luminous, really. Having children is also an exercise in vulnerability and surrender because our sense of trying to protect our children is infinitely more painful than just trying to protect ourselves.

The kids in *Shelter* are dealing with their own versions of grief. And during the years that I was writing the book I lived with that shadow, because my parents died two years apart, after long illnesses. I didn't think about this at the time but I find it interesting that I, as an aged orphan, was writing a book about children who were on their own, who were set apart from their families. There's an old tradition of setting children apart from their families — everything from *Huckleberry Finn* to Walt Disney movies. And the idea of a child in the world alone, or a band of children, is an old idea.

WACHTEL You have said that you wrote this novel in order to understand its opening paragraph. What did you mean by that?

PHILLIPS I think everything in the book is there in the first sentence, the whole book is there in terms of its weight and its gravity. I feel that about all books. Although writers don't always write the first sentence first, I did in this case and I think I actually have in all my books.

WACHTEL Did you come to understand that paragraph after writing the novel?

PHILLIPS I think understanding for the writer is a process and perhaps it can't be summed up verbally. What I was saying about vulnerability has to do with my understanding of the book. I see it as a kind of passion play, in which the children are first witnesses and then participants. I see them as passing through a dark night of the soul and encountering something that will change the way they view themselves for ever, and the way they carry other burdens. I don't think of them as passing through unscathed or undamaged, but I see them as emerging in some ways stronger.

My first idea of the book was very different from what later happened in it. I almost have the sense that a book knows all along where it's going and the material exists in a mist, to use a visual image, and the writer moves through it or descends into it and it begins to take form. My understanding of the issues in the book have to do with those issues of vulnerability and darkness, that whole question of evil: Does evil exist? Is it just a function of damage? And the question, too, of why some souls move through a terrible darkness and yet emerge from it whole, changed perhaps but whole, and why others shatter and explode. I wanted to think about intervention, what intervention is and how it happens between people.

WACHTEL Before we get to some of these issues, I want to ask you about language. *Shelter* is very atmospheric, sensuous, at times ominous — I think you've described it as "subterranean." Can you tell me more about the kind of world you wanted to create?

PHILLIPS In the same way that I use time as almost a character in itself in *Machine Dreams*, I wanted to use place in a very alive, sensual way, as a kind of illumination that shoots through the characters. Whereas *Machine Dreams* took place over a long period of time, I wanted to do a book that took place in three days. I wanted to use children as the characters, and I wanted to telescope their lives with their families into those three days, which meant all that information had to come through a kind of internal monologue, and that made the book rest very heavily on language.

I wanted the reader to experience what the girls are experiencing in that physical place. I wanted the reader to be isolated from the rest of the world. I wanted the book to close off other phenomenon. I wanted the reader to really think into the language and have a sensual feel for the heat and the buildings. The girls' memories and the rest of the world that sifts into that physical place take on that same sensual edge.

WACHTEL *Shelter* takes place in a girls' camp in West Virginia the summer of 1963. Is it significant that it's 1963? It seems to suggest the last days of American innocence before all the political assassinations.

PHILLIPS It does and it doesn't. I wanted the book to take place before the world changed. But part of the point is that it wasn't so innocent before the assassinations. Also, this area in particular is very isolated; in a way it's ten or fifteen years behind the rest of the country. Nineteen sixty-three would be one of the last years in which a kid like Buddy — eight years old, the son of the camp cook — would have lived up a dirt road in that very isolated way and not had a television set. The physical world is truly a spiritual domain to him, yet it's a very real, physical place that he senses he owns, partially because of his isolation. He's lived with his mother alone, and she's a very big presence in the book, although her point of view isn't represented. Buddy, of all the children, has been the most nurtured and protected, but he also has such a close identification with his mother that when they are threatened by Carmody — who returns from having been in prison for five years, gone since Buddy was three (he's Buddy's stepfather rather than his real father) — Buddy senses that this all-powerful woman, his mother, can't in fact protect him and can't protect herself. He begins to feel that somehow it's up to him to save both of them, although he may not articulate that to himself in so many words. His pull towards the girls in the camp is instinctual. Together, they drift towards an almost inevitable encounter.

WACHTEL You were eleven in 1963. Do you remember that summer?

PHILLIPS Oh, very much. I remember Kennedy's death very strongly. Kennedy was mythically heroic to people in West Virginia. The state is heavily Democratic, working-class and Protestant, and the West Virginia primary was a major hurdle in Kennedy's election; if he could win West Virginia, which was rabidly anti-Catholic, anti-everything, he had a good chance to go on and win the Democratic nomination. There were later charges that the election was rigged. But Kennedy was admired, especially by working people and miners, because his concerns were democratic enough that he offered people hope, and yet he came from a princely background, so in a way he provided them with something nobody else did. He provided illusion and story and fairy tale: all these are versions of hope.

WACHTEL You were saying that you remember the summer before the assassination very well. Do you know why? Why is that vivid to you?

PHILLIPS The Bay of Pigs invasion led to air-raid drills in schools and the idea that the Cubans might launch nuclear missiles. People were talking about bomb shelters. I remember all that. I think the sense of the physical world that runs through the novel is something that accrued in me because I grew up in rural, isolated mountains, and I really didn't leave there until I was eighteen, so my entire childhood feels immersed in hot summers. I was trying to re-create that in a dense, seductive way.

WACHTEL In your novel *Shelter* there are two pairs of girls who are fifteen and eleven respectively, and then the eight-year-old boy Buddy. There's a lot of ambiguity about how innocent children are. It's as if these children have foregone innocence, or haven't really been given the chance to be innocent. Is that part of what you wanted to examine?

PHILLIPS I don't know exactly what innocence is. I think things are more complex than that. For instance, there's a sexuality between the two pairs of girls that's very natural and sibling-like. Some people who've read the book have said, well, this isn't so innocent, and what are these relationships between the girls about? Their bonds are intense partly because of what's been going on in their families. But I think this is common; all families go through periods of crisis. And kids who are moving into adolescence typically forge strong friendships as a way of separating from their families, even if their families aren't having problems. But these girls in particular sense that their chances lie more with each other than within their families, at least right now.

Children are seen to be innocent, but in fact they sense a great deal of what goes on in their families, even if they aren't able to remember it later or articulate it to themselves. I think we absorb family dilemmas in a way that becomes part of our souls or part of our identities, and we carry them with us and work them out in some way. These are the patterns of our obsessions, and our obsessions lead us to the centre of the spiral. I suppose what happens in that summer to these children, and the fact that it happens to them together as a group, is a kind of shorthand, in that it pushes them through some of the issues their families have made them face. My sense of the book when I started was that each of the children would enter this primal landscape with a secret that they felt they couldn't tell anyone else, a burden that they were more or less aware of, and that what happened at the camp would change that.

WACHTEL You described it as "a passion play." In what sense?

PHILLIPS There is a moral struggle going on. I suppose I see Buddy, the little boy, as the moral force in the book and also as the agent of change. He is, one would say, the most innocent because he is the youngest; he also has an almost extrasensory way of viewing the world. What happens in the book really begins with Carmody's return to Buddy's household, and the danger he carries. Buddy moves through a darkness, and he enters it with nothing as solace but the world itself, the world around him and everything that he's experienced. I wanted to look at how people deal with sustained danger, or sustained threat, and what they draw on when it seems there is nothing to draw on. I think that happens in the book rather consistently; there are almost miraculous interventions at every turn, some of them having to do with what happens between the children themselves, and some of them having to do with the natural world and their ability to see it.

Perception becomes quite censored within a particular society and era. Buddy and Parson are outsiders whose perceptions are deeper and larger than those recognized or accepted by the society in which they find themselves. Parson understands his awareness within the context of fundamentalism — a fire-and-brimstone story quite understandable to those living in a culture of extremes: extreme poverty, extreme isolation, and a fear of the unknown partly engendered by a landscape of extreme physical beauty and mystery. Buddy is being steered in the same direction but his sense of the world is still naturally and intuitively luminous, and quite pantheistic. The girls begin to apprehend that power in the natural world, the world enclosing the camp.

WACHTEL We were talking earlier about just how innocent or not innocent the girls are. Certainly with the fifteen-year-old girls, Lenny and Cap, there's a sense of their being tantalized by their own sexual awakening, especially in a scene early on in the novel where they go skinny-dipping at night. That scene sets up a sense of sexual danger in the novel, a kind of foreboding. Why do you cast this budding sexuality in such dark terms?

PHILLIPS I don't exactly see it as dark, I see it as big and real and inviting and unfamiliar. I think there's always a shadow around something that's worth doing. You have to give up what you were before, change the limits of things, and you have to surrender to something you may not understand — go on instinct. In a way, the connection between Lenny and Cap lets them walk into the water. If they'd been alone, they might not have behaved in the same way.

WACHTEL *Shelter* is told from inside the heads of different characters and when I was inside Buddy's head or at times with some of the other characters, I was reminded a little of Faulkner's *The Sound and the Fury*. I know it's facile to talk about Southern Gothic, but to what degree do you identify with other Southern writers?

PHILLIPS I identify strongly with some of them but it has more to do with the risks they take as artists. I love Faulkner's work because he seems to be unaware of any rules; he just moves out into new territory every time he speaks. As for Southern Gothic, the term has never made that much sense to me. That's just life, that's everyday life to people in the South, because, particularly at the time that Faulkner was writing, it was a very isolated area, a kind of outlaw country.

I'm in the peculiar position of not really being Southern. No one in the South considers West Virginia the South, and no one in the North considers West Virginia to be anything. It's a third world country, in a way, within the United States; it didn't have the genteel qualities of the South, or the money that the South had in terms of agriculture and plantations. It's completely mountainous and it really has no resources but mineral resources, that from the beginning were owned by outsiders. So the state was exploited — first as timber land and then as mining land. I think my sense of isolation, a kind of sensual isolation, comes from the fact that the land itself is so overgrown — verdant, mysterious valleys and mountains. I think that the isolation itself is a sort of common ground. Any time you have an isolated area that is physically beautiful and yet materially depressed, you'll have what people might term "Gothic consciousness." You could say this exists in Dublin, too, I think.

West Virginia was also displaced in time; for many years it remained less mobile than other parts of the country. People didn't move in or out of West Virginia. There was no work there, and the people who lived there were intensely rooted. They didn't leave just because they didn't have a job, or at least not until my generation.

WACHTEL You have said that although you fled early, you're one of those people who never left home. Why is that?

PHILLIPS My identity began to take form there, and my family on both sides had been there since the 1700s. The way I look at things, the way I think about things, the way I dream about things, was really mapped out in that place. Like all writers probably, I also felt from the beginning very much an outsider, and I always knew that I would leave, but my concerns move back there often.

WACHTEL Family is very much at the centre of your work. I think one critic said that in your writing the real source of darkness *and* light belongs to the family.

PHILLIPS The family is an extrapolated picture of the personality, or the soul, of the individual, and we're all familiar with the ways that families project onto each other. We're familiar with the idea of family therapy in which the whole family is involved because particular individuals are acting out whatever issues there are within the group. My sense of the way writers develop has very much to do with the family. I think the kid who turns out to be a writer is often the kid who was the confidante of one or both parents. He or she is often the one who was the most responsible in some way, the one who remembers, who took it all in unconsciously as well as consciously; who somehow took responsibility for keeping the family alive, psychically. I think for these kids the survival of family becomes a kind of quest, and it very much influences what they try to do as adults. It's not even something that ends with the death of family members. Whether we maintain contact or not, that primal unit does end, and all of us deal with the loss of it as adults. It may feel to us like a good

loss in some ways, but I think we're always struggling with whatever our first sense of home was, and the fact that our first sense
of home has to be betrayed as we move out of it.

WACHTEL You were obviously that kid, the one who was the
confidante, who had a sense of responsibility for, as you say,
maintaining the psychic life of the family. Were you conscious of
that even as a young child? Were you the designated writer?

PHILLIPS No, not really. I was conscious of having a very strong
relationship with my mother and I was conscious of a kind of
female legacy within my family, but I didn't see it in terms of
actually writing. Yet, when I was a child, my mother gave me my
grandmother's poems. She'd had an eighth grade education, was
a great reader, and died long before I was born. She and my
mother decided upon my name when my mother was twelve.

WACHTEL You have written about how desperate you were to
escape from your home town; how you plotted your own escape
and also your mother's because, as you put it, "I am her and she is
me." Can you talk about that?

PHILLIPS I think a common identity exists between mothers
and children for a brief period of time. If the mother takes care
of the child, there's a kind of infant-mother bond that really
doesn't respect identity. There is a melding of self. And we begin
to move out from that and we don't experience it for the rest of
our lives, except in certain peak moments. I think that's what sexuality is about. Sexuality is not about trying to be maternal, necessarily, but about letting go of the boundaries of the self for a
moment, and really not being alone. It's nurture, protection, the
paradox of safety and danger, the edge, the risk of trust. The melding of identity is not always sexual; it's something that people
experience when they're passionate about something. People can
experience it in religious terms. I think that sense of *I am her and
she is me* has to do with almost an unconscious sense of the
mother's life and what the daughter is meant to do. I think we
often have a sense of completing what our parents weren't able to
complete. Children inherit from their parents not only physical
characteristics or certain gestures, but also their unresolved con-

flicts. I suppose you could think of family connections as a kind of karma. We move through not only our own issues, but we carry with us what our parents gave us.

WACHTEL Why was it so necessary to get away?

PHILLIPS I'm not sure. When people get away they have the illusion that they're moving; they change their outward circumstances, and sometimes those changes can be so abrupt or so striking that they compel the individual to take in new information. I think people leave because they're trying to change. You're going to be the same pretty much anywhere, but I think the sense of wanting to move has to do with wanting to move psychically, with wanting to be larger or different and wanting to understand more.

WACHTEL I get the sense that escape, or at least travel, has been important to you: you travelled a lot in the 1970s and ten years ago in Nepal you talked about wanting to be a Buddhist nun. How have you managed to come back and stay put and settle down?

PHILLIPS It hasn't been easy. I think it gets back to what we were just saying, the idea that travel is a kind of illusion. It's easier than living life in one place because you have the sense that things are always changing and you can concentrate on your internal ground a little less. It's been interesting to stay very much in one place and be involved with the identities of other people in the way that I'm forced to now, just as I did as a child, in that I'm living within a family. The difference for me now is that I'm aware of family as an exercise in surrender, which is how parents must experience it. Surrender is not something children have to do, if they're well nurtured, because they're defining themselves within the shelter of relationship. Parents are trying to make a space in which kids are safe and even thriving — part of this is the sacrifice of self-interest — we move ourselves around, allow ourselves to change, in loving our children. But I think the exercise in surrender is luminous as well as dark. I'm interested in moving between those two poles in every way.

WACHTEL How is it luminous?

PHILLIPS I think parenting is an experience in love that is very different from anything else I've ever known. I'd written about being a daughter, and I felt that if I didn't become a parent myself I'd be a daughter all my life, and that the way to move through it was to be a mother as well as a daughter. It's luminous because you do move out of your sense of self in a way that you probably don't otherwise. It's also dangerous because you become vulnerable on behalf of your children in a way that you aren't as an individual. There are no guarantees and that becomes a very different proposition when you're thinking about your children's lives.

It's a lot like writing. You have material that in a way contains everything for you at that point, all your obsessions and hopes and all kinds of things that you're unconscious of, that you experience as just shapes or forms, and you begin to move into that material. You have no guarantee that you're going to come out the other side, but it's a process and you just move through it. You let go of your children, though, in ways you never have to let go of your work — you let go, and let go, and let go.

WACHTEL Calling your new novel *Shelter* and setting it in a place you call Shelter County does raise the question of where one can find shelter or who can protect others. Did you find answers for yourself?

PHILLIPS I think we find shelter in relationships, imperfect as they may be, and I think that is evident in the book. But I think there's also a sense of miraculousness in the book that is bigger than any of the individuals. People perceive things in an almost psychic or telepathic way which hints at something that connects us, that we may not be aware of, that we may actually fight against.

WACHTEL Ultimately the most reliable bond seems to be between the children themselves. The odd adult is okay but not completely safe. For instance, Buddy's mother, with all the will in the world, still can't keep him safe. Is this your own conclusion?

PHILLIPS That's reality. Safety is a temporary situation, just like happiness or sadness. I think the relationships between the children do provide safety and shelter in the book, and that was my sense of it from the beginning. The whole point of setting it in an isolated place, where the children were set apart from their families, was to let those bonds develop in an unfettered way, in which family was no longer present, and then to see what happened.

WACHTEL I really like the tender affection that occurs, not only between the friends but also, and maybe especially, between siblings. Near the end of *Machine Dreams*, there's a reminiscence about a brother and a sister who find comfort and companionship in the darkness, under a bed, or in a big pile of leaves. It's not the same in *Shelter*, but this seems to be something you come back to.

PHILLIPS Relationships between siblings have always interested me. I think childhood is a period in which we're all outsiders; we see things with "beginner's mind," if you know that Buddhist term, in which we don't perceive things in context, we read things as they are in themselves. If we grow up with siblings, we share that period of time with other people who become part of us in a way that probably doesn't happen again until we have children of our own. I see that as very interesting and I've worked with it in several ways.

At the same time, there are elements of that sibling connection in all love relationships. We do speak of "brothers and sisters," "he's my brother," "sisterhood," "sisterhood is powerful." We nurture our lovers. We forge those kinds of bonds all the time — it's not only blood that comprises intense relationship, it's an exchange of identity, and it should characterize relationships of any depth between any two people.

WACHTEL I have to ask you an irreverent question: are you going to send your children to summer camp?

PHILLIPS Camp will be tough. Overnight camp, that is. I probably will, but I'll check it out very carefully. Writers are usually control freaks and separation is probably difficult for them. Separation from their manuscripts, separation from their children, separation from their rooms sometimes. Writers know too much.

January 1995
*interview initially prepared in collaboration
with Larry Scanlan*

CARLOS FUENTES

Described as "Mexico's most gifted storyteller," Carlos Fuentes has also been a diplomat, professor and activist, as well as the best-known Mexican writer in the English-speaking world. That his acclaim extends beyond Octavio Paz, his older compatriot, who won the Nobel Prize in 1990, is partly because Fuentes has spent so much of his life abroad — starting when he was not quite six years old and his father was a diplomat in Washington, D.C. As Fuentes has said about himself, he was "the first and only Mexican to prefer grits to guacamole."

A contemporary of his, the Chilean writer José Donoso, met Fuentes when he was fourteen and they were both attending a posh, Anglophile school in Santiago. Donoso calls Fuentes "the first active and conscious agent of the internationalization of the Spanish American novel." As if by way of illustration, Carlos Fuentes' *The Old Gringo* (1985), was the first novel written by a Mexican to appear on *The New York Times* bestseller list. The book was later made into a movie with Jane Fonda. Gregory Peck played the Ambrose Bierce-character who early in the century follows the revolution to Mexico and disappears. In leaving North America, "the land without memory," Fuentes' hero is the man who crosses the border — in this case, the "scar" between the U.S. and Mexico. But *The Old Gringo* is more straightforward than Fuentes' usual fiction. As one critic said, Fuentes writes such a book as if with one hand; "his major fictions are projects of the bizarre and the uncanny." Experimental, baroque, as in *Terra Nostra* (1975), his stories often revisit historical events.

In the early eighties, Carlos Fuentes delivered the CBC Massey Lecture and called his talk, "Latin America: At War with the Past." In 1992, to mark the 500th anniversary of Columbus' voyage, Fuentes hosted a BBC television series and published a book called *The Buried Mirror: Reflections on Spain and the New World*.

Born in 1928, Carlos Fuentes has been publishing fiction for more than thirty-five years. His recent works include *Diana: The Goddess Who Hunts Alone* (1995), a novel inspired by his 1970 affair with the actress Jean Seberg, and *A New Time for Mexico* (1996), a non-fiction analysis of Mexico's recent political crises. When I spoke to him in April 1994, he was on an American book tour for a collection of stories called *The Orange Tree*. It was only months since the January 1st uprising in Chiapas, Mexico's poorest state, and weeks after the assassination of then-President Salinas' chosen successor, Luis Donaldo Colosio. Fuentes now lives in London and Mexico City.

WACHTEL In your novel, *The Campaign*, which is set in the nine-teenth century, a cynical and brutal man predicts the future of a Latin America lurching from one dictatorship to another, unable to bridge the gap between the imaginary nation constituted by law and an impoverished and corrupt reality. Do you see the potential for this happening even now in Mexico?

FUENTES Yes, it is happening in Mexico and throughout Latin America. Our big problem is that the political institutions do not coincide with the economic, social and cultural reality of the country, both in the sense that we still have so many underdeveloped and backward regions in Latin America that are easily forgotten — as the Chiapas rebellion has proved — and that there is a new society which is rapidly advancing, a civil society, that is not represented by anachronistic methods and institutions and practices. And this is notably the case in Mexico, where the dominant political party no longer represents the most dynamic elements of the society, nor does it take care of those who have been left behind. So it's a bad situation and it has to be solved somehow.

WACHTEL Were you surprised by the peasant revolt in Chiapas?

FUENTES I was. I think everybody in Mexico was. Nobody can claim that we had foreseen it.

WACHTEL You've been accused in the past of romanticizing revolution. Is that the only way for the poor or the dispossessed of Mexico to win justice?

FUENTES I don't think that anybody can invent a revolution. I would have to romanticize the history of the world in order to say that I'm romanticizing revolutions. Revolutions occur when they have to occur. No amount of theorizing or romanticizing is going to change that. I think that if the peasant and Indian population in Chiapas took up arms, it is because they had no other recourse. I'm not in favour of violence or taking up arms, but when all the doors are closed — and in Chiapas they have been closed for five hundred years — then a moment comes when a spark ignites. It's not the first Indian and peasant rebellion in the state of Chiapas. They generally have been smothered in blood and repression; this was not the case this time. It has to be said to the credit of President Salinas that, instead of encircling the Zapatistas and exterminating them, he decided to establish a peace process. But the fact is that if the Zapatistas had not risen on January 1st, the country would not have heard them. Their uprising brought our attention to all that still needs to be done in

Mexico, all that we had forgotten, all that we have yet to aspire to. And this has been extremely important for the country; it has shaken everybody up.

WACHTEL You've talked about how your first Mexico was an imagined one, conjured up by your diplomat father, as you were growing up in Washington. What image did you have then of your homeland?

FUENTES It was a very heroic image because those were the times of the Mexican Revolution under Cárdenas, who was the president — F.D.R. was the president of the United States — times of high hopes, of the conviction that ideals and practice could coincide both in the United States and in Mexico. My father was a diplomat and a defender of the revolutionary policies of President Cárdenas, such as land reform and the creation of workers' unions, and above all, the expropriation of oil in the hands of British, Dutch, and American interests. My vision of Mexico was of an ideal country, a country that was at the vanguard of Latin America in creating better conditions for its people, and with a heroic history. Then of course you go and live there and you find that there is a dark side to everything and a contradiction to everything you believe, and that is, I think, very healthy. It made a novelist out of me, the contradiction between the ideal and the real.

WACHTEL How? How did it make you into a writer?

FUENTES Since I had imagined the country so much and given it such heroic dimensions in my child's mind, actually living there and finding that many of the promises had not been kept, that great injustice was accumulating in the process of developing Mexico — all of these things made me take a very close look at the new classes in Mexico, which became the subject of my first novels. There was a new class in Mexico, a bourgeois class, a class made up of bankers and industrialists, and it hadn't existed before the revolution. A new bureaucracy came out of the revolutionary years, a new politics emerged. All this was subject matter for my imagination and for investigation in my first novels, *Where the Air Is Clear* and *The Death of Artemio Cruz*.

WACHTEL Going back to your growing up in Washington, the natural impulse of children is to try to fit in. When you were a child in Washington, did you feel almost American?

FUENTES Yes, the children of diplomats have to be adaptable or else. If you're shifting from one country to another, from one language to another, from one set of friends to another, you have to adapt or you will be miserable. So I learned to adapt quickly and felt very happy in my school in Washington. By the way, public education was first-rate in the United States in the 1930s; it is not so now. I owe a lot to my schooling in Washington. I fitted in very well, until the expropriation of oil came in 1938 and there was a tremendous anti-Mexican campaign in all the U.S. papers, accusing Mexico of being communist and of stealing oil and that sort of thing. My situation in the school deteriorated very quickly. Backs were turned on me; old friends said: "My father and mother say all of you Mexicans are communists and we shouldn't talk to you." It was quite a shock.

WACHTEL Tell me about your father. He must have been a powerfully influential figure in your life.

FUENTES He was extremely influential, especially because he surrounded me with books and gave me a sense of the pleasure of reading, even of handling books. He subscribed to various book clubs in the thirties and, when we received these packages every month, there was great excitement in opening up and seeing the books, commenting on them, reading them and building up a library — my own childhood library. I think my father was immensely hurt by the death of his elder brother, who was an extremely promising young poet and a publisher of a literary magazine in Mexico. He died at twenty-one of typhus, which was then an incurable disease. My father named me after him — he was also called Carlos Fuentes — and I think that my father saw me as a resurrection of his brother in a way.

WACHTEL Yet he didn't really want you to be a writer; he wanted you to study law.

FUENTES He wanted me to be a writer but *first* to study law, which has been the tradition in Latin America. Families say, if you're a writer you'll die of hunger; first be a lawyer and then become a writer — my father was no exception to that.

WACHTEL Language is something that is fundamental to any writer, but it seems of particular importance to you. Do you understand why you embrace Spanish with such fervor?

FUENTES Yes, for many reasons. First, because I had to fight to maintain my Spanish language, living in countries of another language — French, Portuguese or English — then, because I felt that it was a challenge to be a writer in the Spanish language. I felt that the English and French languages had very powerful and uninterrupted traditions. There has been no break in the English novel since Defoe's *Robinson Crusoe*; there has been no break in the French novel since Madame de La Fayette's *La Princesse de Clèves*. I was always puzzled by the fact that in Spanish we have the great founding novel of Europe, of Western literature — *Don Quixote* by Cervantes — and then we have nothing. We have absolutely nothing until the second half of the nineteenth century, when Pérez Galdós and Clarín appear. We have no great poets in the Spanish language after the great baroque poets of the seventeenth century, until Rubén Darío, the Nicaraguan poet, appears at the end of the nineteenth century. This vacuum, this great void in a tradition, fascinated and preoccupied me and made me feel that there was far more to be said, to be explored, to be experienced, in the realm of the Spanish language than in English or French, the other two languages I have managed since childhood. Besides, I've never had a dream in English or French.

WACHTEL Do you understand why there was such a literary void?

FUENTES It has a lot to do with the political decadence of Spain, the Inquisition, the culture of the Counter Reformation, the impossibility of publishing or even saying certain things, the authoritarian powers — everything conspired to make it very, very difficult to have a living literature. There was no erotic literature, for example; the language had been expunged of any erotic elements in the sixteenth, seventeenth century. All of this meant that there was a challenge there, and that is what I found so attractive about writing in Spanish.

WACHTEL I sense that it also meant a way for you to connect to a larger community outside of Mexico. You talk about language becoming the centre of your being and enabling you to shape your destiny, and your country's destiny, into a greater shared destiny.

FUENTES Yes. Finally, no matter what your nationality, if you're a writer, you're dealing with two universal elements, which are imagination and language. The beauty of it is that in your own society, your real political contribution is in maintaining the vigour of the language and imagination. When a nation loses this, terrible things happen. Look at Germany under Hitler; the kidnapping of the public discourse of language and imagination by the Nazi party almost ruined the culture of Germany. It took an enormous effort after the war to re-create a public discourse, to re-create a language that was not blemished by National Socialism. But beyond the society in which you live, universally, it is language and imagination that identify literature as a work of art. I don't think anybody reads Gabriel García Márquez because he's Columbian or Milan Kundera because he's Czech. They're read because of the power of their language and imagination.

WACHTEL You also seem to argue for a pan Spanish-speaking connectedness. What is the appeal for you in that notion?

FUENTES I think that we belong to a community of language and that we impoverish ourselves if we start balkanizing the regions of the Spanish language. If you have only Mexican literature or Paraguayan literature or Peruvian literature, you come up with a rather poor stack of chips; whereas, if you sum the totality of the Spanish-speaking domain, then you have quite a treasure.

WACHTEL There's also power attached to language. In the first story of your collection, *The Orange Tree*, the hero is an interpreter with the power to decide peace or war through the ownership of words, and I thought you were saying something beyond the specific or strategic situation of the interpreter.

FUENTES Yes, but the folly of it is that this interpreter — who is telling lies all the time in order to further the awareness of the Indian people, make them conscious of the conqueror and preserve the Indian world — finally fails. The language of lies, which the interpreter uses, actually becomes the historical truth. When Hernán Cortés, the conqueror, says, "I come in peace," the translator, Aguilar, says, "He lies. He comes in war. He is going to subject you," and it turns out that the lie is the truth.

WACHTEL You also comment on how Spanish is the language of the conquerors, the language of Cortés, but that Moctezuma, the Aztec emperor, had as his official title "He of the Great Voice," he who has the monopoly on speech, the monopoly on language. There's almost a war of language.

FUENTES I think that the conquest of Mexico was more than a fight between gunpowder and obsidian knives; it was a struggle of words, a struggle of languages. It is extraordinary that the title of Moctezuma, the emperor, was "He of the Great Voice," he who speaks, he who has the right to speak and only he, and that he's defeated by an Indian woman, La Malinche, who captures language, who transforms language, who unites the language of the conqueror and of the conquered. Plus something else: Moctezuma is a theocratic despot; he believed only he should hear the voices of the gods, the language of the gods, whereas Cortés, who was a very pragmatic, Machiavellian European of the Renaissance, knew he had to hear the words of men. What the words of men through La Malinche told him was that the peoples of Mexico were against Moctezuma, against his tyranny, and would join the Spaniards to overthrow the Aztec despot. Of course they only exchanged the Aztec tyranny for the Spanish tyranny, but that's another story.

WACHTEL *The Orange Tree* also has a story about the sons of the conquistador, the sons of Cortés, and they talk about which language? which god? as if everything is to be invented.

FUENTES When you go through a trauma as extraordinary as the conquest of Mexico — where a great empire of several million people, with a magnificent capital larger than the island of Corvo, or larger than Venice, is completely razed and destroyed — a trauma ensues. How do you re-create a society after such a blood-letting, such a defeat, such a thorough-going demolition of all the symbols, the temples, the buildings, of the defeated culture?

I think the solution was *mestizaje*, the mixing of the races. You have the fact that the Spaniards did not have the puritanical repugnance of the English settlers of North America and mixed very freely with the Indian women and probably created a mestizo population. And then the fact that through Christianity the period following the conquest generated a new society, both paternally and maternally determined — in the name of the father, because the figure of Christ imposed itself on the Indian population. Here was a crucified God who, instead of demanding, "You shall die for me," said, "I shall die for you." That made a tremendous impression. And then there is the maternal factor when the sense of orphanhood to be found in the Indian population after the conquest was transcended by the appearance of the Virgin Mary, the mother of God offering roses in December to a very humble Indian fardelbearer; she is brown-skinned and has an Arab name — she's called Our Lady of Guadeloupe — and she becomes the symbol of unity and purity for Mexicans. All these things followed from what I would call the conquest to the counterconquest, the creation of a new society with mixed blood, new dreams, new forms of expression and a new language. So these stories in *The Orange Tree* are dealing with this process of the creation of a new society out of the ruins of an old one.

WACHTEL Your first visit to Spain was in 1967. You were almost forty. You've said that it was an extraordinary experience for you. Why was that?

FUENTES First, because I won my first big literary prize in Barcelona, the Biblioteca Breve Prize given by the editorial company of Seix Barral for my book called *A Change of Skin*. This novel was awarded the prize and immediately it was "awarded" the censorship of the Franco regime. The publisher was forbidden to publish the book. The reasons officially given were quite extraordinary: the book was blasphemous and pornographic, and — the most extraordinary reason of all — it was pro-Jewish and thus anti-German, which is really one of the most fantastic reasons I'd ever heard, until I met the censors and they continued to give the Nazi salute; they were very much a part of the fascist movement of Spain. It was a tremendous shock to arrive at the other side of my culture and find it captured in this sterile, dogmatic fascism of the Franco years. Yet there it was — it was my culture. I went to the *escorial* and I had the first conception of my novel *Terra Nostra* there. I went to *El Prado* and I saw the wonderful paintings by Goya and Velásquez and felt that this was all mine, too. I read the books of Spain once more, and there was this tremendous contradiction again between the culture and the politics of Spain.

WACHTEL I was struck by your having to cope once again with dissonance, with contradictions.

FUENTES That's nothing new in literature, and especially in the literature of the Americas. So many American writers have found that there is this great division between their ideal America and the real America of the Babbitts; so many have found it necessary to leave the United States: Fitzgerald, Hemingway, Gertrude Stein. Henry James saw two faces of America. So did Edgar Allen Poe: He saw it was not all sunlight; he saw the night image of the United States. So I don't think it's anything new.

WACHTEL Why do you identify so strongly with Don Quixote?

FUENTES He's a founding figure of my culture, of literature, of fiction in general. The figure of a man who leaves the security and order of his village, and the certainty of his books. Don Quixote is a character who believes in what he reads; he goes out into the world and expects it to correspond to his readings, but finds out that it does not. What he has read is one thing, what the world has to offer is another. And he refuses this cleavage. He decides that what he has read is true and that even if reality offers him a windmill, for him it is a giant because his books say so. So he is the emblematic figure of writing, of imagination, of fiction, and also of the transition from one age to another.

I know no better explanation, no better symbol of the passage from the Middle Ages to the brave new world of modernity than the figure of Don Quixote. The medieval world was an organic world, unified around Christianity; there were no nation states and there was an absolute certainty of your place in the world and your beliefs about heaven and earth. Suddenly you're thrust into a world full of rogues and tricks, you get beaten up and your ideals are mocked, and you have to improve, invent. And what do you invent? You invent a novel, you invent literature. Don Quixote is the first character in literature who knows he is being written about as he lives his adventures. He is informed that there is a book about him being sold and that everybody knows about it. There is even a sequel being written by an unscrupulous man called Avellaneda, who is inventing further adventures. Don Quixote gets very angry and goes to Barcelona. He enters a printing shop — he's the first character in literature to ever enter a printing shop — where his adventures are becoming a commercial product. All of this makes Don Quixote the founding father of the novel, the most emblematic figure of fiction.

WACHTEL You've said most eloquently and succinctly, "I'm not interested in a slice of life. What I want is a slice of the imagination."

FUENTES That's right. You can get a slice of life through a documentary or a statistic, but the imagination is something else. It is what permits you to understand — not only to imagine the future but to imagine the past, which is very important. Sometimes we become amnesiacs and lose our way in history, lose our sense because we forget the lessons of the past or think the past is dead, which is like killing ourselves, because if we think that way, one day we too will be the past and we'll be thrown on the garbage heap.

WACHTEL What are the lessons from the past? I feel as if there is something you want to rescue from history.

FUENTES The continuity of life. Death is inevitable, but can we ensure that life continues? That is the challenge we all face as individuals and as members of a society. If we forget the past, we are ready to condemn the future, and as there is no living future with a dead past, we condemn ourselves. We condemn what we have created to death. That would break the continuity of life. Indeed we would be at the end of history, as Fukuyama says, and that means the end of the history of the novel, of music, of love, the end of the history of everything. So I'm not about to give in.

WACHTEL The only way to imagine the future is to revisit the past?

FUENTES Yes. You cannot have a future without a past. Of that I am convinced.

WACHTEL Although you've also said that literature does what history can't do, that you write everything that history has *not* said and will otherwise be forgotten.

FUENTES Imagine, that enormous period with no novels in the Spanish language, the things that were not said, that were left unwritten; it's fantastic, it's incredible. We have to re-imagine. That is why so much historical fiction has been written in Latin America. Because of this tremendous void, many novels are being written about periods that didn't have novelists. It's as though we want to rescue the silence of the past; there's nothing that dooms you more than silence. I think this is further proof of this power of the past as an element for the future.

WACHTEL There's a line in *The Orange Tree* where a character says, "I wonder if an event that isn't narrated takes place in reality."

FUENTES I think that what you do not narrate you forget; or, you permit others to mishandle it and create oppressive myths. It's extremely important to be a writer and to be an alert writer — and here I don't mean only writers of fiction; I mean political writers, journalists, economists, sociologists, as well. Everybody has a role to play in order that this sense of the past be kept alive and the gaps of the past be constantly filled in and that we establish a continuum of experience between the past, the present and the future.

WACHTEL At the same time, though, memory is something that's important to you.

FUENTES Memory is extremely important, and the fact is that Bernal Díaz del Castillo's book [*The True History of the Conquest of New Spain*] is important because it is an act of memory. I think it's the founding novel of Latin America, this chronicle of the conquest made by an eighty-year-old infantry man, who is blind and poor and living in Guatemala, who reacts against all the books glorifying Cortés as the principal actor of the conquest of

Mexico. He says, No, I was twenty-four years old when the conquest took place and there would have been no conquest without the artillerymen and the gunners and the shipwrights and the
infantry, and all of us who arrived in Mexico in 1519: 508 men,
eleven horses. It's a great song to the memory of an heroic deed,
an epic that unfolds in a very literary manner because you feel, as
you read it, that you are awaiting the results, that you don't know
what's going to happen. There is a great deal of suspense even if
you know how the conquest of Mexico ended. So this assimilates
a sixteenth-century chronicler like Bernal to a twentieth-century
novelist like Proust. The magic of Proust's novel is that the narrator, Marcel, already knows everything that has happened; he is
aware of how it will all end, yet he has to write it and relive it as
though he ignored the outcome in order to communicate this
great sense of life to us. And the same thing is done by Bernal
Díaz in his very powerful chronicle of the conquest of Mexico.

WACHTEL Memory is related to time and to how time is perceived, and you've said that "time is the subject matter of all my
fiction." Can you elaborate on that?

FUENTES It is very much the axis of my fiction. There have been
times without novels but I don't know of a single novel without
time. No matter which novel you wish to mention, it happens in
time. It happens in time and it happens in space; but time is more
important than space. In my case time is the axis because I am
relating a saga that begins in the pre-Columbian times of Mexico
and comes right to our present day. The whole *corpus* of my novels is now assembled under the title *The Age of Time*. It is twenty-
seven titles; I've written eighteen up till now. I hope I have time
for the other nine.

WACHTEL How do you know that it's twenty-seven titles?

FUENTES That can change. There can be more novels, or there
can be fewer, but right now my plan is for twenty-seven novels,
and time has to be the axis. I'm very conscious of the variety of
times in history. The way we conceive history depends on the way
we conceive time, and time can be very different according to
different cultures, different ways of thinking. For the Aztecs time

was a succession of suns that destroyed themselves and from this destruction a new creation came forth. For the ancient Peruvians it was a constant fusion of horizons, horizons succeeding other horizons and blending into each other. For the West it has generally been rationalist linear time, which is one of the challenges to the modern writer, to break the linear succession of writing itself. As a revolt against the purely linear time of the West, the responses are as varied as Nietzsche's eternal return or the circular times of Borges. What I prefer is the definition by Plato that says that time is the movement of eternity. This movement of the eternal that we call time is very much at the axis of my historical feeling in my novels. I'm not interested in historical anecdote but in this experience of time as a way of movement.

WACHTEL You play with time. For instance, in the last story of *The Orange Tree*, Columbus meets up with some Japanese investors and tour operators, and after a five-hundred-year absence, Columbus wants to return to Spain.

FUENTES He is being sent back to Spain because he's disloyal to his Japanese employer. He's not a team player. He starts talking to German ecologists and probably Canadian human rights groups.

WACHTEL What do you want to do there? You're clearly enjoying this mix of history and time.

FUENTES I would say simply I think that when we celebrated, or did not celebrate, the five hundred years of Columbus' arrival, we all thought, what if this continent of ours had remained a paradise, a totally pristine region of uncontaminated waters and flora and fauna and not the cesspool the Americas have become? It's an idea, simply. It could have happened but it couldn't have happened because eventually you get a Japanese consortium and a pizza parlour and motels and gasoline stations and all the rest.

WACHTEL Do you despair of that inevitability?

FUENTES Do we want it or don't we? You know, in the jungles of Chiapas the Indian women are saying in their demands to the government that they want refrigerators and vacuum cleaners. Would they be purer and happier in their shacks if they didn't have these refrigerators and vacuum cleaners? What will the refrigerator do to their style of life, the purity of their traditions, even the way they cook their food? Who knows? But history is made of movement, you see, and movement brings with it things both good and bad, and civilizations are made of clashes, cultures are made of encounters, not of isolation. Columbus could have kept mum about the discovery and maintained this wonderful paradise in the Americas, but inevitably someone else would have come.

The question is, in the face of progress, what can we do to maintain a dimension of basic decency in our lives, to protect the diversity of species, to protect the purity of things? We can't avoid the presence of progress, but what we can avoid are the excesses of progress. What we can strive for is to have an ecological balance, to see that our water is pure, that our rivers flow well, that our air is clean. All these things we can achieve. We can't stop technological advancement, but we can ensure that there is at least what I would call ecological rationality. That we can do. Of course, in the story it's presented in dramatic and extreme terms. But in reality, the whole ecological movement is showing that there's much to fight for.

WACHTEL I see some recognizable Fuentes obsessions in *The Orange Tree* — not only the re-imagining of history, but also the primacy of desire. In one story you describe a woman's breast with the nipple being the highest part and closest to heaven.

FUENTES You know what? That is an actual quote from Christopher Columbus. It's interesting that that should have caught your attention. It's one of the two or three quotes from the diary of Columbus I included because they seem so natural and modern.

WACHTEL And also clearly something that you can relate to. In *The Campaign*, the hero is driven by his desire for the wife of his political enemy. Desire often fuels your characters.

FUENTES It is part of the passion of living, it is part of the throb of the world. Sometimes I tend to intellectualize things and sacrifice passion. But I think if we don't desire, we're in total subjugation — dead.

WACHTEL In some ways your book *The Orange Tree* is quite dark: there's a lot of death and destruction; there's loss and disappointment. But the images of the orange tree and orange seeds run throughout the book, in every story. What does the orange tree signify to you?

FUENTES It is simply nature. It is the witness of our follies, the witness of the destruction we're capable of inflicting on each other, on the world, on nature herself; yet nature survives and witnesses our passing, our death, our folly. My worry is that this time around we will drive nature into the grave with us, that we'll deprive nature of her ancient privileges and say, now I have the means through nuclear holocaust or ecocide of killing you, nature, along with me. And the arrogance of humankind is such that we just might achieve that.

WACHTEL But in this book you also seem to be affirming because the very last line of the very last story is "I shall plant the orange seed again."

FUENTES I have that hope, but as you say, it is in many ways a dark book with a few flaming oranges here and there in the countryside.

WACHTEL Why is it so dark?

FUENTES I think that history in general is not the place where you find happiness, that history and happiness rarely coincide, and that we fool ourselves when we think the contrary. The history of the twentieth century has taught us that we'd better watch out: there are holocausts and gulags and repression and murder, and we're seeing them today. We're witnessing what is happening in the Sudan and in Sarajevo and Grozny, and it's still there, the blind fury and capacity for destruction and enslavement and punishment of each other that is so terrifying. Yet we have to go on struggling. That is the sense of our being here: that we must bequeath life to our children, in spite of the horror of history.

April 1994
interview initially prepared in collaboration
with Larry Scanlan

NICOLE BROSSARD

Nicole Brossard is one of the most influential, avant-garde writers in Quebec. She's internationally renowned — both for her imaginative writing and her literary theory.

I first met Brossard almost twenty years ago when I was involved with a feminist literary magazine in Vancouver. At that time, virtually none of the new writing by Quebec women was available in English — or was even much known about in the rest of Canada. In Quebec, Nicole Brossard was at the forefront of an extraordinary wave of literary and cultural activism. She was one of the founders of a feminist monthly newspaper; she edited a literary journal, *La Barre du jour*, or "the first light of dawn." In fact, she had just put together a special issue on women writers, called "le corps, les mots, l'imaginaire" — or "body, words, the imaginary." We decided to translate some of those pieces for our West Coast publication.

I have to say I didn't quite realize what I was getting into. Talking to Nicole Brossard is an engaging, stimulating experience. She approaches words and concepts in a forceful, imaginative way. She makes you think. Back then, it was daunting to have this material translated and — even in a minimal way — make it accessible to an English audience. I remember warning readers with cautionary notes like: "the writing translated here must be approached with the same patient care as that summoned for poetry."

Nicole Brossard doesn't worry about all that. She says, "I write to understand the process of writing, words, words, travelling back and forth between reality and fiction. The mind is too fast for words. Fiction is a very old-fashioned word to express a holographic body spiralling into space." Twice winner of the Governor General's Award for poetry, Brossard uses language to explore the boundaries between fiction and reality, between gender and politics. Her innovative energy reminds me of a line by the poet Muriel Rukeyser (quoted by Jeanette Winterson in *Art Objects*):

What would happen if one woman told the truth
     about herself?
The world would split open.

Born in Montreal in 1943, Brossard has published more than twenty books of poetry, fiction and theory. Some of her best-known works are *Le Désert mauve* (1987; *Mauve Desert*, 1990); *L'Amèr ou le chapitre effrité* (1977; *These Our Mothers Or: The Disintegrating Chapter*, 1983); and *La Lettre aérienne* (1985; *The Aerial Letter*, 1988). The new novel Brossard refers to when we spoke at her Outremont home in February 1995 — an airy house decorated with art and high Italian design — is *Baroque d'aube* (1995; *Baroque at Dawn*, 1996).

WACHTEL You one said that you became a feminist, a mother and a lesbian virtually at the same time, which sounds like a radical transformation. Before we talk about that transformation and its implications, can you describe your life before that time?

BROSSARD I was a student, a poet, a writer, a revolutionary. Except for a few women friends, I lived in a men's environment. I was a woman but didn't feel it really mattered. I saw my freedom coming from the fact that I was a writer. I was very active in the students' association at the University of Montreal, writing in *Le Quartier Latin*, the university student newspaper. Then, in 1965, I co-founded the literary magazine *La Barre du jour*. There was action, discussion, and I felt I was part of the exciting changes going at that time in Quebec society.

WACHTEL Your first book of poetry was published when you were only twenty-two. How did you become a poet? What kind of poet were you at that time?

BROSSARD I became a poet by reading poetry and by surrounding myself with young poets. Michel Beaulieu was one of them. Later, he became my first publisher. I guess that in my first two books of poetry I was influenced mainly by Quebec poets Anne Hébert and Saint-Denys Garneau. It was only with my third book *L'Écho bouge beau* that I started to think about language in relation to emotion. I thought that what made the poem was how you behaved in language. It seems funny now, but I used to say that poetry should be about being neutral in language. I now know that "neutral" hides one gender, the feminine. I also used to say that I had no imagination, but that imagination would come from language.

WACHTEL *L'Écho bouge beau* could be translated as *The Echo Moves Beautifully*. It's an evocative title. You're saying that before the transformation, you were a revolutionary. What does that mean?

BROSSARD It means that I became a young adult in an environment of transgression, of subversion, of political turmoil. There was a desire to make space for sexuality, imagination, for a rupture with poetic and cultural tradition. So very early on, I was connected to the idea that writing was "to make trouble" in order to change people's attitudes towards pleasure and towards consciousness, as if there were an equation between pleasure, lucidity and political awareness. I believed that it was socially responsible to encourage disobedience to authority, especially religious and political authority.

WACHTEL You talk about being a rebel or a subversive and you use words like *transgression*. Was there any of this in you as a child?

BROSSARD I think so. As a young child, I remember at church or in class, listening to some priests and teachers and finding myself arguing with their logic, especially when it had to do with justice. Very early on, I was questioning figures of authority, their thinking and their attitudes. I could not tolerate their contradictions or lies. As a teenager, I guess I was something of a delinquent, not conforming, especially to what was expected of a girl. Later on, as a young adult I reacted in the same way to the contradictions, lies and irrationality of politicians.

WACHTEL But you were basically a good girl going to *collège* and to university, *collège Marguerite-Bourgeois* and the University of Montreal.

BROSSARD Yes. I was a good and busy student. Part of me wanted to be responsible and honest, and the other part wanted to be irreverent and to subvert bourgeois thinking.

WACHTEL What kind of household did you grow up in? There's a line in *The Aerial Letter*, where you write, "Dad, Mom, you haunt me like two strangers," and it goes on to say, "My mother is sweet and understands me, my father has nothing to say." How much of that is fiction and how much is real?

BROSSARD Here I am referring to a literary image of the Quebec father. A silent man with no political or economic power. Not really the man of the house. As for reality, I grew up in Montreal, in Snowdon-NDG, in a nice environment, with good, open-minded and caring parents. My father gave me a sense of fantasy, of dreaming, of imagining: he was always talking about New York, about films. I guess he could have been an artist. I probably got my love of cities like New York and Montreal from him. My childhood was happy; it consisted of having friends, going to school and enjoying the summer and Christmas holidays.

WACHTEL Let's talk for a moment about the father and the mother in Quebec society. That quote goes on to say that the fathers keep quiet and the mothers whisper. There is something so recessive — in retreat — about the father as presented in literature here.

BROSSARD I think that the image of the father in retreat has to do with the fact that in "French-Canadian" literature, the man of the house is often portrayed as not being in charge but as acting out of nostalgia and a longing for the past, a time before the conquest. He also holds on to his revolt against the colonizer because he is somehow subdued by the clergy. He is an historical loser with no political or economic power. As for the mother, she is often portrayed as courageous and strong — which analysts have confused with being authoritarian and powerful. Of course, the mothers didn't have power to change reality, but they were often more educated than their husbands and the only power they had was to find ways to survive poverty. Definitely in Quebec rural society, father did not know best. In fact, the only man who had moral authority was the priest. That image of the father is an image of the colonized.

WACHTEL Do you remember when you became conscious of being, as you say, colonized?

BROSSARD The consciousness of being colonized as a Quebecer came through reading articles written in the magazine *Parti Pris* as well as reading books of Frantz Fanon and Albert Memmi. I could feel what they were saying was true, but I did not experience it as strongly as when I realized how deeply we women had been colonized. What characterizes the colonized is that you don't know you are colonized until you identify with the group you belong to. Identifying with a colonized group leads you to understand how, why, and by whom your people were made losers.

WACHTEL When did you realize that? What changed for you?

BROSSARD When you understand what is happening of course you are angry, in revolt, and you become active in projects to change reality. For example, it was only when I became a mother that suddenly I realized I was a woman and that I was being required to do what is required of most women. At the same time, when I was pregnant, I started reading feminist books. *The Second Sex*, by Simone de Beauvoir, *Women and Madness* by Phyllis Chesler, *Three Guineas* by Virginia Woolf, *The Dialectic of Sex* by Shulamith Firestone, *Sexual Politics* by Kate Millett. Of course, like many women, I say that feminism changed my life.

WACHTEL You say you only realized you were a woman when you became a mother. How did you manage to avoid thinking of yourself as a woman up to that point?

BROSSARD Probably because I did not want to act as a woman should. I did not identify at all with the interests women in general had: men, children, domestic tasks. It was probably also a useful mechanism for making space for myself. And most of all, I was interested in poetry and the "revolution."

WACHTEL But you got married?

BROSSARD Yes, but I didn't make a fuss about it. It was not a priority. It happened. For nine years my husband and I enjoyed being together. We were involved in the magazine *La Barre du jour* and I was writing my books. Marriage did not change me; maternity did. Suddenly, I was two bodies to care for, two bodies to nourish, and I realized that I had entered the clan of mothers. This time I couldn't pretend any longer that I wasn't a woman.

WACHTEL So where did that lead to? You became a feminist when you became a mother — how did that change your life as a writer and as a troublemaker, in terms of using language?

BROSSARD I believe that feminist consciousness changes your perspective on reality, the way you look at language as well as fiction. It transforms the image of yourself and of your gender, and it makes you focus on details as well as on systems. At the same time I fell in love with another woman. That's why I say, mother, feminist and lesbian — they all came together. Being a mother is the most common experience of women, being a lesbian a marginal one. The two realities combined in a discourse on women, love, culture and language where I found myself exploring way beyond what I had expected. It was as if I were writing on two pages at the same time. On one page I was trying to figure out the tricks the patriarchy uses to make women feel confused, ambivalent or guilty. On the other page, I was writing with the energy of love and solidarity which produces utopias and audacity. I feel privileged to have been able to link those two pages in a political and poetic project.

WACHTEL You're putting a very positive construction on something that at the time must have been quite anguished — to feel part of the mainstream but also marginalized.

BROSSARD Yes, there was a lot of anguish. But we know that anguish can be fertile for writers and artists. Trying to figure out the patriarchal system and trying to make space for yourself not only as a woman but also as a subject is a difficult task. Understanding paradoxes, double binds and guilt requires a lot of concentration. You also need to envision a positive image of women who throughout history, mythology and religion have been "framed" as inferior, evil creatures.

WACHTEL You were saying that there are these two pages — on one page is the mother and trying to understand the place of women in society, and the anger; and on the other page is joy and desire and your identification as a lesbian. Is there any connection between writing about taboo areas of sexuality and writing in taboo styles of literature? For some time you have been pushing the boundaries of conventional expectations, in terms of writing novels, poetry, texts, even in terms of the way the words are arranged on the page.

BROSSARD I think there has always been a connection between using sexual taboos or simply sexuality and "avant-garde" literature. As an example, French writers of *Tel Quel* magazine combine their *avant-garde textuelle* with comments on the work of Sade and Masoch. And of course, the more it's "subversive," the more a woman's body becomes a means for their transgression.

For me, writing within lesbian eroticism is not really dealing with a taboo. It is writing out of enthusiasm, desire and pleasure. What is subversive in lesbian eroticism is the fact that a woman turns to another woman for pleasure. And even in our open-minded society that is subversive, a luxury.

WACHTEL In one of your books, I think it's *L'Amèr* which is translated as *These Our Mothers*, you wrote, "Were this text not lesbian, it would make no sense."

BROSSARD Yes, in the sense that I was trying to reach for what I felt in me was the essential. I was writing from a lesbian's point of view, which took me further than the notions of equality and equity. I think that lesbian daring in written language has allowed feminism to reach beyond equality and equity, and it has made space for women to become whatever they choose to be. It has allowed them not only to demand justice and respect but to link their anger to imagination. It seems to me that I was able to write this book the way I wrote it because I had a lesbian's perspective; the sentence you're quoting is an acknowledgment of that. To put it simply, some of my best thoughts came to me because of my lesbian sensibility.

WACHTEL The sensibility that you describe in *The Aerial Letter* and elsewhere seems almost religious in exalting your sexuality, in using it to define yourself as a writer and as a person. If it were religion you might be called a zealot.

BROSSARD Sexuality in action as well as desire gives us vital information about who we are, what's important to us, how we use our imagination. Part of the sexual response we give to the *other* is constructed within a heterosexual framework that is taken for granted. I think that what I have been writing — whether in *Lovhers*, a book of poems, in the novel *Picture Theory* or in the essay *The Aerial Letter* — is definitely inspired, shaped by my passion and love, by my inclination toward *she*. At the same time those books also deal with the relentless curiosity I have about language and creative writing. Everything that happens to me only becomes meaningful to others if it can be processed by language into something that expands imagination and memory, personal and collective. I don't think I would have been able to write those texts without the emotion of love or without the environment of lesbians and women. This is important, the interrelation, the exchange of energy among women, and between the woman writer and her community. That exchange of energy is *reconnaissance*, it allows each woman to be acknowledged but keeps the focus on women as a group. This focus requires a lot of concentration and attraction, because women as a group are usually hidden within the other groups they belong to, based on ethnicity, social class, race, etc.

WACHTEL I was hoping we would come back to language because that is in a sense where you began. You said that before you had these transformations of consciousness, language was the most important thing. But language has often been seen as a barrier, too. In her preface to *The Aerial Letter*, Louise Forsythe writes that the normal practice of language stands as an implacable barrier to all women in their writing.

BROSSARD This is what *The Aerial Letter* is about. Trying to figure out what the barriers are and how they prevent women from becoming who they aspire to be. The first barrier you have to overcome is to give yourself permission to be a writer. Then you have to allow yourself to invest your subjectivity, your perspective, in language. The usual meanings that we give to words have been filled by masculine subjectivity throughout the centuries. Language has reflected this masculine subjectivity because men appropriated the public arena. They were the only ones to publish, to make laws. For me, going beyond the barriers of language meant working very closely with words, decomposing them, opening up their taken-for-granted meaning to other possibilities. In fact, once you make room for a feminine or a lesbian subjectivity in language, it belongs to you.

WACHTEL A long time ago you said that "to write *I am a woman* is full of consequences," and you said quite recently that you still believe that to be true. Why?

BROSSARD To write "I am a woman" is full of consequences because you take along with you the past, the present and maybe the future of women — you take along a destiny. It means you have to think about what the destiny of being female is. Then you have to question history, institutions, tradition and religion, which have always undermined women. The *I am a woman* forces you to at least pay attention to the way women have been treated throughout cultures and centuries. Of course, you cannot complain all the time; you have to make propositions. I believe that this sentence will be important as long as women give birth and are "the second sex." I know that when I use the word "woman" in a sentence, that sentence grows ideas in a different direction. The same applies when as a reader I encounter the word "woman." That word is full of special effects. It sparkles. As an author sometimes I wonder if I use it too much, if that erodes the reader's response to it. I don't think so. To write *I am a woman* is to change the course of your thoughts and at the same time of your emotions and memory. It can also move you into some unknown territories of meaning.

WACHTEL In *The Aerial Letter* you write that reality is always true but that women's reality is not men's reality. This question of reality and whose reality is to be reflected in writing seems central to an understanding of your work.

BROSSARD Yes, it has been very important. Again, we go back to the feminist consciousness because normally we take reality for granted. We take for granted the organization of society, habits, traditions; and suddenly you realize that your daily gestures, your daily experience as a woman, are not included as evidence of reality. For example, when women started saying "I don't think this is right" or "I don't agree with that," they were told "Oh, it's in your imagination, you're seeing things." Trying to understand why women's angle of vision was always dismissed as unreal led me to ask: What is reality? How do we construct reality? How do we construct fiction? Finally I ended up believing that we do not construct fiction differently from the way we construct reality. "Fiction" is only the underground of reality. For a long time it hid violence against women. By telling the shameful, the unbelievable, women have changed part of reality, part of fiction.

WACHTEL Do you still feel that women's reality and men's reality are different?

BROSSARD Now women can play more roles in society but they still experience those roles within the rules set by men. In politics, in business, it's difficult to change the rules of the game.

Of course more and more, women's version of reality is making it into the public arena. Laws and services are changing to accommodate women, mostly mothers; some men, mostly fathers, are experiencing a fraction of women's daily work. But on the whole, I believe to be a boy or a girl still makes a difference in the way you view the world and respond to it. After all, physical violence as a response to frustration is definitely not a girl's habit.

WACHTEL In terms of fiction you've said that you don't like novels because they're mostly anecdotes. Do you still feel that?

BROSSARD I'm now writing a novel and I guess I am still debating my relationship with that genre, which is somehow about a relationship to prose and time, because the novel is about time; it can only develop in time: three, four years, or even more. When you write a novel, you are bound to write "*La marquise sortit à cinq heures*," which is to say, to write banal sentences and link them until a whole universe surges from them. You have to wait until you're finished to say okay, that's it. In poetry you get gratification almost instantly although you might need to work for many hours on a poem. So they are two different ways of relating to time and to the pleasure of writing. While I say that, I realize I have to take into account that it has been mainly through novels that women have expressed themselves. Telling stories is human nature. Maybe it's too natural for me.

WACHTEL I thought you found that novels are too easy, that they're just stories, they're too undemanding.

BROSSARD They are too undemanding! Most of them are absolutely undemanding and unchallenging. In the late nineteenth century the novel played a major role because through their stories authors were discovering subtle laws of relationship between individuals. Today we know more and more about human motivation. To enjoy a novel I need to be surprised, astonished by what I read, and very few novels give me that pleasure.

WACHTEL The desert is a strong image in several of your books, in *Daydream Mechanics* and of course in *Mauve Desert*. What is the appeal of the desert for you?

BROSSARD It is an important symbol, the desert. It is a place of life and death. A dangerous place, where you might lose your way but at the same time you are always facing the horizon. It is a beautiful place, full of life. Also, in the desert you are by yourself, in direct relation with nature. The desert is a place of meditation, of *recueillement*. I chose the American desert to create a contrast between beauty and a certain decadence that you find through the traces people leave in the desert: bottles of beer, rusty cars. I also chose it because it was in the American desert that the first atomic bomb was exploded. It was important for me to inscribe my North American reality. It's strange to talk about the desert since I am now working on a novel in which the sea is a major theme. But maybe it's not all that strange since in Sanskrit the words *maru, mari*, desert and sea, have the same origin.

WACHTEL There already have been puns in your work about *la mer*, the sea, *la mère*, the mother, *l'amer*, bitterness.

BROSSARD Yes, it is interesting that you mention that because in this new novel the sea is very important, and the mother reappears as a character but in a very different way from in *These Our Mothers*. I think it's almost impossible not to relate the sea to the mother as the origin of life. The question I am now working with is: Is it possible to change the symbolic dimension of certain words? As a woman writer, can I behave differently from a male writer in my relationship to the sea?

WACHTEL In *Mauve Desert* there's a point where two women have a discussion about the body. One asks, "Could you have loved me without my body, leaving out my body?" What is that about?

BROSSARD I have noticed that sometimes women living together as a couple don't seem to have a sexual life that is very important. So in that dialogue I wanted to raise the question: Are you a lesbian because of your inclination toward another woman or because you make love with her? Are you a lesbian because you value another woman symbolically; or is it what you learn by making love with her that makes you a lesbian? I like that dialogue because it is at the core of lesbian emotion. Is that emotion coming from sexual desire, or from a longing through a woman for her gender?

In that dialogue, one of the women says, yes, I would have loved you even if I'd had to go around your body, and the other replies, but love is about kissing, touching; sex is vital to love. I personally agree with the one who says: do it. Desire and love-making mobilize imagination. Desire is a powerful and creative emotion. It is a key word in my writing because it is energy, and with energy we can transform language. Language does not transform itself only by intellectuality and rationalization, it moves and changes because of desire trying to make its way through it.

WACHTEL I was drawn to that dialogue between the two women, because in a sense we are misrepresenting your work if we talk only about its seriousness and experiments with language because there is also joy and eroticism and playfulness.

BROSSARD Oh, absolutely. I always used that expression, "the emotion of thought and the thought of emotion" to describe the seriousness and the pleasure of writing. I think that it takes both emotion and thought to be sharp. I don't believe you can think properly without emotion, pleasant or not, and if you are too emotional then you're "absent minded."

WACHTEL When you talk about the emotion of thought, the thought of emotion, I'm reminded about all the other contrasts in your writing. In *Mauve Desert* there's hot passion and cool detachment; there are cities and then there's the desert; there's the intuitive but also the theoretical.

BROSSARD I guess I'm like that myself. For example, usually a novel starts to become a necessity when obsessive images offer paths to a narrative. But at the same time I need something, a question, an enigma to be at stake in that novel. I like to explore in writing, and that exploration is made up of emotions, pleasure, fear. Exploring also means playing and learning from the process and the new ideas that come along. The same thing happens in poetry. The beauty of the language, the sound and the rhythm are very important for me, and at the same time I want to make propositions of thought. We have talked about desire as being a very important word in my work but I think that the word "question" now also figures prominently, especially in the novel that I am writing.

I want to keep questioning about the society in which I live, but even more about the shift of civilization which I feel we are entering. I find this very troubling because I want to be a contemporary subject. I don't want to exist in the past, historical or personal. I want to be able to understand all the dimensions of the civilization to which I belong. When I say that, I am of course thinking about new technologies — how they will affect the mythologies, the beliefs we have been relying on to figure out our place in the universe as well as to give meaning to life.

WACHTEL Is that what you refer to when you say "the shift of civilization"?

BROSSARD Yes, it is. I feel that somehow we have lost our poles of reference, as if we have entered a state of non-gravity, and this gives us the feeling that we have lost our sense of orientation. Our notion of time and space are changing. Beliefs which we have lived with since the Renaissance and the Enlightenment now seem obsolete. We are moving from the civilization of the written word to the civilization of the electronic image: from memory to instant future, from emotion to sensation, from human speed to electronic speed. I want to understand that shift. One way or another I am part of it, so I might as well try to understand. It's part of the task I assign myself, to be a contemporary subject.

WACHTEL There is widespread admiration for your work, for its passion, its brilliance, its depth. But occasionally there are grumblings about its inaccessibility: it's too difficult, too theoretical or too post-modern or too lesbian. How do you respond to that?

BROSSARD It's hard to respond to that. If I were trying to write in a much simpler way I don't think it would help anyone — neither myself nor the readers. The main thing for me is to be honest with myself in the writing, and whether the text is difficult or not, readers — lesbians, feminists — will recognize what is going on. I don't think that I should make any concessions. On the contrary. If you are a writer, then you have to go as far as you can think and desire, and this is what readers usually like about "their" writer. For me, writing is freedom, and freedom means to explore.

WACHTEL You were saying you want to be a contemporary subject. When you look back over several dozen books, how do you think your style has changed?

BROSSARD There is definitely a rupture between before being a feminist and lesbian, and after. I think the writing has changed formally; it has become rounder, more accessible and, with *Mauve Desert*, it has also become more linear, at least in the sentence — of course the structure might still be *déroutante* — but the sentence has become more fluid. In my current writing I see something changing in the rhythm. It's slower. Sometimes I have the *nostalgie* for those little very short lines, verses that you find in *Daydream Mechanics* or for the crazy sentences full of puns in *French Kiss*. I like the electricity in that writing. I definitely like the libidinal electricity which accounts for the glorious word-play and the tiny sharp moves in language. Like tattoos on the straight skin of "language as usual."

At the same time I think my changes in style have to do with the difference between the energy you have when you are twenty-two or thirty, and the energy, knowledge and experience that you have when you are fifty. Is there a relationship with libidinal energy? It's an interesting question because, if I am right in saying that writing is energy, energy obviously changes, and is spent differently over the course of one's life. The main thing for me is to keep the focus on questioning and on consciousness and, at the same time, on beauty.

WACHTEL Is death more important now? Does it have a more immediate presence at fifty-something than it did twenty years ago?

BROSSARD The word death has been in my poems since *Le Centre blanc* in 1970. But it was a word, an abstraction, a cultivated, philosophical, literary device more than a thought. Now death means that some friends have disappeared, a generation is gradually moving into old age. It makes me look at time in a different way. To think that we are just passing makes one more humble. Things which are so vital when you are twenty or thirty later become part of a movement, a flow of objects, of reality, of memory.

WACHTEL In a funny way you're a good girl again now; you're very established, you win a lot of literary prizes, there are films made about you. Do you still feel that you can make trouble?

BROSSARD I would hope that I can still make trouble and for the same end — greater awareness. I will follow my inner rhythm, my own questioning about society. I will take my time, because I think that everything goes very fast, and taking your time to write and to be lucid about what is going on inside yourself and around you is part of a writer's task. I want to give myself as much freedom as I can in order to be as honest as I can be in my writing, and at the same time keep in my heart that quest for beauty and for lucidity.

WACHTEL It's more than twenty years since those transformations that we were talking about. Have your preoccupations changed?

BROSSARD I think that in *The Aerial Letter* and in *Picture Theory*, I came to understand a lot about women and our interaction with the patriarchal system we have to deal with. Now I seem to be preoccupied with that shift of civilization we were talking about. I'm trying to understand what's going on and what's happening in Western culture, in ethics, values and science.

There are all these questions about the purpose of the writing, the purpose of the written word when the written word is failing. A lot of people are still reading and will be reading again and again, certainly, but we are entering a civilization where mainly you will be arguing with images; you will be looking at your screen more than looking at the horizon or at the weather, or being on the *terrasse*. There are things changing about the written word, about the library as a huge symbol of human knowledge. These are all thoughts which are with me whether as a proposition or, as I say, a question.

February 1995
interview initially prepared in collaboration
with Larry Scanlan

MARTIN AMIS

Martin Amis has been described as "the cleverest and most entertaining English writer of his age." Or, as *The New York Times* put it, "Mr. Amis is his generation's top literary dog." He is also its most notorious. Not only did the young Martin Amis *look* a little like Mick Jagger, he also had some of the bad boy's swagger.

The son of novelist and poet Kingsley Amis, who died (after this interview) in October 1995, Martin Amis wrote his first novel when he was only twenty-one. Around the same time, he got a first-class degree from Oxford. He wrote raucous books about adolescent sex, drugs and communal living. In his later novels, Amis took on class, nuclear weapons and environmental apocalypse.

Martin Amis is a satirist, which means he's serious about his laughter. His works include *London Fields* (1989), *The Moronic Inferno* (1986), *Money* (1984), *Other People* (1981), *Success* (1978), *Dead Babies* (1975) and *The Rachel Papers* (1973). His 1991 novel,

Time's Arrow, was a slender but ambitious book — tracing the life of a Nazi doctor backwards through the century, reversing "time's arrow." It is intense, inexorable and dark. But then Martin Amis came back with renewed ebullience, with a big comic novel called *The Information* (1995).

Revelling in irreverence, scathing in its satire and dazzling in the sheer energy of its language, *The Information* is about literary envy and the male mid-life crisis. What was unusual was the hype and gossip associated with the publication of this novel — what Amis himself referred to as being "caught up in some post-modern joke." First came his own mid-life crisis and the breakup of his marriage, along with a very public attachment to a glamorous American. Then came the book deal. Amis was looking for a £500,000 advance, or more than a million dollars upfront. In the process of negotiations, he jettisoned his long-time agent, who also happened to be the wife of his long-time friend, Julian Barnes, in favour of an aggressive New York agent, Andrew Wylie, whom the British papers dubbed "the jackal."

And just to keep things interesting, amid allegations of greed, A.S. Byatt jumped in and accused Amis of "male turkey cocking" and brought up the story of Amis' spending £20,000 on dental work in the United States. In my fifteen years of perusing literary news, I've never seen as much print devoted to any single story comparable to the ink spilled on Martin Amis in the spring and fall of 1995. There were features in *Vanity Fair*, *The New Yorker*, *Esquire* and virtually every English newspaper and magazine.

When I first met Martin Amis a couple of years ago to talk about *Time's Arrow*, I was struck by how thoughtful, sensitive and reflective he was — in other words, how *un*like the tone of his books. He saves his mockery for his characters. We spoke again in June 1995, this time about *The Information*.

WACHTEL You're known as an edgy, satirical writer, with a critical eye on society and a number of dark subjects that you've made your own. In *London Fields* there was decadent London and a sense of impending apocalypse; your story collection *Einstein's Monsters* concerned nuclear power; *Time's Arrow* focused on a Nazi doctor operating at Auschwitz. Maybe *drawn* isn't the right word, but are you drawn to exemplars of evil?

AMIS It's not something you set out to do, but yes, there would seem to be an imaginative attraction, which is tied up with repulsion. You are drawn to what most repels you as a writer — not every writer, but it certainly seems to be how it is for me. For instance, in *Time's Arrow*, I'm interested in what happens to the doctor who decides that he will start killing and stop feeling — a place perhaps not everyone wants to go to.

WACHTEL In *Time's Arrow* you change the direction of that arrow, you create a world that runs backwards, and at one level it's an interesting intellectual exercise to try to write a book backwards, but there also is a deeper purpose here because it's as if you're trying to make sense of a world that doesn't make sense going forwards, so you've got to try some other route. Is that why you wanted to tell the story backwards?

AMIS That's exactly right. I'm saying that Nazi Germany and Nazi ideology would have been what they thought it was, would have been a healing process, which was the term they always used — they were excising the gangrenous appendix of Jewry to make Germany whole, to heal the open wounds of the First World War and so on. And I'm saying that if you do turn time's arrow around, you come up with a world that is pathetic, meaningless, pointless, above all senseless, and the only thing in this inverted world that makes any sense is the Holocaust because in such a world it does become a healing process, a rejuvenation, a way of redeeming the country from its sins.

It has to be taken on board that as the Nazi idea formed, as the final solution formed, it wasn't just a gang of psychopaths getting together, saying, let's kill a lot of people, let's have an orgy of violence; they really did think they were doing something good and this is the way that great wrongs are committed, in the name of good.

The German medical profession, which emerges from the story with eternal disgrace, allowed itself to be persuaded that the way to heal was to kill, and this began with a euthanasia program run by the doctors, and in fact the more control the doctors had the wilder the euthanasia became. It started off with insane children. They were the first to be killed. No racial emphasis at that point. But by the time the doctors had taken full control of the euthanasia program, malingerers, grumblers, clubfoot, cleft palate — "unworthy mouths," as they were called, life that is unworthy of life — they were all being gassed. And this was a kind of dry run for the Holocaust. It showed that technically it could be done, and also that German society, as Primo Levi says, must accept general blame for this because it's inconceivable that people didn't know about these things. At these centres where euthanasia was being committed, there were locks of hair floating through the evening air.

But the innocent eye in a backwards-in-time world can be confronted with the Holocaust as a kind of magical event. The narrator of my novel, who starts to talk in a kind of stirring, Nazi-ish ideology language, can say that what we're doing here is dreaming a race down from the heavens, the race that will moreover make a huge contribution to German culture. They come down as smoke, they're transformed into women and children and men, they're then fattened up and given a lot of exercise; they're then reunited with their families on the ramp, they're then sent back to their homes or ghettos; the ghetto walls come down, they're taken back to their villages and normal life resumes, or starts, as it were. So the inversion is complete and it looks like a deed of full philanthropy when done backwards in time.

WACHTEL What did you learn from this backwards-in-time world?

AMIS There's an important image in Holocaust studies of the façade of Treblinka, I think — the façade of a railway station. This façade had the clock at the top of it frozen at four o'clock — because it was painted; it could never move to an earlier time or later time. This façade was very convincing and expertly done. A lot of talent was expended on, for example, signs saying Change

Here for Eastern Trains, Telephones, Changing Room, Ticket
Office, an arrow pointing — again, time's arrow. But in fact it
was just a prop and the arrow led to the gas chamber. This was
how an industrial intelligence, a modern capital-M intelligence
went at this "problem." It wasn't a question of drunken horsemen
galloping to a village with swinging swords, it was special trains
and manifests and quotas and lists and all the apparatus of an
industrial society turned to a reptilian end.

WACHTEL You chose a narrator who is a naïf; he's the voice, or
maybe the soul, inside the body of this Nazi doctor who's getting
younger and younger and who's heading back to his destiny from
death in America to birth in Germany. Who is this narrator?

AMIS I did intend him to be the soul that was, as it were, absent
during the doctor's life, or cancelled forever, after an hour in
Auschwitz. I tried to write about this Nazi doctor without much
human sympathy because I felt none for him, but as soon as the
book arrived at Auschwitz towards the end, I found it impossible
to write about this doctor as if he wasn't paying a huge human
cost for what he was doing, and I do very firmly believe now that
people who submit to the herd instinct that brings about atroci-
ties of this kind are finished forever as soon as they start doing it.
It's as if their soul is banished.

In this novel it's the soul who has to analyse and judge, the
soul that, in the last sentence of the book, wonders whether he
just came too late or at the wrong time, because he was never a
guiding presence in real life. The reader is in the position of rewriting, as it were, everything that happens from his own historical knowledge. The narrator says that the dental work on the
Jews was done before the reviving process to spare them unnecessary suffering, but the reader knows that the opposite was the
case, and so the reader has to become a kind of soul or conscience
and has to do the moral reordering from his chair.

WACHTEL Why did you want to take on such a difficult and
loaded subject as the Holocaust?

AMIS I was thinking of writing a story of a man's life backwards
in time and then I read a book by a friend of mine, Robert J.

Lipton's *The Nazi Doctors*. Before he handed this book to me, I would have said that of all living writers I was the least likely ever to take on the subject of the Holocaust, which has fascinated and appalled me, gripped me for many years. I just thought, this can't be for me. But after a couple of days of reading Lipton's book, I saw that in fact I was going to write about it. I thought if you did this world backwards, there would be a real point — the inversion is so complete. And the inversion that Lipton talks about is "the healing-killing paradox."

I felt I was in a forest of taboos throughout writing this book. This is the most difficult and sensitive subject ever, I think, but I do believe, as a writer, that there are no "No Entry" signs. People say, legitimately in a way, what am I as an Aryan doing with this subject? But I'm writing not about the Jews, I'm writing about the perpetrators, and they are my brothers, if you like. I feel a kind of responsibility in my Aryanness for what happened. That is my racial link with these events, not with the sufferers but with the perpetrators.

For someone of my age, mid-forties, the Holocaust dawned on me when I saw these images that we all have in our heads — the chimneys, the bulldozed corpses — and I remember saying to my mother as a child, "What was that all about?" And she said, I think quite sweetly really, to protect me, "Oh, don't worry about it. Hitler would have loved you, you've got blond hair and blue eyes." I remember feeling a sigh of ignoble relief at this. I thought, "Phew! At least it wouldn't happen to me." That perhaps was the germ of *Time's Arrow*.

WACHTEL Let's shift now to your new novel, *The Information*. Why did you choose to call it that?

AMIS It's one of those titles that presents itself early on. It refers to about half a dozen things: the information *on* someone, the dirt on someone; the information revolution; one character informing another, like a succubus; and the certainty or the knowledge that you're going to die, and how this affects the male ego. It means a concatenation of things. The most central meaning has to do with this inimitable information that you're not going to get away with it. Around about the age of forty you realize the jig is up and this long-delayed realization, that in fact death means business with you, provokes an overreaction known as the mid-life crisis. Then it passes and you're left sadder and wiser and also you're a bit more grown up and liberated in a way by this tough knowledge. But for a year or two you're in the overreaction stage and that's why men buy sports cars and run off with eleven-year-old girls and all the rest of it.

WACHTEL I'm interested in several aspects of information that you raise, and in an essay of yours called "Nuclear City" you talk about how there's no understanding to be had, only more know-ledge or information. Is there any way that knowledge *can* lead to understanding?

AMIS There are certain kinds of truths that are hard to take but are liberating. You might even say that the Renaissance was pow-ered by Copernicus and Galileo, who were telling us that the earth orbited the sun and not the other way around, thus demot-ing us from centrality in the universe. This notion was savagely resisted, but its effect was liberating. You think, no one knew this before we came along, all your precursors laboured under a pathetic, egotistical illusion of centrality. That kind of realization makes you grow up and gives you some energy. I think the equiv-alent thing will happen in the next century with the discoveries of our time, discoveries about the size of the universe, and so on. I think there are certain kinds of salutary knowledge that one is quite flattered to learn.

WACHTEL I was thinking before about one of the aspects of infor-mation, the information revolution, the notion that we live in an information age. You said that it changes the way we see our-selves. What were you thinking of there?

AMIS I'm not talking so much about the Internet and all the rest of that, I'm talking about the great proletarian art form of tele-vision, which gives us hourly disasters but also gives us various kinds of crude drama. After a generation of that, I think people have fallen into the habit of seeing themselves from the outside. They don't have just the usual pangs and urges, they wonder about

the shape of their lives; they think, am I a victim, am I a preda-
tor, am I being used? The language of crude drama is how we
have come to interpret our own lives.

WACHTEL In *The Information* there are a lot of allusions to the
physical universe, and how the planets are related, the sun is
dying, time-in-space formulations. What got you interested in
astronomy?

AMIS I've always been very interested and as I started to read, I
realized that this was a subject that thrilled me. I read very unsys-
tematically but I read a lot. Astronomy gives you a sense of how
incredibly isolated, remote, vulnerable and rare this planet is, and
it makes you feel that in the future perhaps, if everyone shared this
understanding, we would pull together as a species more, and the
kind of barbaric border war that we're seeing in Bosnia would
look stupid in this vast context of the universe.

I expect something of the kind to happen in the next century, that there will be a revolution in consciousness about our
place in the universe. We've taken a terrific pasting in this century. In 1920, you know, even people like Einstein thought that
the galaxy was it, that the Milky Way was the extent of the universe. Then with Edwin Hubble and his observations we realized
that those little cloudy bits in our galaxy are not nebulae but
other galaxies beyond the Milky Way, and since then, since the
twenties, the universe has been bounding out away from us at
many, many times the speed of light. Intellectually, we've had to
wrap our heads around an hysterically expanding universe, and it's
beginning to look as though there are an infinity of parallel universes too; this is what people are now more and more unani-
mous about in this branch of knowledge. So we're getting tinier
and more remote all the time. This will have an effect, I believe.

WACHTEL You're suggesting a fairly positive outcome, that our
species might bond together better in relation to the vastness of
the galaxies and the ever greater universes, but at one point in *The
Information*, your central character, Richard, as the failed novelist,
invokes the planets to develop his theory of the history of increasing humiliation. Can you elaborate on that theory of his?

AMIS The history of astronomy is the history of increasing hu-miliation. We have gone from amply filling the centre of the uni-verse to a remote outpost on an average galaxy. You begin with gods — this would be around Homer's time, when they thought the world was flat; then demi-gods, Virgil — Virgil knew the world was round; then tragedy, failed heroes. And then after Copernicus and Galileo you get social realism, which is about you and me, and then in the twentieth century you get the age of irony, low-life. And then what? Are we going to write cockroach novels or rat novels? The character poses the question, which I have fre-quently posed myself: How can we go on like this? It's crying out for renewal, isn't it, this cycle? That might well be what happens; we'll go back to gods and work our way down all over again.

WACHTEL So you agree with Richard in his analysis of the decline of the literary protagonist?

AMIS I think it's an intriguing possibility that, as we get smaller in the universe, as our centrality is questioned and then abolished, our opinion of ourselves goes down. I think these things do not progress in a straight line forever and we've run up against a brick wall. The investigation in the twentieth century has not been into how good someone can be, it's been into how bad someone can be. We've done very well and, as we reach the end of the century and the end of the millennium, we've pretty well exhausted tur-pitude and evil. You can't just go on making people worse and worse, so some sort of turnaround seems in the air, seems likely.

WACHTEL It's interesting to hear *you* say this because turpitude and evil have been your subjects.

AMIS Absolutely. I've often set out to create the worst characters I possibly could, just to see how bad I can make them. You keep on being surprised by how even your worst characters get a fol-lowing and people like them. Updike said that it's very mysteri-ous who we like in fiction. And by *like* I don't mean want to have around for the evening, I mean enjoy the company of on the page, protected by these nice hard covers. And it turns out that the sophisticated reader doesn't like goodness. Perhaps only Tolstoy has made goodness swing on the page so that it's fun to read about.

And Updike says, what it turns out we like is life, and if a character is alive it doesn't really matter what they do, we're going to want to read about them. If vigour is there, we will follow vigour.

WACHTEL You've said yourself you haven't ever created a character that you've hated.

AMIS No, because your characters are rather like your children in that you don't like your children for their qualities. It's not because they're so cute or they say such funny things; they come equipped with your love.

WACHTEL *The Information* is about, among other things, a literary rivalry. There are two friends, initially they're friends, writing books. Gwyn writes novels that are simple, unsophisticated, New Age pap; Richard writes novels that are modernist and impenetrable. Gwyn is extremely successful. To what extent are you creating an indictment of contemporary standards?

AMIS There is a suggestion that the culture is or will be capable of liking literature that does nothing except not give offence. The cultural political euphemism is certainly pointing that way. I call it that rather than "PC," or politically correct, because that label is going to be dead in a couple of years. But the impulse towards political euphemism has been around in America for a long time and will continue.

Euphemism is the enemy of the novelist. In this book I have a black character who is a driving instructor, and whose driving and whose personal rhythm are affectionately satirized, and I have a Jew who is mean — I'm almost programmatically saying I must be allowed to have these characters; such people do exist. That's a way of holding out against processed fiction. It's now common practice to go into the past and savage writers for not having modern attitudes, which I once compared to a school of seventeenth-century Italian art critics spending all their time jeering at their predecessors for not knowing about perspective. What kind of occupation is that? The self develops; the trouble with political euphemism is that it denies that fact. It doesn't see that this is all a process, an evolution. We're never going to get to the point where we have these cleansed personalities that are free of atavism; we're all racists and we hope to get less racist. We're racist because we like our families, because we're clannish. But the political euphemists proclaim that they have succeeded in cleansing their natures of these ancient atavisms. And it's bullshit, it's a lie, and it creates great anxiety in them, which is why political euphemism is so open to a thought-police attitude, always checking up on each other's progress and standards.

WACHTEL To bring it back in terms of your novel, though, you obviously create quite amusing extremes. Richard's novel is not only impenetrable but it makes people physically ill when they try to read it. You also comment on today's audience for literature. For instance, when Richard is on an airplane the people in Coach, or as we call it Economy, are reading George Eliot and Homer and the people in Business Class are reading thrillers and the people in First Class aren't reading at all.

AMIS Or they're reading perfume catalogues. But I have no worries about the health of the novel. It's pronounced dead every ten years and then every eleven years we go into the hospital ward and find that the novel is sitting up in bed and having a cup of broth and feeling much better. When you read a novel you're communing with the author in a very intimate way that's hard to duplicate, and I think people will always want to do that in book form. This somehow answers to the experience of communing with another mind. You have this little oblong, heavy shape on your lap and you can pause and reread and go back a page and write in the margin. This communing is inseparable from the experience of reading.

WACHTEL But in terms of the literary standards that you're satirizing or questioning in your novel, you say that when talking about beauty in the heavens and the flesh we can quickly agree about it, but not on the page. Why?

AMIS There's absolutely no way of establishing whether one line of poetry is better than another, although we all kind of know, don't we? A great deal of very high-level intellectual energy has gone into trying to establish ways of separating the excellent from the not-so-excellent. The last word on all this has been written by Northrop Frye, who ripped up the literary value judgment and threw it out in the fifties in his book *The Anatomy of Criticism.* The introduction to that book spells the end of the value judgment for ever. You cannot tell whether one book is better than another; all you can do is labour the point. But what does happen, or has always happened, is that time sorts this out, and after a few centuries it's very clear that Milton is more rewarding to study than Lascelles Abercrombie or Shackerley Marmion. The more this strikes you, the less you are going to want to labour the point, it's just evident.

WACHTEL You have said that comedy is really the only form left. Why?

AMIS On the whole I do feel that comedy is the only form left. The reason why comedy looks so odd is that tragedy doesn't exist any more, it doesn't resonate — no one's going to believe in it any more. So comedy is having to take on all the real ills, the refugees from other genres. The original butts of comedy used to be buffoonery, pretension, pedantry, but now they have to include murder and child abuse, the decay of society. Dickens, a comic writer of another age, dealt with his villains by either tritely punishing them or improbably converting them. But the old schema no longer work. We know that evil isn't necessarily punished any more than good is necessarily rewarded. I think now we can deal with iniquity only by sneering and laughing it off the stage. It's all you can do because you know that in real life it's not going to be converted or punished, it will go on. There's a lovely bit of Nabokov in one of his lectures where he said: You do not punish the criminal in his armchair by having a conspirator tiptoe up behind him with a pistol; you punish him by watching that little finger of his probing in a profitable nostril. You watch him picking his nose, that's how you get your own back as a writer. You use ridicule, not an obsolescent machinery of punishment and conversion because that just doesn't convince any more.

I also feel that the old nineteenth-century views about motivation have exhausted themselves. Motivation is now nothing more than literary convention. I don't think people in the real world are coherently motivated. Timothy McVeigh, the Oklahoma bomber, thinks he's got motives but they're not cogent — they're very much of someone who sees himself on the outside, as a kind of Rambo figure, full of second-hand paranoid fantasies. Whatever the power of these images, they definitely got into his head and kicked the place apart some time ago. Motivation in the A.C. Bradley nineteenth-century Shakespearean criticism sense has gone, in my view. It's absented itself from human action.

WACHTEL You're a moralist and you write about bad behaviour and sleaze and decline, but you've said that your touchstone — that's not exactly your word but something like that — is innocence. What does that mean?

AMIS I was trying to grasp the difference between my father's moral scheme and mine, and it occurred to me that what he prizes is decency. And when I look for the positive values in my books, I find they are always represented by innocence, by a child — the metaphor always seems to be the sky, clouds, things that are guiltless, and that seems to be what I prize. Innocence is definitely what the world is losing. It's an illusion to think that the world is getting worse; everyone has always thought that. Scraps of papyrus six thousand years old when translated say children no longer respect their parents. Where have they gone, the good guys? That's a recurring human illusion. But we do know for sure that the world is getting less innocent all the time simply because of the accumulation of experience. And you'll notice that children now lose their innocence increasingly early.

WACHTEL Certainly innocence is hard to find in your writing. I think in *The Information* the only tenderness, which is perhaps a close relative, is towards children — for instance, Richard in relation to his sons.

AMIS Yes. In fact without that he would be hard to sympathize with at all; it is the only time when he's kind of off-duty, and grosser feeling is replaced by gentle feeling.

WACHTEL I'd like to go back to the questions of literary rivalry, jealousy, envy, competitiveness. Why are these subjects so important to you?

AMIS I don't think they necessarily are very important to me, but once I began writing, they became important to me for the purposes of this book. I never thought about it in the early years of writing this novel, but I've since come to the conclusion that I am uniquely placed to write about this subject in that I don't think there's ever been a case of father-and-son writers who have both had a body of work out there at the same time, who are both, to quote my father, "some good" and are contemporaries as well. I grew up in a household that had a writer in it, and nothing is less exotic than what your dad does. So writing has never been exotic to me. I think, why isn't everyone doing it? It seems to be a very natural thing to do. But I do have all these writerly envies and ridiculous flashes of megalomania and all the rest. I can run with these feelings and thoughts, but I can also detach myself very quickly from them and inspect them for their comic value, as I do in this book. I have a take on it that's different and I perhaps am more objective about it than any other writer could be. So it was my duty to give my version.

WACHTEL Although hearing you talk about detaching yourself from it, with all the discussion about your seeking a large advance for this novel, one of the things that struck me was where you said, "It's not the money, it's to see what I'm worth." Is that the measure?

AMIS No, it's the measure of the market for literary fiction, it's not the measure of me. One of the strange locks that operate on a writer is that you're never going to know how good you are, because that all gets decided when you're gone. No review, prize, gong, sash, bauble, advance is going to tell you what you want to know. So the advance doesn't tell me anything about myself, but what my rate is in the marketplace. And for some reason to do with my own mid-life thrashings, I did want to know that. But it's not the case that I fetishized this figure out of the air [£500,000] and demanded it. It was a rollercoaster, the whole thing, and as soon as it was being aired in public, as it was within seconds of the first meeting, I never felt I was in control. I was a pincushion from then on.

WACHTEL I was thinking about the whole theme of pairs and doubleness in your work. There are two rival novelists in *The Information*. There are also twins in this novel, two young boys who are at each other's throats, and then in your story "Career Move" there are two opposing characters, a screenwriter and a poet in tandem. In your novel *London Fields*, there's the good lover, the bad lover. Why are you drawn to doubles?

AMIS I've wondered about that too, and I think it probably goes back to childhood and my having an older brother, Philip, who was very close in age but a lot bigger than I was, and the obsession of small differences comes in. My father once found me in floods of tears, lying on and beating the floor, and he asked what the matter was, and after several husky intakes of breath I managed to say, "Philip had a biscuit."

It's there all the way through. As you say, in *London Fields* there is the good lover and the bad lover. I think it's a comic device. Many writers would have just one lover who was sometimes good, sometimes bad, sometimes vicious, sometimes romantic, sometimes lustful. Similarly, in *The Information,* many writers would have had just one writer character who sometimes felt neglected and sometimes felt over-rewarded. I'm not that kind of writer. I write of huge disparities and vicious invidiousnesses. It's been said that my writing deals with banalities rendered with tremendous force. I've always liked that verdict, I'm quite happy with it. There are plenty of people writing novels about subtle gradations within one mind. Comedy comes into the gap that you create between people when you force them apart, when you make the division extreme — that's where comedy lives. And that's what I'm always in search of — the comedy of the disparity. So for instance, Gwyn sells hundreds of thousands of books and gets the whole treatment and Richard doesn't sell one book, and when he thinks he's sold one book, the guy returns it on the last stop of his tour. That's how sharp the division is.

WACHTEL But Richard is in a way the vehicle for your own mid-life crisis, and he is the failure.

AMIS I depended on the crucible of the imagination for that aspect of it, because the only aspect of the mid-life crisis that I *haven't* had is what I'm sure is the most universal of all: waking up in the night thinking about all you haven't done and all you were hoping to do when you were nineteen, and realizing nothing is going to happen now, this is more or less it, and there are going to be no sudden expansions from here on in. This is the verdict, this is the information on your life performance. I don't have that because I've done more than I thought I was going to do. But we all live in our failures; we never give ourselves credit for a damn thing. And funnily enough, success is a drag. As a subject, success is just cornball. It's not interesting — it's always the same. But failure is rich and complicated and plangent.

WACHTEL In *The Information* you play with the omniscient narrator, with the initials "M.A."

AMIS I'm present for the first half of this book. I make perhaps a dozen appearances, and I'm present in the first sentence in a phrase like "I said, so I feel." And then I absent myself from the book and, as it were, let them get on with it without me. It's hard to give the artistic justification for that. In some ways I felt I had to tell the reader where I was coming from in this book, I don't know why. It's not at all autobiographical, but it is very personal. The other thing is that as I absent myself in the novel, the information is telling me to stop saying "hi" and to start saying "bye." When novelists arrive, they're saying to their readers, Hi! you know, I can do this, I can do that, I can be funny, I can amuse you, entertain you, delight you, instruct you, all these things. They're saying: I notice this about the world. Have you ever noticed this about the world? After your mid-life visit from death, you realize that in a sense you've stopped saying "hi" and now the world has a different coloration because you are making your very earliest preparations to leave it. And so halfway through the book I say "bye." That's kind of a cheat and a play on words but it had to do with that feeling.

WACHTEL How do you prepare to leave the world?

AMIS You ready yourself, brace yourself. Like the history of increasing humiliation, at least it's gradual, the news is a long time coming. There's a beautiful phrase in *Herzog*, Saul Bellow's novel, where the character goes to see an ex-girlfriend, five years after their affair, and he's describing her face and talks about the lines under her eyes, and he says, "Death, the artist, very slow." The funeral-parlour director is already putting on your dabs of make-up for the last appearance. You've got to get on sober terms with it, that's all.

WACHTEL Is there something gained as well as lost by passing through a mid-life crisis?

AMIS You definitely come out the other side of it thinking, well, that's not so bad, I've still got one leg and this arm sometimes works. You think you've got life taped at thirty-eight, it's almost boringly transparent to you, and then suddenly you don't know anything at all. You're in a strange land where you don't know how to use the currency and you don't know how to get around on the subway, you don't speak the language, your knowledge is wiped out. Everything you knew beforehand is of no use to you, and what you have to do is learn the P's and Q's of the second half of life. Conrad said every ten years we have to learn a new set of rules, and that's why we're children all our lives. I think that's a great remark but I feel that actually you have to learn a whole new textbook when you're forty. You actually notice things that you couldn't have noticed earlier.

My favourite example in the novel is where Richard is on an airplane and he sees two or three women crying, and he realizes they have always been there, these women, but before he had thought they'd had rows with their boyfriends. Now, at forty, he knows that women on planes are crying because someone they loved is dead or dying somewhere else on the planet. The death awareness wasn't there — you weren't ready — and then suddenly at forty-odd you think, Jesus, why couldn't I have seen that that was what it was? So it's exciting learning these death tips.

WACHTEL There's a moment in the novel when Richard's wife suggests he give up writing because it doesn't pay. Richard's response is that he couldn't because then he would be left with experience, untranslated and unmediated experience, because then he'd be left with life. This was a moment where, even though you hadn't been calling yourself M.A., I felt it was you.

AMIS Yes. I don't know how people get through life without being artists in some way. Life would seem terrifyingly thin to me if I wasn't constantly reshaping it in my head. Life's just not shapely enough, it would look like a mess of days to me if I weren't a writer. It needs this other dimension, which is the shape and form and humour you give it in your thoughts. I really do feel that and it fills me with terror to think of not being a writer, not having that dimension, not communing with yourself about the world in this way.

January 1993/June 1995
interview initially prepared in collaboration
with Sandra Rabinovitch and Mary Stinson

JAMAICA KINCAID

I first came across Jamaica Kincaid's work in *The New Yorker*: powerful, moving stories about a young girl and her mother on the Caribbean island of Antigua. Kincaid recounts an intense relationship and in story after story she probes its force, its fragility and her own profound ambivalence.

To write about mothers and daughters is not particularly unusual, but Kincaid's stories have an obsessiveness, a lyricism and a poignancy that sets them apart. As the daughter in one of these stories says about her mother's withdrawal of affection, "For ten of my nineteen years, I had been mourning the end of a love affair, perhaps the only true love in my whole life I would ever know."

Kincaid's growing up stories were linked in a novel called *Annie John* (1985), one of three finalists for the international Ritz Hemingway Award. Her next book, *Lucy* (1990), follows her alter ego to New York, where she works as a live-in nanny for an affluent, liberal family. Kincaid herself left Antigua when she was seventeen (in 1966). She'd grown up in a house without electricity or water, and she too started off as an *au pair* in New York. As Kincaid recently put it, "Everything in my writing is autobiographical — down to the punctuation."

She chose the name Jamaica Kincaid when she was in her early twenties. She'd been born Elaine Potter Richardson, but she changed it when she started writing because she thought a new name would free her to say fierce things about the people around her. Kincaid still writes fierce things but doesn't care any more who knows or recognizes themselves. Her most recent novel is *The Autobiography of My Mother* (1996). It's narrated by the seventy-year-old Xuela Claudette Richardson and, while it continues some of Kincaid's earlier themes, it goes further in its uncompromising portrait of a woman determined to take hold of her life and resist the comforts of a more conventional existence.

Jamaica Kincaid is married to Allen Shawn, a composer who's the son of *The New Yorker*'s late editor William Shawn. She once said that when she first started working for *The New Yorker*, people at parties would ask her how she got the job. "Oh, my father is the editor," she'd joke. The couple live with their children near Bennington, Vermont. Kincaid has written about her house and about gardening — cross-cultural gardens, historical gardens, and just plain planting and thinking about gardens — for *The New Yorker*, pieces to be collected in a book in 1997.

This interview took place in two parts — both, unfortunately, over the phone — in June 1993 and February 1996. Not only does Kincaid speak with remarkable candour and without affectation, but you feel she's someone who would really say *anything*.

WACHTEL You've now lived in the United States longer than you lived in Antigua, but your writing continues to come out of that early experience. Would it make any sense to say that you have an American life and an Antiguan imagination?

KINCAID I suppose you could say so. I seem to have most of the values that are considered American, and even if I don't have them, even if I, for instance, don't support war in the Persian Gulf — which I don't — I enjoy the fruits of the war in the Persian Gulf just as much as the person who was for the war. So I suppose I have an American life, for good or bad, and I still write about the place I am from. But I would just say I am in exile somewhere, which is a wonderful thing about America: You can place yourself in exile in it. You can live in America for the rest of your entire life and remain the person you were. It allows you that. There isn't really any one American identity that all Americans agree on, except, I suppose, the Bill of Rights. But that's not an identity: that's a frame of mind, and anybody can have it, anywhere.

WACHTEL What you're saying sounds different from what is commonly thought of as the American melting pot.

KINCAID I think in some ways that's always been a myth, but when the American melting pot works, it does so because everyone agrees to melt into a European. The melting is into an Anglo-American person, but more and more people defy that. They've decided that that's not attractive — and it really isn't. Even as I live in America and can vote and do all the things an American can do, I don't feel I'm an American in a certain way. I feel that a lot of American things have collected on me, like driftwood or something in the sea.

WACHTEL So you're an exile with American barnacles.

KINCAID Yes, with American barnacles.

WACHTEL You've been writing about gardening in *The New Yorker* magazine — pieces to be collected in a book. In one, you analyse the way that flowers and plants in Antigua reflect its colonial history, and at the same time you confess to enjoying most of the seasons in New England and planting your own garden in Vermont. Do you feel any sense of balance between the two places, between your current and your past homes?

KINCAID Balance implies a kind of satisfaction. No, I don't feel any balance. I live this life of contradiction. I am someone who comes from the bottom of the world. And I now find myself at the top of the world and I take my place quite nicely and with no regrets, and I hope I have a conscience but not enough to stop myself from enjoying more than my share of the world. I have lots. I have far too much! I live in a very big house, I have land, I have a garden, and I grow things organically, and I'm sure each tomato costs ten dollars the way I grow it, and I'm debating with myself whether I should grow food that is the diet of some poor Indians in Peru. But I just go right ahead and do all these disgusting things. I like my life; I only wish I had more of it.

Balance? No. I hope never to have balance. I suspect if I have so much as balance, the next thing I know I'll be voting Republican or something criminal like that! No, I'm totally unbalanced.

WACHTEL Antigua was originally a slave colony and it remained in British hands until 1981. You've written that the Antiguan character is influenced by and is inherited — by conquest — from the English. Can you describe the legacy of that character?

KINCAID I think I'm actually in the last generation to be that influenced by it. In my generation, we are very English in some way, certainly through literature, and we see the world not in a European but in an English way. The legacy of conquest is mostly in forms of cruelty: not love and sympathy and charity, but brutality. Part of that legacy is the way people abandon their children and go off.

WACHTEL What do you mean abandon their children and go off?

KINCAID People would leave their children and go and work in Canada or England. It's very much a theme in a lot of writing — not my own, because I had this unusual mother who I knew would not abandon me. But there's a great deal of abandonment in West Indian literature and in West Indian life. In Antiguan life people leave each other, people who you would normally think would love each other, they just go. The legacy is in the cruelty between ordinary people. I would say that typical of all colonial life or colonial existence is a legacy of not really being interested in who you are or who you might be, so that the things you would normally think of as culture — an interest in each other and how you live — doesn't really exist. To put it in one word, cruelty is the legacy of this experience.

WACHTEL I'm surprised to hear that because usually when people write about their own society — independent of the colonial enterprise — there's a tendency if anything to romanticize their own people rather than discern something as uncomfortable and unpleasant as cruelty.

KINCAID Yes, there is a tendency to say that in spite of this history we remain marvellous and wonderful, but it's just not true, in my experience anyway. All you have to do is go to places where colonial rule was very strong and very successful: Africa, the Caribbean, certain other parts of the world. Africa is a disaster. I don't know if it will ever be healed. To say once the colonizers left that they hadn't touched the African people's spirit — well, it's not true. Africans are very cruel to each other; you only have to look at all those starving people. How can any African leader look at the faces of his or her people and not be very moved? Well, they don't seem to be very moved; they continue, and actually in a worse way, what had happened when colonialism existed. The truth is that the legacy of colonialism everywhere is cruelty and brutality and theft. What the colonizers did in a mild way we now do to each other in an exaggerated, grotesque way. We do it full force, you know. So maybe under colonial rule, Africans ate very little; under African rule, Africans eat not at all — and so on. In the West Indies, it's not as exaggerated as the African situation and the West Indies was never run as cruelly as Africa — there wasn't as much there to exploit, I suppose. But after colonialism ended, the rulers in the West Indies ruled people somewhat worse than the colonizers did. There had been certain things that Antiguans could take for granted, such as health care, education, the things you call infrastructure; they wouldn't be as good as the things in England, but they were there. Well, they aren't there any more under self-rule. Hospitals are bad, very bad, if they exist. I never saw malnutrition when I was a child. There is malnutrition in Antigua now. There's no reason to romanticize it unless you wish to perpetuate it.

WACHTEL Was there a particular event or moment that you can remember when you first recognized and refused the colonial inheritance?

KINCAID I remember, and I don't know how, that I thought "Rule Britannia" was odd to sing because it has in it those words, "Britons never shall be slaves." I remember finding that odd, and so I suppose that was the beginning of something. It is true that my mother did get very excited at the thought of Princess Margaret visiting the West Indies on a famous trip she took. Her family wanted to divert her from an affair with a married man and sent her on a tour of the West Indies, and the entire West Indies got very excited by her presence. I think there was a moment when she came and I was forced to become a Brownie or something; I think that must have been the beginning of realizing that there was something wrong. Ever since I can remember myself as a person, I've had very anti-colonial feelings and very anti-British feelings. But it's very odd because the only language I can express it in is the language of English, or the language of my tormentors. It's sort of delicious in some way.

WACHTEL Like your characters, Annie John and Lucy, you left Antigua as a teenager to make your way in the world; you were only seventeen. Did it feel like an escape?

KINCAID No, because I couldn't have handled that. To have realized it was an escape would have meant that I understood where I was going. It would have meant that I understood something about myself and I couldn't have tolerated that knowledge then. In retrospect, yes, it was an escape and somehow I knew I would never return. I think I felt I would rather be dead. Yet I risked a great deal, you know. I went to this country where I didn't know anyone, I went to live in places where I didn't know anyone. I decided to be a writer and I had no credentials. I just took all these chances and I didn't know how it would turn out. The one thing I did not have was self-consciousness. I didn't want to know what I was doing. So I would not have wanted to know that I was escaping, because I couldn't take that. I could only act on instinct. If I had stopped to think, I would have fallen into a precipice.

WACHTEL Do you know why that was?

KINCAID It was an enormous undertaking. Too much for a seventeen-year-old, I think. I'd grown up with love, certainly, and people had placed an unusual amount of faith in me. I had been given so much support, and I think to have wilfully removed myself from it was ultimately destructive to me. I couldn't have spoken to anyone then, the way I'm speaking now to you. Certainly not to myself. I was sort of moving into thin air. When I look at it, even now, I sometimes want to faint; it's like showing me a picture of someone walking across Niagara Falls on a thin wire. I don't know how I did it. So if I don't know how I did it now, and I have all this — a loving family, wonderful friends, a somewhat successful career — if even now I don't know how I did it and want to collapse, imagine what it was like when I was actually doing it, when I didn't have any of this. I couldn't afford to know!

WACHTEL In your novel *Lucy*, the narrator is a young Antiguan woman working as a nanny for an affluent American family, and there's a sense that she's shedding her skin. She's left home and now finds herself alienated from the values of white America. Did you feel between identities, like Lucy, or is even that too conscious an experience?

KINCAID That was too conscious an experience and I must say that, then and now, I don't make those distinctions about white America and black America, and that's not the distinction I would have made. I would have made the distinction between privilege and power and no privilege and no power. Those words — white Americans, black Americans — they're not the correct words to describe what it is that goes on. Skin colour is ultimately of no importance — it's a shorthand. So I didn't make those distinctions, and to me there are no such things as white values or black values: people do what they can when they can do it, and if they can get away with it, they do it. In *Lucy*, not once are the words "white" and "black" used for racial identification. It would have been false to have someone from her background be race conscious but not false for her to be conscious of the disparity in power.

WACHTEL Yes, in fact there is a scene when Lucy is travelling with her employer on a train and she does observe that all the people in the dining car look like her employer or her employer's relatives and all the people serving them look like her or her relatives.

KINCAID I think what people mean by white values are material things, and I've never seen anything wrong with having a very nice refrigerator — I now have one myself, thank you. I have all of it. And I don't support the means for getting it, like oppressing many people around the world, but once we've successfully done it, I simply line up and enjoy my share of it.

I'm not really interested in race. When you begin to think about race, you immediately diffuse what the real issue is, because when you talk about race what you are saying in fact is that there's a powerful group who can enforce the idea of race and there's a powerless group who has to *accept* the idea of race. But ordinarily you get out of bed in the morning and the first thing that comes to you isn't, now, my race. The first thing that probably comes to you is how queasy you feel, the shock of reacquainting yourself with the cold world, or the warm world; no matter what your circumstance, the world is incredibly uncomfortable when you first step out of bed. And unless you are deeply psychologically deranged, the first thing you think about isn't your race, you think about being human and how hard that is.

WACHTEL But maybe the third or fourth thing that you're forced to think about is your race.

KINCAID Well, there you go: *forced* to think about. But in a normal world you don't think about it. In the world that I grew up in, which was quite a normal world, I did not think of race when I first got up, but my normal world was that everybody was black. So to me it's black people who are normal. I now live in a place where most everybody is not black, but since they don't mention that I'm black and I don't mention that they're not black, I forget that we are different, because we live in this small place, it's a little village, and we're all very nice to each other. It's possible that when they see me they're thinking, "Boy, she's black," but they never mention it, so I completely forget it.

I've always been fascinated by what would have happened to Africans if they had not accepted the beliefs of their conquerors. Even a simple thing such as, who made you? is a weapon. When people say someone is too political, what they're saying is that you are thinking about the everyday too much and you won't let anything slide.

It comes back to what would have happened to African people in this part of the world if they had not come to believe in Christianity, if they had continued to hold on to their sense of reality and insisted on its right to exist.

WACHTEL What would have happened had that been possible?

KINCAID I don't know exactly but I think about it all the time. The example we have is of course the Jews, who continue to believe what they have always believed. So what would have happened? I don't know. We all come to the same conundrum: how to live. I don't know what would have happened but from my privileged position, I think I would have liked it very much, since I can *choose* not to like it. It must be a great thing to see the people you've humiliated and defeated and destroyed come to believe in the same source of forgiveness and redemption that you, who did the horrible thing to them in the first place, believe in. Oh, it must be marvellous!

WACHTEL The character Lucy is emotionally ruthless in carving out an identity for herself. She won't be weighed down by her past, she won't answer to her family or friends or lovers; sometimes literally she won't answer her own mother's letters. Is that necessary in order to free oneself?

KINCAID I think so, unless you plan to be a saint. I don't think one should live that way one's whole life, but it's entirely understandable and forgivable when you're young. If that's all you remain in a very long life, then after a while it turns against you, but it's a very useful thing to do at the beginning of your life, and I speak from experience.

WACHTEL This is something that you felt you had to do?

KINCAID Yes. I felt I had to ruthlessly carve out some space for myself. If someone had shown me the family I left behind, who had nourished and nurtured me — if someone had shown me them in a capsizing boat, and had said, if you sacrifice this turn you are about to make, which will bring you great self-assurance and confidence, if you sacrifice this one turn to save them, well, when I was twenty there's no question that I would have said "Let them go over." I wouldn't have made one sacrifice in my life to help. But that's not true any more. It would be a tragedy if I had remained like that.

WACHTEL But even to hear you say it now, it does shock a little, it seems quite extreme.

KINCAID Well, it may be shocking, but it's true. I try to be as true to my memory and to myself as I can, and I don't mean to make a mountain of how truthful I am — because I'm not really — but I know this to be true and I don't flinch from it. This is true and this was true of me. As I say, it would have been a terrible thing if, at forty-four years old, I would say that now. But I don't say that now. I *would* forego a turn in the road if I could help my family, my family that I left behind in Antigua. I would forego every good turn for the rest of my life for the family I now have, my children and my husband. What I mean to say is, I hope I'm not the same self-serving, self-absorbed, self-obsessed, ruthless person — ruthless on my own behalf — that I was when I was twenty. I believe that I am not; but I was such a person, and I do not, speaking to you, regret for one moment that I lived like that when I was in my twenties. If I were twenty again, and those choices were available to me, I would take them.

WACHTEL You were born Elaine Potter Richardson and over twenty years ago you chose the name Jamaica Kincaid. Why did you choose that name?

KINCAID I wanted to write and I was going to say brutal things about myself and my family and I did not want them to know it was me. But of course they immediately recognized themselves without my telling them and said, "Isn't this Elaine?" I've since legally changed my name. It's very odd to hear myself referred to as Elaine, and I always flinch whenever I meet somebody with that name. I can't imagine they're a nice person.

WACHTEL How did you find the name Jamaica Kincaid?

KINCAID I was experimenting. It does occur in literature, I think it may be Shaw or something. I was with friends and we were all calling ourselves different names, and I thought of that name and said, "That's my name." There were other versions of it, involving other islands, but that was the name that stuck. And you know, it being America, from the minute I said "This is my name," none of my friends ever called me anything else. And no one ever reminds me of it, everyone just accepts it. It's America: you just invent yourself. It's a great gift to the world, America is, at the expense of the people who used to live here.

WACHTEL The voice in your work, in *Annie John*, in *Lucy*, and in the non-fiction, is very distinctive; it's strong, it's poetic, and it certainly seems absolutely uncensored in its honesty. I think Susan Sontag talks about the emotional truthfulness in your voice. How did this voice emerge in you?

KINCAID I wish I knew. I'm glad it seems true, because it seems true to me that I'm being honest. I think I learned something in my life about shame. I think that if you're ashamed of something you must say it, because if you don't it gives people power over you. I try to say the things that I am ashamed of because I can't bear to be subject to anything. Again, this must come back to my obsession with powerful and powerless. There aren't too many bad things anyone can say about me; I've already said them about myself. If you're ashamed of something, it holds you in its sway. It can bring you to your knees. And I don't mind being on my knees, I just want to be the one to bring myself there. I search out in myself the things that I'm going to be ashamed of, and I say them.

WACHTEL That's interesting because in *Annie John* there's an instance where the girl is writing an essay in school and she censors it because she can't bear to show her mother in a bad light, but then she also admits that she couldn't bear to have anyone see how deeply in disfavour she herself was. She holds back from revealing what you — as the author — are prepared to reveal.

KINCAID She may not want other people to see, but *she* sees. I have really told everything in fiction. Sometimes even I'm surprised at some of the things that I've said. In some writing I'm doing now I say these very frank things about my family, and my husband, who reads everything I write, has said to me, "Oh, darling, are you sure you want to say this?" But I do, I try to be very frank. There are things I write down that are very deep family secrets, but then when I leave the typewriter I'm no longer that person. I don't go around standing on a street corner saying things about myself. I try to write down all of these things that have happened to me. I think I must have suffered greatly from shame when I was a child. Actually, I know I did, I was very ashamed of not only the perceived loss of my family's favour, when more children came into the family, but I think that as I grew older I began to be ashamed of various parts of my heritage and my family life. It turns out that my father wasn't my father, and I must have known but I didn't know because it was too shameful. I must have suffered a lot; it made me feel powerless. So now I've just written it all down.

WACHTEL We talked earlier about Lucy and her need to carve out her emotional independence and her refusal to let anyone lay claim to her. In just about all of your fiction the most powerful feelings of love or hate are centered on the relationship between a mother and a daughter. Can you talk about the power that this holds for you?

KINCAID As I grew older that hold between my mother and me lessened, and I suppose it's because I've become a mother myself. I'm at a stage of my life with my mother where I see her much more clearly than I ever did. But it's not as great as it used to be because it's been replaced by another kind of love, by other kinds of holds. I have two children and I have a husband, and so there's very little room in my life now for my mother and me.

I would say my daughter has a tremendous hold over me and I'm very interested in articulating it. I feel I know my daughter very well, which may be a mistake, and she, I'm sure, will find that a great burden, but I do feel I know her. The hold my son has over me I don't quite understand. I love him completely, but in a different way. He's more mysterious to me. I don't understand men, really, or masculinity. I often look at him with a kind of curiosity that I don't feel with my daughter at all.

Because I haven't known my daughter very long — she's only eight years old — I don't really know how to articulate the hold she has over me. I find it very interesting how much I love her and how much I depend on her, on seeing her, on being near her, and how much I worship her in some way. I think that it will be a very absorbing thing for me to see how that kind of hold develops. I think it may be quite difficult for me. I identify so strongly with her in her little ups and downs and ins and outs. Recently, she'd been away at camp and I hadn't seen her in a few days, and when I went to visit her I was stunned at how speechless I was in her presence, almost in awe. Maybe I'm just doomed to be in awe of these two powerful women at various times of my life — first my mother and now my daughter.

WACHTEL Listening to the way you talk about your daughter, how you worship her, and thinking about the way you write about your mother and your attachment to her, it does sound similar, even in the language you use.

KINCAID I do think of my daughter in that way. But she is worthy of it, as was my mother. You should ask my daughter — I don't know how she feels about me. We went somewhere and someone recognized me from my writing, and the person was very complimentary; much later my daughter told her father what had happened. I heard her and I said, "Oh, did it embarrass you?" and she said, "No, I was very proud of you," and she's eight years old. I can only tell you my feelings about her. I don't know what hers are. Maybe she feels a little bit overwhelmed.

WACHTEL The way you describe your relationship with your mother, it becomes mixed and turns on itself. It starts off almost paradisal, like the Garden of Eden, and then there's a kind of expulsion from the garden and there's a feeling as strong as hate and a desire to see her dead. When you talk about your daughter, are you worried that that might come back at you?

KINCAID I'm not worried about it; you can't worry about these things, they have a whole life of their own, and if it turns out to be that way, so be it. But I rather doubt it. My feelings of hatred for my mother did really have some basis in fact and I didn't just make it up. But the other thing you have to remember is how things get complicated in a person's psychology. I read *Paradise Lost* at a very early age and I did identify completely with Satan. It had been pointed out to me, long before I had this realization, that almost all of my work centres on the beginning of a paradise from which one falls and to which one can never return. When I was a child, I used to enjoy and torment myself at the same time by reading the Book of Revelations. It's quite possible that if I had read something entirely different I would not have modelled my entire literary life so far on *Paradise Lost*. You are articulating something that you didn't even know was an influence on me, but it was. When I was bad in school, I had to copy out verses of *Paradise Lost* as a punishment.

WACHTEL You didn't see your mother for nineteen years after you left home. Obviously you were a different person when you went back, but what was that like?

KINCAID I wasn't entirely a different person. I was older, but not altogether different. We picked up where we left off, and it's only been since then that I've actually grown up as, you know, as a child. It's incredible to me that if I hadn't had children, I might not have seen her again. I wanted to see her because I had become a mother and I didn't want to make the same mistakes. I didn't want my children not to see me for twenty years or however long it had been, so I went to see her. We resumed our relationship and I would say that phase of our relationship ended about three years ago, after she came to visit me and I had what might have been a nervous breakdown — I can't really tell. When I left Antigua for the first time I was a hundred and seven pounds, and I think when I saw her again I was a hundred and thirty pounds. Plus I had written two books. But I wasn't terribly different. There's more of a difference between that time and now. There's ten worlds of difference, because I am now no longer my mother's daughter, really.

WACHTEL You have a line at the end of *Annie John*, where your mother says, "It doesn't matter what you do or where you go, I'll always be your mother and this will always be your home."

KINCAID Yes, that's a very nice thing for a child to hear. You must never reject your children, but you have to allow them to reject you. In fact it's absolutely necessary for children to say, what art thou to me? It's required. If you do a good job, that's one of the rewards you get, they ask you, who are you? what have you to do with me? Absolutely nothing, is the answer. My husband and I went to visit my daughter in camp, as I told you, and she didn't quite say that but she was on the verge, and I thought, yes, we're doing a good job. She actually felt our presence was an intrusion in this wonderful world she had created for herself, and we were reminding her that she's our daughter. She was distant and almost dismissive, and we were thrilled!

WACHTEL The heroine of your novel, *Lucy*, says at one point that her creative assets are memory, anger and despair. What would you say are yours?

KINCAID Memory certainly. I'm not living a life that takes in more than simple sympathy for the person I used to be and for the person that I might still have been if not for some miracle that I'm living the life I lead. I don't know if many people in my position retain memory, but I do have memory. And anger.

I think that people are ashamed of anger. It's all right for a European man to be angry and perhaps now that privilege extends to European women. People find it rather upsetting when someone with my complexion and my gender gets angry. We start to say things that no one wants to hear, and if on top of that you have memory, it's really terrible. I still have memory and I still have anger. I don't have despair, but that just happens to be today. From time to time I have it, and I've written a great deal out of despair. That's another thing perhaps one's ashamed of, to be despairing or to be in a state of despair or to be unhappy somehow. But I'm often unhappy and I'm often in despair, not about things in my life today, though sometimes about those things too. I don't mind it. It's a part of life and sometimes it's crippling and sometimes it's not. Sometimes it's the greatest thing. I rush to my typewriter in such a state, in despair or in happiness. I don't have despair every day, but I think I have memory every day, and I certainly have anger if I think about things long enough. And I hope always to have those two things. I don't see why even a person with everything desirable in the world shouldn't have anger — after all, one will die. That's enough to make me angry.

WACHTEL The title of your latest novel is intriguing, *The Autobiography of My Mother*. Why did you decide to call it that?

KINCAID From the very beginning I knew that's what I was writing, the life of a certain kind of woman from the British-ruled West Indies. It wasn't my life and it wasn't my generation, but I wanted to say all sorts of things in a voice that seemed autobiographical. The tradition of autobiography of course is that it's your own life you're talking about, but I believe that I can trace my line legitimately through the maternal, and that all the female lives that came before mine are part of me, so I can think of it as my own life, my own biography, though strictly speaking it's not that at all.

WACHTEL Is it meant to be the life of your mother?

KINCAID Not at all, though it is her generation. I don't know that much about the intimate details of my mother's life, but some of the sense of self, a feeling that the woman in this book has of being in control of her own destiny — which is of course totally elusive — I sense that in my mother. Having authority over your own narrative, I feel that particularly in her. As I say, it's completely an illusion; no one has that kind of power, but one likes to think so.

WACHTEL You set up a puzzle for us because the woman in the story decides not to have children and yet it's "an autobiography of my mother." So already there's a paradox.

KINCAID Yes. I imagine a life in which I do not take place. None of us is sorry we were born; perhaps we wish for other beginnings. That's one of the answers to that question.

WACHTEL You've written a lot about mother-daughter relationships in your fiction. In this novel why did you decide to kill off the protagonist's mother in the first sentence of the book?

KINCAID I'm never thinking of my other writing when I write, I'm only thinking of what I'm writing at the moment. You put it in a much more pronounced way than I thought of it. That her mother dies sets up the whole point of how her life came to be. At her beginning she was living with her end, because in the natural progression of things, your parents make the inevitability of your own death seem impossible because you're still a child. When your absolute progenitor isn't there to protect you from your own end, then you live constantly with the reality that it's your turn next.

WACHTEL So you have the protagonist's mother die giving birth to her.

KINCAID Yes. And in a way it's the beginning of sterility, really, because there isn't any fertile ground being set up for her. No one is a mother to her, so she's incapable of continuing the progression. It ends with her.

WACHTEL Early on she decides that if no one loves her she will love no one —

KINCAID But she does love herself. She's perhaps narcissistic and self-centered, but that kind of narcissism is harmless if you don't have children. She does love herself, and if you can love yourself, really, the possibilities for extending it to other people are quite great. And you would have to admit that she is not unloving. She views everyone else with great sympathy. You have to be very careful; when someone can know themselves that clearly, they don't know themselves at all. I think she so often says that she's incapable of loving that you have to be suspicious.

WACHTEL Ah, another unreliable narrator.

KINCAID Exactly! Like most of life.

WACHTEL Language, or differences in dialect, seem to play a large part in your character's perception of the world. She doesn't speak until she's four years old and then her first words are spoken in English, not the French *patois* that the people around her speak. What does speaking English mean to her?

KINCAID Well, it's not so much what it means to her as what it means in the place she is. English, and proper English, is the language of legitimacy and the language of reality — all the things that are not described in the proper European language are not considered real; they are unreal and not to be taken seriously. And she recognizes instantly that the tongue that one speaks in is a weapon. She is aware that everything, even being allowed to breathe, is an act of power, an expression of power.

WACHTEL Your writing is wonderfully evocative and powerful but the vision of Caribbean people, both black and white, is quite bleak in *The Autobiography*. Do you think there is any way for this part of the world to overcome its legacy — of cruelty and brutality, as you say — left by the colonial masters?

KINCAID There's always hope. One lives for the future, when injustice will be wiped out. I think it's possible for everybody everywhere to overcome these difficulties. But the way you say it makes it sound as if we live happily ever after and the credits roll. I think life is complicated and up and down. The problem of injustice is not black and white or, as I say, racial, it's about the powerful and the powerless. One of the horrible things that black people in this part of the world have had to face is that their presence here would have been unimaginable without the help of their fellow Africans. So life is incredibly complicated. One longs for justice but it doesn't end with black people and white people kissing each other on the cheek; it's much more universal and complicated *and* simpler than that.

WACHTEL I'm not sure I was looking for happiness before the credits, but *The Autobiography* is not only a fine book, it's a fierce book.

KINCAID I wouldn't write anything but a fierce book, I hope never to write a book that makes you want to curl up and go to sleep nicely. I hope I'm never capable of such comfort.

WACHTEL I know you've cautioned me that the narrator might be unreliable, but very early on she says, "Almost everything in my life to which I am inextricably bound is a source of pain." That's very, very tough.

KINCAID But it's true, don't you find? Everything has six of one and half a dozen of the other. I would never expect anything to be straightforward, or not have different sides. That's the way life is. I hope to fully accept that, as the narrator does. It is a very tough thing to live with, but I would really like to be able to live with that. I'm not sure in my own life that I can. Perhaps she's a bit too realistic for all of us, but I rather like her.

July 1993/January 1996
interview initially prepared in collaboration
with Sandra Rabinovitch and Paul Wilson

JOHN BERGER

Novelist and art critic, John Berger, radicalized a generation with his provocative television series and book, *Ways of Seeing* (1972). He's written about photography, painting, and about peasant life in the French Alps.

I've admired John Berger for a long time. I came to him through his essays, and used his pieces as course material when I had the occasion to teach. I remember a four-page article called "Photographs of Agony," which somehow fused an astute media analysis with morality and politics. I remember a line from another book, where he says: "You can't talk about aesthetics without talking about the principle of hope and the existence of evil."

Berger has an extraordinary, capacious mind, fuelled by an ardent sensibility. In an introduction to one of his collections of essays, this is how the editor enumerates Berger's themes: "Love and passion, death, power, labour, the experience of time and the nature of our present history."

Born in London in 1926, John Berger began as an artist. In fact, he says that "if the world were more human, I wouldn't write at all. I would only draw." He went to art school at the age of sixteen. He later taught drawing, and in the 1950s he became an art critic for *The New Statesman*. Seeing comes first, he's always said. It's primary to how he understands the world. Storytelling may be about paintings or about people, but he starts with the eye.

In 1972 John Berger became famous for two reasons, first for his landmark BBC television series and book, *Ways of Seeing*. By illuminating its social and political context, Berger changed how people thought about art. For instance, his chapter on women as visual objects became a cornerstone of feminist theory in the 1970s. *Ways of Seeing* sold a million copies.

The second thing to happen was that Berger won the Booker Prize for his novel, *G*. He became renowned not only for winning the prize but for his acceptance speech, in which he denounced the Booker-McConnell Corporation for its labour practices in the Caribbean. He donated half his prize money to black revolutionary organizations, and used the other half to finance his next book, about immigrant workers in Europe.

It was also around this time that Berger left England. He's lived on the continent ever since and, for the last twenty years or more, in a village in the foothills of the French Alps. It's here that he wrote his peasant trilogy, three novels called *Into Their Labours*, starting with *Pig Earth* (1979). At the same time he's written plays, screenplays, poetry and collections of essays — more than twenty books now.

I talked to John Berger by telephone in July, 1995, when he was at his Paris apartment after hay-making season. His novel, *To the Wedding*, had just been published. It's an eloquent prose-poem about the triumph of love over death, about a young woman who's HIV positive.

WACHTEL In a recent essay, where you talk about your brief stint as a film actor, you say that you've always tried to lend your imagination to lives other than your own. Not as a virtue, but as a compulsion. Why do you think that is?

BERGER I don't think that's something I acquired with experience. I have the feeling I was like that even as a small child, and when I was an adolescent. Now I'm quite old and it's the same. It was something given to me and probably like most things that are given it springs from a weakness. It's quite wrong to think that capacities are strengths; they are ways of overcoming weakness.

WACHTEL What would the weakness be?

BERGER I'm very suspicious of psychological analyses and, if you notice, I almost never use them in my stories or my novels because I think those analyses are a closed circuit and have very little of the breath of life in them, even though they can be very elegant and quite neat. But having said that, to try to answer your question honestly, it may be because I have a very fragile sense of my own identity. It may seem strange — especially when people meet me because I know I have quite a strong presence — but nevertheless in fact my *own* sense of identity is extremely fragile. Quite often it almost dissolves and I feel that I am nothing.

I think that began in my early childhood. I had a quite close relationship with my mother and my mother had a very close relationship with me, but during my early childhood she was seldom there. So there was no one to say all the time — as mothers say to their children — "John. Our John. John!" I think perhaps it began there. In some ways I had a childhood which was, without being pathetic, a little bit like an orphan's.

WACHTEL Why was that? When you say your mother wasn't there, you mean literally, physically, she wasn't there?

BERGER Yes. She wasn't there because she was working. She was working a great deal, because we didn't have much money, so I saw her very little. Then I was sent away to boarding-schools and, obviously, she wasn't there. Nobody was there. That was for me a quite traumatic experience. What happens, if you have a rather weak sense of your own identity, is that it may be easier for you to perceive or to take on in some way the identity of the one in front of you. Whether they are physically in front of you or only in front of you in your imagination.

WACHTEL I'd like to go back for a moment to what you were saying about feeling like an orphan. Could you talk a little more about what that felt like?

BERGER I suppose that the first thing that an orphan experiences, compared to other children, is a sense of solitude and a realization that you have to depend upon yourself. Those two things go together: a kind of self-dependence, which perhaps can also be called an independence; and also a sense of being, as it were, ontologically alone — not necessarily physically alone.

WACHTEL You started off as a painter. You went to art school, but you gave it all up in the early 1950s. It wasn't because you didn't think you had any talent, but you turned to words, to the printed word and art criticism. Why?

BERGER That was political. We're now talking about the early fifties, the height of the Cold War. For those who didn't live through it, it is somewhat difficult to imagine the monstrous intensity of that historical time. It's very important to remember that at first the Soviet Union did not have nuclear parity. Therefore the proposition made by philosophers and politicians — not by all but by some, and by some quite important ones — was actually to start, as it was called, a "preventative" war. That is to say, to make a nuclear attack on Moscow. This seemed monstrous. Hiroshima hasn't been forgotten even now, but the horror of it was then quite fresh in people's minds.

Then the Soviet Union gained nuclear parity and there was the risk of mutual nuclear war. This risk was very real. Those of us who were particularly conscious of that were living from day to day. It wasn't our own deaths which were in question but millions, and maybe the death of the planet as well.

In that situation, to go on painting pictures to be put into galleries and to be sold, as some of mine had been, and then to be hung in drawing-rooms, seemed absurd. It didn't seem absurd to all painters — many continued, thank God — but it did seem absurd to me. To write seemed a little less absurd, especially to write journalism and especially to write about these issues. I didn't write only art criticism; I also wrote precisely about nuclear war, about politics, about the Cold War. And so the sense of political urgency, or historical urgency if you wish, was what made me decide to begin writing publicly. I'd previously written privately.

I think from the beginning I knew it probably wasn't possible to continue to do both seriously, so I abandoned painting. Although as I'm sitting here, on the wall are three drawings and two are by me — one quite recent of a mule and a ram who were inseparable friends in Spain. Next to that is a drawing I did in the Hebrides, so I still draw.

WACHTEL You've described writing as a continuous struggle, yet you seem to find so much pleasure and immediacy in the eye, and seeing is so primary to your way of understanding the world. Was turning to writing a kind of wilful sacrifice in some way?

BERGER No, I don't think it was a sacrifice, but it did require a strong will. It required a lot of determination, because I didn't have much facility. I didn't think of it as a sacrifice, because we thought we were all going to be sacrificed. And if that were the case, we were going to be sacrificed protesting.

WACHTEL In the late 1950s, in 1958, you published your first novel, *A Painter of Our Time*. Why the move to fiction?

BERGER I don't think it was such a move. This is said in retrospect when now, at my age, I can look back and see continuities in my life which at the time I didn't see. If I look back now, it seems to me that I was always very closely connected to stories, even when I talked about painting. When I was an art critic my approach was always that of a storyteller. I was not a literary art critic who was always wanting to drag stories into paintings or to find the story in the painting. No, not at all. Sometimes it was about the subject of the painting, when the painting had a very definite subject, let's say, Rembrandt's *Prodigal Son*. But more often the story was the story of the painter's life, both his or her personal life, and the painter's relationship to that historical moment, to his or her time.

When I then wrote a novel about a fictional painter, this time to *tell* a story, it wasn't really such a shift. I think it was only a development. With *A Painter of Our Time*, I discovered that I did have the stamina to write a whole book, to produce what people call a novel. Having proved to myself I was capable of that, I began to become interested in trying to tell other stories.

WACHTEL That novel — *A Painter of Our Time* — is about a Hungarian expatriate painter in London. You seem always to have been drawn to exiles, emigrés, the displaced.

BERGER Yes, in London at that time and even a little earlier, during the forties, most of the friends I made were considerably older than myself. I don't really know why they accepted this kid as their friend, but they did. Most of them were emigrés from fascism — Austrians, Germans, Hungarians and others. I felt at ease with them. And I learned so much from observing and listening to them.

If one wants to link that autobiographically — it wasn't conscious at that time for me — my father's father, my grandfather, was an emigré also. He came from Trieste. He went from Trieste to Liverpool. So although my father had the air of being very English — in his manner and so on he was an almost ideal English gentleman — in fact he was a first-generation emigré.

WACHTEL That's interesting about Trieste, because it shows up in your work as a pivotal place.

BERGER Yes, the first time is with G and that choice of Trieste was conscious — I was thinking of my grandfather. In fact, when I went to Trieste to do research for that book, I tried to find relations, members of the family. I didn't have any clue about them because I had been told very little about my grandfather. I was just told that he was dead. Later, I discovered that he wasn't dead until I was about twenty-six or twenty-seven, but he'd left my grandmother and was living with another woman and so the family said that he was dead. So when I was in Trieste, I looked in the telephone directory and went to several families to see if they were related to my grandfather. Mostly they reacted with great suspicion because the only reason imaginable for my doing this was that I wanted money or support in some way.

WACHTEL I'm struck when you say your father was the quintessential English gentleman, because I get the sense that *you've* never felt that English or comfortable as an Englishman.

BERGER That's true.

WACHTEL It's the classic immigration pattern.

BERGER Exactly! My father took on the appearance of being English, and English of that particular class, but in fact, in his soul, he wasn't. He was a man deeply marked by World War I, like so many of the men who survived that war.

He was an infantry officer. He spent the whole four years on the Western Front, as a lieutenant and then as a captain. The number of lieutenants and captains of the British Infantry who survived four years were very few. He was a brave soldier; he was decorated several times. One of my earliest memories is hearing my father in his bedroom, screaming and shouting; he had many nightmares, nightmares always about the war.

WACHTEL When you started out as an art critic, Marxism informed your aesthetic. Has that changed?

BERGER No. What I knew as an art critic about aesthetics was from painters, from teachers, from painting and drawing myself. That at the same time I was a Marxist, is of course true. Marxism seemed to me to be a tool with which one could explain parts of history, including parts of the history of art. But Marxism was not the determinant of my aesthetics. Marxism — and this is very important, and is something I realized even a long way back — doesn't have an aesthetics itself, any more than it has an ethics. This is the lacuna in Marxism. There were Marxists who behaved disgustingly, but there were also millions who behaved with incredible self-sacrifice and with great ethical nobility. But this came from themselves; it didn't come from Marxism. Also behind that there was a political allegiance that I had for socialism, a hatred of capitalism, a conviction that capitalism is finally doomed. Which I still believe.

WACHTEL I think I was probably extrapolating from something you wrote, that you judged a work of art according to whether it helped men in the modern world claim their social rights.

BERGER　I remember writing that. Like many things that I wrote at that time there was a kind of defiance. That comment has to be placed in a context in which all official thinking was saying that art was a completely autonomous activity, to do with sensibility and taste and so on. So I was defining defiantly my own practice as a critic. But I do think that somebody who is now unemployed, and who comes upon a work of art that speaks to her or him, can receive a certain sustenance from it, which will make that person more aware of their own dignity, and will therefore make them perhaps refuse or struggle against their fate. I think the concept of dignity and the sustenance that dignity requires can never be simply individual. Dignity is a question, above all, of how people treat you and how you treat other people. So if art is about human dignity, one can also say that it is about the relations between people, and that those relations are social.

WACHTEL　Whether you're writing essays or criticism or novels, as you have said yourself, stories are at the heart of what you do. You're a storyteller. But you say that when you came to write your trilogy about peasant culture — starting with *Pig Earth* — you had to almost relearn how to write. What necessitated that?

BERGER　It was about the experience those stories tried to tell. If you find a story — I say find, because stories are half-found, half-invented. When there is a story there, this is only the beginning of the task because then the voice for telling that story has to be found and that's the most difficult part of all. Each story, ideally, has its right voice. Sometimes voice can actually mean the voice of the narrator who takes over the telling of the story. But even if the story is told completely in the third person, the story has a voice and that voice has to be found, and only that voice can do justice to that story. I think this question of voice is so important because stories depend not only on what is said, but maybe even more on what is *not* said. They depend upon silences. And every voice has its own kind of silence, jumping over the unsaid.

The voice for telling stories about peasants had to be a voice that came from peasant experience. Even so, in different stories the voice changes somewhat, though perhaps they're all, to some degree, peasant voices. That means having to learn.

For example, as I understand it — from the peasants that I know — they very seldom use the word "but." The word "but" is a word of intellectual discourse, based upon a sense of polarities: "He was handsome but mean-hearted." The peasant uses the word "and." A more graphic example might be: "We liked Doris our pig, and last January we killed her." The more familiar, the more intellectual discourse would say: "We liked Doris our pig, *but* last January we killed her."

If you see the difference by taking just one word like that, then when one comes to things that are much more complicated — such as syntax, different words, the things which are taken for granted and not taken for granted — you can see how much I had to learn again — or not again, but for the first time, when I started trying to tell stories about peasants. Previously, the books that I'd written were either about bourgeois people or about workers or intellectuals or artists, but not about peasants.

WACHTEL How did you find yourself among peasants? What made you decide to live there?

BERGER Chance. I think most of the big decisions that one makes in life are made intuitively and without a great deal of reasoning. Afterwards one tries to rationalize them, and one starts distorting the truth. I don't think this was something where at that moment I said to myself: "This is a way of living cheaply." Or: "This is a good place to live." I didn't say: "I like being surrounded by animals." But in fact I do like being surrounded by animals. And animals recur and recur both in my drawings and in my paintings, and maybe also in my writings.

Before I wanted to be a painter, what I wanted to be — this was when I was really a kid — was a veterinary surgeon. If I just talk off the top of my head, I suppose some of the pieces of writing that most deeply marked me when I was in my early teens were all the D.H. Lawrence poems about animals.

WACHTEL When we were discussing when to have this conversation, we had to plan it around hay-making season. Do you like hay-making?

BERGER Making hay is very tough, especially when it's hot. It's dusty and tiring. But because there are always two or three or four people working together, there is this mutuality, this small community of work, and of protecting one another because it's also somewhat dangerous in the barns when the hay gets really high. And being together is a pleasure, I like that. At the end of the day, the kind of fatigue one has, which really means that everything else is totally brushed out of your mind, one comes to enjoy that. And in the mountains, there is a spring where the cows drink, which is always cold and never dries up, it's flowing all the time. And when you come out of the barn between hayloads and you put your whole head into that cold water, it's very good.

WACHTEL When I hear you talk, I think about the first volume of your peasant trilogy, *Pig Earth*, which describes some of what you're saying. It's not exactly celebration — I think that would be too romanticizing — but it's about this community of work and the interrelations between people.

BERGER One shouldn't exaggerate the conviviality. But yes, when all the loads have been brought in, except one, which is already in the cart but not yet unloaded, we stop and go into the kitchen. We make coffee, and get out the cheese and the wine, we cut the bread, sit down at the table. It's very dusty and there are quite a lot of flies, but that's always a kind of celebration. We drink wine, maybe have a glass of *gnole*, cut the cheese and eat. And that is a ritual, a positive one.

WACHTEL You describe this in such sensual detail, but — not but, *and* — the movement in your trilogy, which you call *Into Their Labours*, is inexorably towards loss; it's away from this kind of close connection amongst people and to the land.

BERGER Yes, absolutely, because that's what's happening all over the world. The new economic powers of the world have decided that peasants — whether in Mexico or the European Alps — are obsolete. To varying degrees the peasants resist, but even when they resist they usually fail. So this isn't a question of my mood, it's a question of a world development.

WACHTEL I'd like to talk about your novel, *To the Wedding*. In a sense, what we've been discussing is almost preparatory to it, because the question of vitality in the face of death is very much at the centre of this novel. In most of your work, the forces of capitalism or political oppression or inexorable urbanization have been the destructive elements. In *To the Wedding*, HIV is the agent of tragedy. Why did you want to write about AIDS this time?

BERGER It seemed to me that I had to write about it. One of the reasons for writing such a book is that there's a grave danger of those suffering from this terrible scourge being put into a ghetto. One of the functions of writing stories is to take people or to remove them from the ghetto that other people have built around them. When people are put in a ghetto they become "them" instead of "us." When they are removed from the ghetto they become "us" again. I was aware of a need. I didn't know that I could meet that need in any way. I still don't know.

WACHTEL *To the Wedding* is very much a love story, and the energy of love, the idea of love, is something that recurs in your work — whether in essays about notions of time, or in your fiction, *Once In Europa*, or in the last remembered words of your mother. To borrow from Raymond Carver, what do we talk about when we talk about love?

BERGER I know he's dead, but ask Raymond Carver; he knew so much. Of course we are talking about something infinitely mysterious and I think something closely connected with the very origin of life. We're talking about creation, not artistic creation but the creation of life itself, or the Creation with a capital C. Perhaps we can say nothing about it except acknowledge its mystery. I hate mystification. Every word that one uses has to be cleaned of its mildew of mystification. But at the same time, one has to acknowledge mystery, which is something very different.

WACHTEL The language that you use, when talking about art and about so many things, is not only specific and practical and sensuous and detailed, it's also evocative and seems to point to or suggest the existence of something beyond the physical, something spiritual. Do you know what I'm trying to get at?

BERGER Yes. I think that is quite true. I can try to answer that. First of all, if we can go back a long way and talk for just a moment, a little abstractly, I think my cast of imagination, from the time I was a child, was at once physical and metaphysical. I think I have a metaphysical cast of mind, in a certain sense. That's why, when people said that I'm a Marxist or that I was a Marxist, I accept it. It's part of the truth, but it's only part of the truth, because coexisting with that — which doesn't exist in Marxism — I have a metaphysical awareness of life and of the meaning of life and of the origin of life. That is very general and very abstract. To put it very simply, I believe in God. I don't want it to appear that I'm a "believer." It's not that at all. But that faith appears between the words with which I write.

Another answer to your question is professional in a way. I write very slowly. The quickest book I've ever written took me two years, the longest took me eight or nine, most take three or four. It's not that I'm lazy, but because I write with great difficulty and I write nearly every page numerous times — probably eight or nine times. Now in that writing and rewriting, I'm all the time searching for the relation of the words to the language as a whole. If the words are rightly chosen and if they have the right relationship with each other, there is a kind of resonance. The whole language to which they belong offers them back a very slight echo. And that very faint echo is perhaps something which is perceived as an element of faith, because perhaps it banishes — no, it transcends — the trivial, which when it fills the whole horizon is so demeaning and so discouraging.

I think that the thing that you're talking about actually comes in some ways from my use of language. But I don't have a sense of using the language; it's more a matter of being receptive, of being open to language. Because finally, just as you have to get close up to experience, you have to get close up to that mother tongue and then she will give you something. If she gives you something, it means that the reader will receive it too.

WACHTEL What I feel much of the time when I read you is that resonance, a kind of hopefulness, but it's tinged with yearning, which maybe is a necessary part of it. I'm thinking of the quotation by Gorky that you use at the beginning and end of your first novel, *A Painter of Our Time*. It must be the bleakest statement on hope that one can imagine: "Life will always be bad enough/for the desire for something better/not to be extinguished in man."

BERGER That's exactly his nobility. I don't think it is bleak. It is the opposite which would be bleak, for that hope to be extinguished. But this depends upon how one views the interlude of life. Viewed from the point of view of any utopia, it is very bleak. But it isn't bleak when viewed from the point of view of the creation of life and freedom — which means that men can do what they wish — and of the inevitable struggle and wrestling and conflict that entails. Included within that capacity for the open choice of freedom, is the open choice for good or evil, and within that context, I don't think that the quotation from Gorky is bleak. It's bleak from the point of view of the Age of Enlightenment, but it wouldn't have seemed bleak to the Greeks, for example.

Another thing that I wanted to do when writing *To the Wedding* (this was part of removing the ghetto), was to try to connect the loss, the suffering, and the pain of those afflicted with this disease — allowing all its terrible specificity and its newness — to place it in the context, in the frame of human tragedy, which has always existed and which we know a great deal about, amongst other things, because of the Greek tragedies.

In the Greek tragedies the chorus is very important. The chorus was played not by actors, but by citizens of the city, which is important because they were the representatives of the public, of the spectators *in* the tragedy. The chorus really has no power. It cannot change events; all it can do is comment on them and lament them, and sometimes praise them. But above all what it does is express pity. And in that there is something quite prophetic about these plays, written four or five hundred years before Christ, because on occasions they prophesy the compassion of the New Testament. In our time the word "pity" is very explosive and in some ways dangerous. Because of the nineteenth and twentieth centuries, it is seen or can be seen as something patronizing. But in its original sense and meaning it was not. It was a way of bearing witness to and sharing the suffering of somebody else. The Greeks would not find that Gorky quote bleak because they were accustomed to the emotion of pity and also accustomed to the actions which sometimes can arise from that emotion; that is to say, the actions of solidarity. So when one sees that quotation as bleak it is perhaps because we are today less familiar than most men and women in other centuries with this emotion of pity.

WACHTEL Given that we probably live in a time when it's perhaps most called for, why?

BERGER I think that's very complicated and something that is changing. I think the banishment of that emotion — if one can call it that — which dominated perhaps two centuries of European thought, is now over. The problem with pity, as it is sometimes understood, is that, okay, so you feel pity, and that means, having felt pity, you can sit back and do nothing. So it becomes a kind of cop-out. But that's a defamation of the idea, not of the idea, but of the faculty, because it is a part of what constitutes human nature. It is maybe the first action of the imagination, and is something that is extremely basic to human nature. One sees it in all children, everywhere. Children identify with those around them, with animals, even with their toys, with the characters in their stories, completely. This is the first act of imagination, to at least make the steps towards getting into somebody else's skin. It is not achievable, of course; it would be very sentimental to say that. But the first steps are made. In my opinion this is where not only ethics begins but also art.

July 1995
interview initially prepared in collaboration
with Mary Stinson